Directors of Photography

"The art and craft of the operating cameraman has never before been explored or analyzed in depth as it is in **OPERATING CINEMATOGRAPHY for FILM and VIDEO**. With great thoroughness, Bill Hines examines all aspects of the technique and practical application of the craft, its historical development and the social skills and 'on set' procedures that previously were left for the individual to learn by trial-and-error."
—John Hora, ASC

"The camera operator is a critical instrument in the collaborative process of cinematography and as an extension of the cinematographer, can be a helpful moderator between the director, the cinematographer and performers. Bill Hines' **OPERATING CINEMATOGRAPHY** illustrates the importance of this relationship."
—Haskell Wexler ASC.

"**OPERATING CINEMATOGRAPHY** is a wonderful guide. In it you'll find everything you need to know to do my favorite job, the best job in cinematography— camera operating."
—Conrad Hall ASC.

"**OPERATING CINEMATOGRAPHY** is a comprehensive 'how to' handbook for success, not only in camera, but in the industry as well. When you finish reading this book, you will know what camera operating and operating cinematography are all about."
—George Spiro Dibie ASC

"In camera operating as in filmmaking, always concentrate on the purpose rather than the method. **OPERATING CINEMATOGRAPHY** is an excellent guide to that end."
—Gordon Willis ASC

"Camera operating—1) as a contributor, 2) as an influence, 3) as a team player, 4) AS AN ART FORM—from A to Z, it's all there in **OPERATING CINEMATOGRAPHY**. *Must reading* if you want to expand your visual capabilities."
—William Fraker ASC

"**OPERATING CINEMATOGRAPHY** is a valuable, well-written, one-of-a-kind book on camera operating."
—Vilmos Zsigmond ASC

"**OPERATING CINEMATOGRAPHY** includes a wide diversity of essential information relating to camera operating, such as on-set protocol, working effectively with other crafts and shot management."
—Dean Cundey ASC

"In addition to the technical and aesthetic considerations in **OPERATING CINEMATOGRAPHY**, Bill Hines emphasizes two important areas often neglected by others writing about our industry—these are set etiquette and communication. Good manners and good communication guarantee the best use of everyone's energy during motion picture production." **—Allen Daviau** ASC

more on next page
& at end of book

Also by William E Hines, SOC

JOB DESCRIPTIONS FOR FILM AND VIDEO:
Responsibilities and Duties
for the
FILM and VIDEO Craft
Categories and Classifications

What Practicing Professionals Have To Say, continued from previous page

Camera Operators

"Each of Bill Hines' '**Operating Tips**' provides a unique perspective that only a working camera operator could give. His extensive experience comes through in each of his monthly columns—and now, in his book."   —**Norm Langley** SOC

"**OPERATING CINEMATOGRAPHY** is the complete guide to professional camera operating. An essential tool."   —**Georgia Tornai Packard** SOC

"In his book, **OPERATING CINEMATOGRAPHY**, the author, Bill Hines, has given us a fabulous primer for youngsters entering our profession and a comprehensive reference guide for old-timers as well. I strongly recommend it."
     —**Howard Block** SOC   *more at end of book*

Experienced First Assistant Camera Operators

"Every camera assistant who wants to learn and know more about their craft, and the craft of the camera operator, as well as set etiquette and safety, should study and keep **OPERATING CINEMATOGRAPHY** at hand for ready reference."
     —**Richard Meinardus**   *more at end of book*

OPERATING CINEMATOGRAPHY

FOR

FILM AND VIDEO

A PROFESSIONAL AND PRACTICAL GUIDE

BY

WILLIAM E HINES, SOC

ED-VENTURE FILMS/BOOKS

LOS ANGELES, CA

Published By
Ed-Venture Films/Books
P O Box 23214
Los Angeles, Ca 90023

Cataloging Data

Hines, William E., date
Operating Tips for Film and Video / William E. Hines
256 pp.
ISBN 0-935873-01-5

784.5
I. Title
II. Cinematography
III. Film. Camera Operating Tips
IV. Video. Camera Operating Tips
V. Motion Pictures. Camera Operating Tips
VI. Television. Camera Operating Tips

1997
Library of Congress Catalogue Card Number 97-90057

Manufactured in the United States of America

ACKNOWLEDGMENTS

This book became a reality as a result of numerous requests from colleagues, coworkers, students and cinemaddicts—who have been following my monthly column, "**Operating Tips**," in *The International Photographer* magazine for the past ten years—that the articles be organized into book form for convenient and long-term reference.

A full production schedule and commitments to the International Photographers Guild and the Society of Operating Cameramen has allowed little time to select, update and organize the articles into book form. Nevertheless, bit by bit, with the encouragement of the readership, friends and family, this volume has taken form and is now in your hands.

Production of a book is in many ways a collaborative effort, somewhat like a film or video production. Many people are involved in achieving its reality: The author and his first-hand experiences, of course; the many craftspeople of varying skills and abilities with whom the author has worked; the editor; the designer and formatter; the copyreaders; the printer; the distributor; the bookseller; and last, but not least, the reader—for it was the input of the readers of the columns which directed the attention of the author to specific interests and needs.

As designer, formatter and editor, Lynn Lanning has done a comprehensive and thoroughly marvelous job in shaping this book into an attractive and useful edition.

My wife, Zee, whose patience, encouragement and participation helped make this publication possible, was there as each article took shape.

The valued input from those practicing professionals who were prevailed upon to read the assembled articles in manuscript form is deeply appreciated. These working associates include: John Hora ASC, Director of Photography; Michael A Jones, Director of Photography; Georgia Tornai Packard SOC, Camera Operator; Jeff Goldenberg, First Assistant Camera Operator; and Kevin Haggerty, First Assistant Camera Operator. Lauren Rhoades, my junior high school mentor, also contributed valued counsel.

Finally, the introductory comments by George Spiro Dibie ASC, Director of Photography, President of the National Camera Guild and Editor-in-Chief of The *International Photographer* magazine in which the "Operating Tips" articles appeared, and the testimonials appearing herein from a number of my valued colleagues—including Directors of Photography: Haskell Wexler ASC, Conrad Hall ASC, Gordon Willis ASC, William Fraker ASC, Vilmos Zsigmond ASC, Alan Daviau ASC, David Quaid ASC, John Alonzo ASC, Sol Negrin ASC, Dean Cundey ASC, Stephen Burum ASC, Jack Green ASC, Steven Poster ASC, Robert Primes ASC, Nick McLean and Brian Reynolds; Camera Operators: Bill Clark SOC, Howard Block SOC, Norm Langley SOC, Paul Basta SOC, Eugene Jackson and Sean Fairburn; and Assistant Camera Operator Richard Meinardus—not only mean a lot to me personally, but are especially pertinent to those seeking to be Camera Operators or to improve in the art and craft of operating cinematography.

FORWARD

I was pleased to be asked by the publisher of this text to write an introduction commenting on its contents and its potential benefit to film and video craftspeople and, not least, to students of the cinematic arts.

As editor-in-chief of *The International Photographer* magazine, I have watched this book grow, column by column, article by article, month by month, over the past ten years into a treasure-trove of practical knowledge shared with its avid readership of professional craftspeople in the film and video industries.

One of the values of this work is its comprehensive and in-depth look at the industry from the highest level to the lowest as it all comes together on the production set. The reader will find that each carefully crafted article deals in detail with a given facet of the business—for example, working relationships with producers, directors, actors, camera personnel, sound, grip, set dressing and other crafts working on the set. The insights provided expose the reader to details never before shared with those not privy to the craft of cinematography. It covers such subjects as responsibilities, duties, attitude, set etiquette, networking, production problems and techniques and the collaborative process as applied to film and video production.

Another value of this text is its basis in reality. Every member of this industry can identify with the problems, challenges, solutions and experiences mentioned. The writer, a practicing operating cameraman himself, has spent forty years on sets and locations observing, analyzing and participating in a variety of production situations. He speaks from extensive experience. Nothing herein is hearsay; everything is based on fact. Anyone used to working on film or video production will experience a feeling of déjà vu in reading this practical manual.

The author uses the camera as the focal point for the collaborative effort contributed to by all production crafts as well as by other facets of the industry. He makes clear that everything the industry does relates to, or owes its existence in some measure to, the images the camera will capture. The contributions of many of the crafts participating in this collaborative effort are thoroughly detailed in this book. And, not least, the importance of caring interpersonal relations and of the pride of craftsmanship are discussed in detail and analyzed from various points of view.

In appraising this book, I feel that it is a comprehensive "how-to" handbook for success, not only in camera, but in the industry as well. It is written on a level that is both easy to read and beneficial to everyone whether heavily experienced or a rank beginner; it is a valuable learning tool for one and all.

When you finish reading this book, you will know what camera operating and operating cinematography are all about. It is my hope that cinema students who aspire to any of the professions in the industry will not only read and study this text, but also keep it as a ready and reliable reference source throughout their careers.

—George Spiro Dibie, ASC, National President
International Photographers Guild, Local 600, IATSE

INTRODUCTION

There is lighting cinematography and there is operating cinematography. Each technique has its important place in the process of image capture. The former prepares the images for capture, first, by appropriately illuminating the subjects and settings, and then, by determining exposure and the photographic look of the imagery by selection of the film stock, lenses and filters. The latter technique is responsible for appropriately following, framing, sizing, focusing and capturing the action.

The purpose of this presentation is to share some of the myriad details that contribute to the art and craft of operating cinematography. Operating cinematography is much more than simply physically operating a film or video camera. It is acquiring the understanding not only of technique but of the aesthetics of camera operation and its emotional and mental effect upon the intended viewer which is essential if the technical craft aspect is to be raised to an aesthetically higher, if not artistic, level.

This handbook contains a compilation of monthly articles which have appeared in "**Operating Tips**," a regular departmental column in issues of *The International Photographer* magazine. The reader will notice that craft classifications, appearing in the text that follows, have been capitalized. That is because caring professionals consider what they do to be not only a job function, but also a hard-earned and well-deserved job title, to be worn with honor and pride. Then, too, the capitalizing will help direct and focus the reader's attention, not only on specific job functions, but also on the interrelationships among the many job functions.

The articles were written not only as an aid to the neophyte to assist the learning process, but to remind established film and video camera craftspersons of the importance of not only performing their job junctions efficiently, safely and well, but also understanding as much as possible about the contributions made by their colleagues in other craft classifications and categories.

Although there are those in the production chain exercising more or less responsibility during the various phases from concept through exhibition, no one individual makes a fully staffed movie, or makes it either a success or a flop. The cinematic media—film and video—said to be Director's media, are processes which are entirely collaborative and which depend upon the cooperation and contributions of each and every individual on the staff, cast and technical crew. The care focused on the attention to detail during the pre-production, production and post-production phases helps insure optimum realization of the project.

Everything that is done during pre-production through production is done directly or indirectly with the camera in mind—in fact, done **for presentation to** the camera. The technical responsibility of the camera crew to accurately, consistently, creatively and efficiently record each presentation—take by take and shot by shot— is awesome: The Director of Photography, for the lighting and coordinated effort of the camera, electrical and grip personnel; the Camera Operator, for the framing and coordinated effort of the operative camera crew during the shot—and in video, for focus, zoom sizing and camera movement, as well; the First Assistant Camera Operator, for focus, zoom sizing and other settings, and the care and placing of camera accessories on the camera; the Second Assistant Camera Operator, for accurate and complete slating and camera reports; the Loader, for carefully loading the unexposed film, downloading the exposed film and keeping accurate records thereof; and the Dolly or Crane Grip, for moving the mobile camera platform while following the action.

While attention to craft category and classification responsibilities and duties is important, there are other factors which may affect job performance and are well to consider. This volume will include not only a section on operating cinematography but sections on various craft responsibilities and duties, production types, production practices, and interpersonal relations.

The revised articles as they appear in this volume have been arranged by category rather than in the chronological order in which they appeared in *The International Photographer* magazine. Consequently, there will be some informational repetition and overlapping in several of the articles herein presented. It was felt that it would be more appropriate to maintain the integrity of each article as it appeared in print and not to excise material simply because it might have been touched on or covered in another article.

The reader will find that the material in this book is not dated. It is as applicable today as it was when it was written and is unlikely to become obsolete in the foreseeable future. Indeed, it will prove to be a handy reference source for those seeking a better understanding of the many elements that contribute to the art and craft of operating cinematography.

If the reader has been helped to understand and/or apply and practice film and/or video operating techniques by material presented in this writing, this manual will have served its purpose.

—William E Hines, SOC
Los Angeles, CA

PROLOGUE

CAMERA OPERATING:
AN HISTORICAL PERSPECTIVE

One hundred years have passed since the motion picture camera and the motion picture projector were invented to, respectively, record and give life to static images, exposed and displayed at 12-16 frames per second.

In 1889, Thomas Alva Edison introduced the Kinetograph, a cumbersome battery-driven camera, and the Kinetoscope, a projector for the so-called "peep show." In the same year, George Eastman produced the first celluloid strips coated with photographic emulsion. The 4-perforation per frame pull-down standard and the 35mm film width was then established by his assistant, William Kennedy Laurie Dickson.

In 1894, the Lumière brothers, Louis and Auguste, brought out the first practical, portable, hand-cranked production camera, the Cinématographe, which also served as a printer and projector, in turn. Louis Lumière called himself an *Opérateur* (an Operative Cameraman) to describe what he did when he set up, placed and lined up the camera view, and then threaded, turned and exposed film in that camera.

From 1895 to 1896 ten Cinématographes were produced in France, while other cameras were being produced in England, Germany and the United States.

Lumière filmed all of his early films outdoors for maximum light exposure on the very slow emulsions. After bi-packing unexposed negative behind the exposed negative in the Cinématographe, he would print his films by the sunlight reflected into the lens off a white board while cranking the bi-packed film through the camera-printer-projector. He made fifty one-minute films in 1895 which were each 17 meters in length (60 seconds at 16 fps).

To maintain the appearance of normal movement, the subject matter was usually projected at the same frame rate as it had been exposed in the camera. However, creative projectionists often varied the hand-cranked projection rate to either speed up or slow down the on-screen movement. Film editing had not as yet been discovered.

During filming, everyone—staff, actors and extras—pitched in and did everything—set construction and placement, costumes, prop acquisition, set dressing, makeup, hair dressing, etc. There were no specialists, as such, in those days. The lighting source was the sun which made shooting motion pictures an outside activity. And this remained so until the turn of the century, just five years away, when Georges Meliés built his glass-enclosed studio in Paris and filmed his interiors and other stage sets in daylight, protected from the elements.

The Cameraman was the technical (and often creative) key to the movie-making process. Then, as now, everything was prepared for presentation to the camera. The Cameraman functioned as Director, Director of Photography, Camera Operator, Focus Puller, Loader, Electrician, Grip, Lab Technician, Optical Technician, and (with filming completed) Film Editor and Projectionist—a veritable one-man band.

The Cameraman then was, and was expected to be, a one-man band—providing his personal camera equipment and the overall technical direction of the recording process. He would set up his camera, load film into it, set the exposure functions, frame the action, crank film through the camera at a given rate, set fades and dissolves and irising, unload the film, develop the film, print the film, and, when early story films required moving the camera from place to place, he would edit and splice the scenes together, print and then project the final result. All of this was really only an extension of what the still photographer did (and does) in getting pictures. Many Cameramen of the day were well-grounded in the techniques of still photography.

By 1899, story-telling techniques developed. Scenarios were written. Film presentations were one reel (1,000´) in length, approximately seventeen minutes at 16 fps. At 8 frames per turn, the Cameraman-Operator would crank film through the camera at the rate of two turns per second in order to maintain that 16 fps rate.

By 1904, the static camera, instead of recording the entire production from a single position, began being purposefully placed at varying distances from, and viewpoints of, the action or subject matter—viewpoints from long shot to medium shot to close up—and somewhat later, was placed on a mobile platform and moved while filming, from a long view to a close view and vice versa, while panning and tilting as necessary to hold the action in frame.

Films were being imported and exported. In the USA, two cameras were being used during production. The principal, or **first** camera, operated by the principal, or First Cameraman, was placed in the optimal position with respect to the blocked action and was used to expose the more important domestic release negative. Next to it, with the same focal length lens and similar coverage, was placed the **second** camera, operated by the Second Cameraman, which was used for the foreign release negative. Hence the origin of the designations, First Cameraman and Second Cameraman.

In the USA, the earliest films were all of exteriors and of exterior events. Even the earliest studio interior scenes were illuminated by sunlight entering floor-to-ceiling windows, controlled by muslin sheeting. Some interior settings were constructed outdoors, or on stages which could be rotated with the movement of the sun.

It was the First Cameraman's responsibility to determine the camera position(s), the lens, the f-stop, the focus and the lighting balance and to adjust the muslin and/or to have the studio rotated to maintain proper relationship to the sunlight.

When sodium vapor lamps were adapted to motion picture use, it made it possible to film on sets in studio interiors. The First Cameraman had to spend much time adjusting or supervising the adjustment of the lamps in order to properly illuminate the studio settings and balance the lighting on the actors. With these heavy lights, he was given an Assistant, a Chief Electrician, to place, connect and adjust the lights. The Chief Electrician would often save himself the trouble of using a ladder to adjust each light by using a boat gaff stick to reach up and tilt, turn or swing each light to a desired position, or to switch a light on or off; hence, the term, "Gaffer." However, there are two differing theories also related to the derivation of this term: One is that the foreman of a railroad rail-laying crew was called a "gaffer"; the other is that the foreman of the circus tent-raising and rigging crew was also called a "gaffer"—so, take your choice.

With the advent of sound in 1926 for major studio production, lighting procedures, handling large crews and the multiple-camera requirements of sound recording finally divorced the First Cameraman from operating a camera. Each camera had a constant-speed electric motor set to run at 24 fps but, because the silent era did not require silent-running, produced an unacceptably high running noise level for production-quality sound. In addition, the strong lights made the studios extremely hot and uncomfortable.

Compounding the problem, the recording of production sound required that all cameras and their Operators be enclosed in sound-proofed, non-air-conditioned cabinets (called "hot-boxes"). Up to ten cameras, two to a booth, were used to film heavily rehearsed sequences in one full-load take (up to 11 minutes per 1,000′ load). In order to avoid this torture, and to make the cameras more mobile again, sound-proofing blimps were soon developed to contain the noise of the silent-era production cameras. Self-blimped cameras were promptly put on the drawing boards.

Microphone and boom shadows were everywhere and had to be controlled. The First Cameraman, now called the "Director of Photography," had to be on the floor, away from the confined cameras, to be able to see what was happening, monitoring his lighting and the action, ready to take immediate corrective action. The responsibility for operating the camera and keeping microphone, mic booms and their shadows out of frame, fell to the Second Cameraman to whom the titles of Camera Operator and Operating Cinematographer were applied.

The Camera Operator, the person looking through the viewfinder, has always been responsible for framing the action which has been established by the Director and set by the Director of Photography, and including essential parts of that action in frame while excluding extraneous matter. In the days before video assist, the Camera Operator saw the framed action first and was the only one able to say accurately whether the take was pictorially acceptable or not until dailies were looked at the following day.

The heavier, bulkier precision production sound cameras with their geared heads required assistance to move, set up and operate. What had been possible for a Camera Operator, operating a smaller camera on a friction head—making adjustments while panning and tilting, such as, focus, shutter angle, irising, sliding diffusion, etc—became impossible or impractical to accomplish with both hands on the control wheels of a heavy-duty geared head. So the Camera Assistant became the First Assistant Camera Operator (focus puller and record keeper) and the Second Assistant Camera Operator helped the First Assistant and slated scenes, while a Loader kept film magazines loaded and down-loaded, properly identified the exposed film and sent it to the film lab for processing

The reflex camera was introduced in 1932 in Germany and used during WWII. When the reflex studio camera came into vogue, the Camera Operator was expected to monitor focus in addition to the responsibilities for achieving smooth camera manipulation, proper framing at all times, with no microphone, boom or their shadows or extraneous personnel or equipment in frame during a take. This expectation continues in practice today.

Today, the Camera Operator may be a man or woman operating a film or video camera, in a studio or on location—domestic or foreign; in the air or underwater; perched on the end of a crane, or on a plane, boat, or dolly; operating a hand-held, body-mounted, or remotely controlled camera; or working on a feature, commercial, an episodic or sitcom series, or on a documentary. No matter where or what the project or tools, good operating practices, which have evolved over the years, are being put to good use by the specialists with the title and responsibilities of Camera Operator.

Thanks to the following (now deceased) International Photographers Guild, Local 659, members for their constructive input: Jimmy King (Camera Operator), Walter Rankin (First Assistant) and Charlie Termini (First Assistant).

Reference material used: **The Liveliest Art** *by Arthur Knight and* **Film Makers on Film Making** *by Harry Geduld.*

CONTENTS

SECTION D — OTHER COLLABORATING CRAFTS ... 155

ILLUSTRATIONS

Section

INTERPERSONAL RELATIONS

Because the cinematic media—film and video—are intensely collaborative processes which require a very high degree of respect, interaction and cooperation among the craftspeople, both above- and below-the-line, on staff, cast and crew, it is important to understand the interpersonal relations aspect. Understanding and abiding by written and unwritten rules, performing one's job efficiently and safely, understanding and abiding by both chain-of-command and lines-of-communication, and respecting the craft contributions of others are important aspects of helping to make the production process flow smoothly, efficiently and effectively. This is especially so on major studio productions, which have large crews of craft specialists.

In addition, film and video productions have become staffed at nearly every level largely by relatively inexperienced freelancers, some fresh out of film or television school, with all the insecurity and opportunity that implies.

During early job opportunities, there is no union connection to protect these innocents from the predatorial effect of non-union work. It therefore becomes imperative that the freelancer works to master his or her craft in all respects and seeks to hone those skills on every assignment. With sufficient production experience and a dedication to the chosen craft, the individual may then consider applying for, in order to enjoy the protection and considerable benefits of, union affiliation.

The importance of attitude, conduct, job skills and networking cannot be overemphasized. The tools and skills used in finding and filling a job opening are essential to the freelance film or video craftperson. The process of networking, properly engaged in, provides an important means to the job-seeking end result.

Experience is a great teacher. Some say, the only reliable teacher. Contributing concerted attention to technical craft detail and to the relationships with one's colleagues and coworkers in a union environment can help make every production experience a rewarding one for all concerned. The alternative, if pursued, can be a very painful and expensive learning experience.

THE WHO, WHAT, WHY & HOW

The old maxim, "**Who** you know gets you in, **what** you know keeps you there" is only partly true. In reality, it is the **how**—how *well* you do the **what**, and **who** sees you do it—that counts.

One can gain access to the **what** (the duties and responsibilities, the methods and mechanics) by going to school, seminars and workshops, observing production procedures and by reading books or articles in trade journals. And that in itself is an important step toward understanding the production process and the niche one might find for oneself as a part of that process. But more important still is the **how** (the craftsmanship—the execution of technique), which is the key to the successful doing of the targeted job, whatever it may be.

The Who. Whether a mentor, coach, teacher, or well-placed relative in the hierarchy of the hiring chain, the **Who** is important, and can be the catalyst in getting a career started by providing the guidance, encouragement and/or entrée for a paid position from which to apply one's craft. This support is important and helps smooth the way, but the beneficiary had better be ready—*really ready*—to assume and perform the duties and responsibilities of the proffered employment. Otherwise the opportunity is lost, and may not be available again for some time.

There is an arcane saying: "When the student is ready, a teacher appears." Since most of us lack a relative in an important hiring position, the question posed is: How to find and/or attract a teacher/mentor—a caring and experienced counselor?

It used to be that, under the guild system, a willing neophyte was brought in and trained by a master craftsman in an apprenticeship system. After a certain fixed length of time under stern and strict mentorship, the apprentice was promoted to the next higher craft level, with continuing tough and exacting supervision until deemed ready to move up to each next higher craft level, until the top craft level of responsibilities and duties was reached and mastered, whereupon this master craftsman became, in turn, a mentor to entering apprentices. And so the wheel turned.

A mentor's relationship can be passive (as a carefully observed role model), or interactive. Mentors can take several forms: An instructor, a counselor, a confidant, a protector, a friend, a working superior or associate, or a combination of these attributes. Ideally, a mentor is one with substantial experience and clout (reputation, position and connections) in the industry who then consents to become a caring counselor.

It requires time, energy and interest to be an effective mentor. Mentors can be attracted and maintained by their seeing a substantial work ethic—interest, energy, dedication and loyalty—being consistently demonstrated by the neophyte. Even experienced craftspeople desiring to move up, in, or across categories, can profit by having a mentor take an interest in their progress. Sometimes it only takes a simple request to start such a relationship.

With such an ally, one is well on the way to meaningful career moves. But bear in mind that one's mentor is there to give encouragement, guidance and support, not to do one's work by proxy. A mentor can critique one's work, suggest a plan for one's advancement and provide guidance to help one realize his/her maximum potential as efficiently and effectively as possible.

It is essential not to abuse the time, energy and interest which a mentor contributes to the relationship. In order to keep a mentor interested in one's problems and progress, one should stay focused on the job and short-term goal at hand and strive to make steady progress toward that goal.

The What. It is quite important to choose and undertake an occupational activity which fully suits one's interests, ability and personality. This can be done by working at various film and/or video crafts while in school or in an apprentice capacity on low-budget independent productions, or by participating in an industry training program. Once the category of work has been decided, the classification goal established and with a mentor's help, the entry position secured, the apprentice can start practicing his or her craft to the best of his/her ability.

The Why. The important element in gaining this experience is the **why**—**why** it worked or **why** it didn't. Even with mentor help, there is still no substitute for on-the-job experience, where trial-and-error is often the best teacher. With proper analysis, it comes clear just what works, what doesn't and why, which leads to what likely will work, and what probably won't. A mentor can be useful in helping point out and analyze these aspects of craft experiences.

The How. Networking can be a profitable activity for anyone working to improve their craft capabilities. Sharing experiences with others in the same category and/or classification of work can be a valuable trade-off. Attending seminars and demonstrations and participating in hands-on workshops leads to techniques which often can be immediately put to the test in the workplace. The production site is the laboratory where technique can be tested, expanded and polished to a very high degree. However, any experimenting should be attempted and refined only during rehearsals, before the viable result is applied to on-camera takes.

How Well? The key to a successful mentor relationship is **how well** the protégé has applied him/herself to the task of mastering craft techniques. And craft techniques are not only concerned with handling the equipment, but equally important, deal with interpersonal relationships experienced with one's superiors, peers and subordinates. The image-making process is a thoroughly collaborative procedure, requiring the best efforts of all the craftspeople involved in order to achieve an optimum result. Each person's contribution to that integrative process is important, if not essential. A weak or missing link can substantially weaken or distort the desired result.

A mentor's reward is in the satisfaction of seeing his/her protégé do well and move forward and upward in the chosen craft. To test the limits. To achieve a real sense of purpose, accomplishment and fulfillment.

A Caution. The mentor-protégé connection may provide a few pitfalls. It may develop into a parent-child, or authoritarian, relationship, which could result in the apprentice being too reliant or dependant on the mentor. Peer resentment and jealousy can also result from an effective mentor alliance. Finally, for any number of reasons, this affiliation often has a built-in time limit on its effective duration.

In Summary. The **who**, **what**, **why**, **how**—and **how well**—of getting off to a good start and continuing successfully in the motion picture-making industry has a great deal to do with interpersonal relationships as well as mastery of the technical aspects of craftsmanship. Although mentors can be of significant help in mastering the craft of choice, not everyone needs a mentor to accomplish this. One can be one's own best teacher. Doing one's job well, whatever it might be, technically and interpersonally, is sure to draw the attention of those who can be helpful in insuring one's job security and advancement.

GREAT EXPECTATIONS

While it is undoubtedly more pragmatic and less stressful to have preferences rather than expectations regarding people and events, nevertheless, each of us has our expectations when it comes to doing our job—expectations about how we do our job and expectations about the performance of those who help us do our job. As a rule, we know what to expect of ourselves, and we know what to expect from our assistants. In addition, it can be of significant help to know what is expected of other key crafts. However, what we need to have clear in our mind is what our superiors expect of us.

The **Producer** is the top dog, the number-one person in the chain-of-command, and has the responsibility of first putting the project together and then keeping it together and running efficiently. His or her prime expectation is to produce a financially successful project which comes in on schedule and within budget. For this to happen, all the elements must work effectively and efficiently—and this is the Producer's hope and expectation. When this doesn't happen, heads will, and do, roll.

The **Writer** is expected by the Producer to deliver a well-constructed and viable scenario which fits the Producer's expectations of being able to be shot on schedule and within budget, delivering a substantial audience and financial profit.

The **Production Designer** is expected by the Producer to design an overall visual production plan which will serve to present the camera(s) with the very best angles with which to capture the visuals for the production. The sets and set dressing are expected to be designed and constructed to facilitate photography and without the expense of non-essential construction or detailing.

The **Director** is expected by the Producer to do extensive pre-production planning and be ready to lead and pace the production effort when it goes before the camera(s). In turn, the Director expects to have the wholehearted cooperation of performers, staff and crew technicians in putting his or her visualization of the final product on the screen.

The **Production Manager**, the Producer's alter ego, is expected (by the Producer) to prepare a realistic budget and efficient shooting schedule and, in turn, expects to receive accurate and comprehensive input from each category Department

Head with regard to specific requirements of personnel and matériel—the equipment, tools, materials and expendables—as a result of each Category Head doing a script analysis and breakdown. The PM is the off-the-set expediter and sees that everything needed on the set or at the location site—personnel and matériel—is provided for and there when it is needed.

The **Assistant Director**, the Director's alter ego and on-the-set expediter, is expected (by the Director) to have the set or location site dressed and the performers and technicians ready and waiting for the Director's touch. The AD expects the technical work setup to be accomplished efficiently and be ready to function smoothly (and quietly) during rehearsals and takes.

The **Director of Photography** (sometimes called Cinematographer) is expected (by the Director and Producer) to work closely and collaboratively with the Director in efficiently producing appropriate and effective visuals for the production. The DP expects to be supplied with the matériel to do the lighting and camera work required. The Cinematographer expects those who assist him or her to work together closely and collaboratively in order to efficiently and effectively perform their functions for the benefit of the production.

The other **Category Heads** are expected by the Producer to promptly provide budgeting input as needed and to run their respective department and its personnel efficiently and well. Each Category Head expects each person in the department to perform responsibilities and duties in a dedicated and professional manner.

Insofar as the camera category is concerned, the **Camera Operator** is expected by the Director and DP to consistently deliver appropriately framed and followed subject matter and to inform the Director forthwith of any anomalies regarding the framing or subject matter contained therein. The Camera Operator expects either to receive from the Director or Director of Photography explicit instructions regarding the desired framing, what elements to hold in frame and which subject to follow, or to determine and frame the subject matter in a logical manner. It is also the expectation of the Operator that the First Assistant Camera Operator accurately follow focus and input correct zoom lens sizing at all times during rehearsals and takes.

The **First Assistant Camera Operator** is expected by the DP to see that the appropriate film stock is properly threaded in the camera, the specified filter(s) placed in the lenticular system and that the designated T-stop is accurately set. The First Assistant expects to get input and feedback from the Camera Operator regarding the precise sizing of the zoom lens, the coordination of the zoom moves with the camera and dolly moves and whether or not there has been any soft focus during the rehearsal or take. The First Assistant expects the Second Assistant to assist in setting up the camera and in handling camera adjustments, when necessary, during a take.

The **Second Assistant Camera Operator** is expected by the First Assistant to have fresh film loads ready and to keep accurate Camera Reports, and is expected by the Camera Operator to present the slate, containing legibly entered information, to the camera in an appropriate manner. The Second Assistant expects the Loader to have an appropriate supply of film magazines loaded and ready to be used.

The **Loader** is expected by the DP to have an adequate supply of designated film stocks on hand and loaded in film magazines, ready for the requirements of the day's shooting. The Producer expects the Loader to be extremely careful in the handling—loading and downloading—of film stocks; the enhanced-valued exposed stock represents the negative costs of the production.

The **Dolly Grip** is expected by the Camera Operator to mark and make fully integrated dolly moves which are coordinated with the moves of the subject matter. The Dolly Grip expects to get constructive input and feedback from the Camera Operator regarding the timing of the dolly moves.

The **Still Photographer** is expected by the Producer to capture on film key moments of production performances and activity. The Still Photographer expects to have adequate cooperation, as necessary, from production management and the camera category to facilitate required coverage.

Summing Up. Since cinematic media productions are collaborative exercises, each production requires ongoing coordinated and interrelated efforts of numerous craft and artistic disciplines. Category Heads are the leaders of these crafts, and their Assistants are the members of each respective craft team. For this organization to work well, each Category Head must be aware of and serve the expectations of the overall leader—the Producer—and the expectations of the team leader—the Director; all production team members must also be aware of the expectations of their respective Category Head and strive to meet those expectations.

TEAMWORK

As we all know, the cinematic arts—film and video—are a combination, a composite, of the established arts, and so, are collaborative in nature and procedure. It takes many diversified and integrated skills to make a cinematic product. It requires every category of craft, raised to the level of art, thereby effectively affecting the emotions of the viewer, to make a top-quality, memorable product. This requires inspired and dedicated leadership, teamwork and performance by each and every category and craft, at the very highest practicable and professional levels.

From concept and development through pre-production, production and post-production, on into distribution and exhibition, the team concept applies. Each craft category has its team of players, preparing its work for integration into the production process, under the direction of a team leader, the Category Head .

Concept & Development. During the conceptual and developmental stages, the team and its leadership may be one person—the Producer. The Writer may come aboard during the developmental stage as a team member, under the supervision of the Producer. An administrative staff, including Associate Producers and Production Accountants, is assembled in preparation for . . .

Pre-production. Thereafter, normally once the script has been completed and approved by the Producer, then the Director as the integrator, the Production Designer for the look, and the Production Manager for the scheduling, logistics and budgeting, will be brought on by the Producer to begin the process of preparing for production. The Director of Photography, the Composer, and the Location Manager are brought in early on in order to give and take input regarding the upcoming production. These will be the leaders, the key players, during the production process. They in turn will each assemble their team of coworkers to begin their contribution to the production effort. Casting, selection of location sites, and hiring of production crew personnel will have taken place in preparation for . . .

Production. Nearly everything done during the previous stages, and everything that is done during the production process, will have been planned and done for presentation to the camera. The focus of production is on the camera and what takes place in front of it, within its view of acceptance. It is here that everything comes together. It is here that the work of many is captured by the camera, on film or tape. It is here, during the process of image capture, that the work of the camera team becomes the focus of attention.

Team Effort. It is during the production process that teamwork becomes essential. Time then is worth big money. The per hour cost of pre-production time may be only one-tenth the cost of production time, during which many more people and production elements are involved than in the earlier stages. So decisions made and work done prior to actual production time are critical to the economic viability of the project. It is well to keep in mind that what you do and how well **others** (those in a hiring capacity) think you do it will keep you and your team working.

Leadership. In order to attain optimum efficiency, it is necessary for the production team in each craft category to have, and to follow, a leader—a leader willing and able to lead; a leader thoroughly skilled in the particular specialized craft—who deserves and has earned the respect of his or her peers and teammates.

Leadership abilities include: A thorough knowledge of the craft; a consistent and highly skilled performance in that craft; an affinity for making decisions under pressure; equitable delegation of work among coworkers; recognizing, encouraging and complimenting top-quality work by the team and team members; an ability to work comfortably and collaboratively with team leaders in other categories; the ability to work efficiently under the leadership of the overall team leader—the **Director**.

In addition, in order to excel, it helps to acquire and develop some of the following qualities or traits: A clearly defined purpose or mission—in order to plan and do the best work possible under the constraints of time and budget; an ability to set, and focus on, goals—completing the work on time and within the budgeted amount; an appetite for challenges—enthusiastically tackling any of a diversity of projects; an understanding of the collaborative potency of consensus among one's teammates—being open to both input and feedback from the team and being prepared to be flexible and compliant when consensus points to a better result; an integral belief in the crafting and production process and in oneself as a contributing participant—knowing that you are in the one activity which, for you, is completely challenging, satisfying and fulfilling.

Team spirit. In order to do the best work, team members should demonstrate mutual respect for one another. This is something not gratuitously given. It is a status to be meritorially earned by demonstrating competent craftsmanship along with a shared feeling of genuine respect and camaraderie and of working together to consistently put out the very best work possible under often varying and difficult circumstances.

It is useful to be mindful of, and nourish, interpersonal relationships among members of one's category team and of those in other categories of work on the overall production team, particularly those with whom you have frequent contact. For camera, that would be: The Director, the First Assistant Director, the Key Grip, the Boom/Crane/Dolly Grips, the Boom Operator(s), the Script Supervisor, the Gaffer, the Key Grip, the Set Dresser, the Property Master, and, less frequently, makeup and wardrobe personnel.

Teamwork. Understanding the team ethic, working together in mutual respect and esteem, performing the responsibilities and duties of the craft with dedication and precision, giving the best effort to, and fully participating in, the project at hand, all this leads to worthwhile, lasting and valued experiences and relationships.

PROFESSIONAL CONDUCT

Since nearly everything that happens during a production is directly or indirectly done with the camera in mind, the camera becomes a focal point of attention. After all, the medium is *moving pictures*, and the camera (as well as the actors) can and does move, keeping the essential action within its framed proscenium, as it moves with the ebb and flow of the movement while recording sequential images of the action.

This attention means that the camera and the camera crew are under nearly constant scrutiny by production management, cast, stagehands and casual observers (or an audience, during multi-camera sitcoms).

It is important that the camera category functions smoothly and efficiently at all times. The camera(s) and crew(s) should be ready to record a take without undue delay. This means the operative camera crew must be on its collective toes: The Camera Operator, First and Second Assistant Camera Operators (and Dolly Grip) should be at their posts "ready to roll" with the camera—the slate ready, the lens and camera controls in hand (dolly prepared to move)—ready to go with **"ACTION!"** A fully coordinated ensemble effort by the camera contingent looks good to either a professional or casual observer.

Personal appearance is another pertinent aspect to consider—particularly when operating before an audience in a sitcom environment. An ungroomed appearance and soiled and/or tattered garb, while appropriate at a gritty/grimy location like Indian Dunes or the back lot, is hardly conducive to a positive image of professionalism when working ("**performing**") on a sitcom.

Arguments should be kept off the production floor at all costs. To "adjust" differences, take the dispute outside, away from the immediate production site and above all, in private, far from attentive third party eyes and ears. Production companies do not want trouble—or troublemakers—around to disrupt production processes.

The above considerations are called *job security.* Since employment opportunities fluctuate with the seasonal employment afforded by television programming, job security must be an area of continuing concern to us all.

RULES OF PROFESSIONAL CONDUCT
PROTOCOL & SET ETIQUETTE

During recent years there have been significant numbers of craftspeople coming into the major film and video production industry who have not had the opportunity of working with and learning from highly experienced film and video craftspeople. Consequently, many of these newcomers do not fully understand their responsibilities and duties toward either their craft or their co-workers. They have yet to learn and properly practice the fine arts of cooperation, communication and collaboration within the parameters ("ground rules") established and developed by their predecessors.

This has resulted in a number of problems for both the newcomer and those with whom the newcomer works. With that in mind, perhaps it is time to give renewed consideration to a few of the time-tested and valued practices developed by industry pioneers and which are observed by experienced production professionals to this day.

All that is done on a production set or on a location site is done, directly or indirectly, for presentation to the camera. Therefore, the camera area becomes the focus of activity and attention and it becomes incumbent upon all camera personnel to deport themselves properly and professionally at all times while on the job.

Making motion pictures, whether film or video, is a collaborative process shared in by cast, staff and crew. In order to keep the process as functional and efficient as possible, each crew member should understand and perform craft responsibilities and duties as effectively and efficiently as possible and have clearly in mind, and adhere to, the chain-of-command and the lines-of-communication as developed and practiced in this industry. This is the established set protocol.

There is no substitute for experience. The practices that have been established during the past exist and persist in the present for good reason—they have stood the test of time.

The following are well-established production practices and are presented as guidelines in order to aid film and video craftspeople function more efficiently, effectively, productively and safely during the collaborative process of film and video cinematic production. Call it set etiquette, if you will.

FIGURE 1
PRODUCTION TEAM
CAMERA CATEGORY—CHAIN-OF-COMMAND

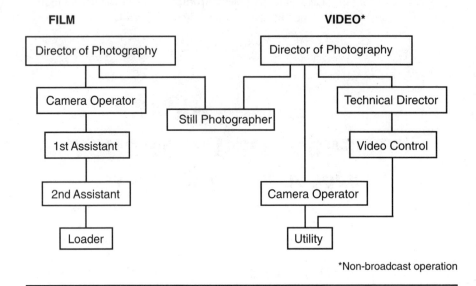

FILM

VIDEO*

*Non-broadcast operation

PRACTICES TO BE ENCOURAGED:

- Knowing and properly practicing one's craft responsibilities;
- Knowing to whom one is directly responsible and adhering to that relationship;
- Thoroughly knowing, understanding and performing one's craft duties in a professional manner;
- Keeping current on the latest equipment, accessories, expendables and production techniques;
- Assisting one's immediate superior to the greatest extent possible at all times;
- Helping one's crew associates in their duties in any way possible, when called upon;
- Always presenting oneself in a professional and considerate manner to crew, cast and staff;
- Being at one's assigned post, prepared to perform craft duties, at all times while at work, unless specifically excused;
- Dressing in attire appropriate to the type and location of the production;
- Maintaining a subdued talk/noise/behavior level on the set or shooting site;
- Having the camera equipment checked, assembled, adjusted and ready to roll at the earliest possible time for each setup;
- Immediately advising one's superior of any perceived technical omission or commission which may have occurred during production and which could have an adverse effect on the image-capture process;

- Immediately reporting any potential safety problem to one's category crew chief;
- Immediately calling one's category crew chief's attention to a possible staffing shortage or irregularity;
- Backing one's subordinates to the full extent during the production process;
- Helping subordinates achieve greater understanding and competence in their work;
- Giving credit where, when and to whom credit is due for superior job performance or other invaluable job contribution(s);
- Recognizing professional competence and showing mutual respect for other professionals on the production.

PRACTICES TO BE AVOIDED:

- Being habitually late in reporting for work;
- Appearing at work in an unkempt condition;
- Doing only enough to get by;
- Engaging in any activity while at work which might cause disruption of the production process;
- Utilizing company matériel for personal use, without permission;
- Leaving one's assigned post, the set, or location site without specific permission from one's immediate superior;
- Passing the buck—allowing or forcing a subordinate to take the blame for a miscue which in fact was one's own or a shared, error;
- Going over or around one's superior or superiors in matters relating to the responsibilities and duties of that (those) superior(s);
- Being openly argumentative with or hostile toward one's superior(s), subordinate(s) or co-workers;
- Using one's position to verbally abuse, or to make unreasonable (beyond normal specified duties) demands upon one's subordinate(s);
- Ingesting any substance which might impair the performance of one's responsibilities and duties or put one's co-workers and self at risk of physical injury or job termination.

Remember, following the *rules* (the established practices—how to get along with others and how to get things done efficiently—set protocol/etiquette) is the essential means of helping keep the production process on track and running smoothly—and safely. Following the rules and getting along with others are effective forms of job security.

PROFESSIONAL ATTITUDE

An inappropriate attitude has been the cause of many lost jobs and work days. Webster defines **attitude** as "1. Posture; position assumed or studied to serve a purpose. 2. Position or bearing as indicating action, feeling, or mood."

We will be considering the second of these two definitions ("position" and "bearing") whereby an attitude transmits to others, through action and/or body language, the way a person feels about his or her work and associates (peers, subordinates and superiors).

We are constantly projecting attitudes which others pick up on and which can be perceived by them as beneficial, neutral, or threatening. We each have an attitude toward our family, our friends, our associates and our work. If beneficial, the attitude can help insure job security; if perceived by higher authority in a negative way, the attitude may well work against the person and result in censure, dismissal, or not being hired in the first place.

When we hear of someone who "has an ***attitude***," we immediately understand that it carries a negative connotation and we may tend to want to separate ourselves from that individual. The so-called "attitude" is usually the result of insecurity on the part of the carrier. Lack of maturity, experience, knowledge and/or patience are usually the causes of a negative attitude. After all, we are part of a team, operating in the collaborative arena of film and/or video production and with all the constant technical, physical and emotional demands made upon us by our work, who needs anyone **with an attitude problem** adding to our concerns?

Among those actions which contribute to the perception of a person having a negative attitude are: Carelessness, absenteeism, tardiness, inattentiveness (requiring constant supervision), and/or being uncommunicative, too talkative, disruptive, argumentative, temperamental, uncooperative, undependable and/or disinterested— a loser's credentials.

We each project an attitude toward work, toward others, and toward life in general which is both personal, distinctive and, at times, variable. In our demanding business, it is essential to develop an attitude which is positive, unwavering and thoroughly professional—that is, that clearly and consistently communicates to others: A deep and abiding interest in one's work and in the skilled performance thereof; a genuine respect for the skills and contributions of one's associates; a craftsman's concern for the proper utilization and care of the tools of the trade; an artist's concern for a creative contribution to the production in process; that one's attention is focused on the production at hand and on one's specific contributory role in that production; a caring and sharing demeanor.

The professional attitude is not uncaring, selfish or inflexible. It allows space for humor and relaxation. After all, we are not, nor should we let ourselves become, automatons, all pressed out of the same mold; we are each a unique being. We should be able to thoroughly enjoy our work. And work well done should bring a sense of satisfaction, fulfillment and well-being.

Just as change is immutable, the attitude we bring to our workplace is continually growing and being modified, based on our daily experiences. We are the product, the sum total, of our lifelong experiences. Each of us has and expresses his or her own perspective on the various aspects of life and on a work ethic.

A thorough understanding of, and participation in, the picture-making process, and particularly, of one's classification responsibilities and duties, goes a long way toward providing the comfort and poise of knowing what one is doing. It's called production experience and, as has been said, **there's no substitute for that kind of experience**. We absorb, filter, then selectively combine and focus those experiences, as needed, from one job experience to another.

Each of us absorbs that experience at his/her own rate. Each of us has varying opportunities to experience and practice the methods and techniques devised by our predecessors and refined by ourselves, our contemporaries and colleagues. We find ourselves on a production with many others, contributing our skills in a cooperative, collaborative effort. Our attitude toward our work and toward our associates is a key to our job performance abilities and how that performance is perceived by others.

A positive and professional attitude and on-the-job competence are synonymous with job security. A person with this attribute shows total involvement with and interest in the job and the particular challenge at hand. He or she considers problems as challenges and approaches those challenges in a positive, get-it-done-right attitude.

A professional attitude is reflective of: A thorough knowledge of the tools of the trade; a comfortable competence in handling and applying those tools during job performance; a genuine respect and appreciation of the talents others bring to the job at hand; a caring vigilance for the safety and well-being of working associates; a free-flowing collaborative cooperation with other craftspeople to help achieve highly efficient and optimum results for the team effort.

A person with the professional attitude is a can-do personality, a person with poise who is stable, balanced and in harmony with him/herself, with no personal need to put others down or to claim the lion's share of credit for a job well done.

A thoroughly professional attitude and bearing is the reward for a substantial length of time of being: Observant, willing to learn, flexible, caring, respectful, sharing, cooperative, self-confident and modest.

ON ATTENDING INDUSTRY GATHERINGS

Never underestimate the power of appearance, of physically being there, where it's happening. Actors and salesmen know this all too well. Their very livelihood depends upon being among the right people, at the right place, at the right time, with the right appearance and pitch—a combination of dress, attitude, experience, knowledge and talent. This also applies to anyone working in the freelance field.

The **right people** are those in the business. They are our peers, subordinates and supervisors in the cinematic crafts. They can be those we know well and work with on a regular basis. And they can be those we have never had the opportunity to work with or for. We are there primarily to profit from the purpose of the gathering, whatever its nature and purpose. Equally important is to see and be seen by those with whom we can share work opportunities and experiences.

The **right place** can be a workshop, seminar, demonstration, screening, membership meeting, awards banquet, or other strictly social setting. The place provides the environment for meeting and mixing and sharing. People like to work with those they are comfortable being with; with those they like and whose talents, attitude, dedication and work they respect.

The **right time** is any time there is an event which will attract people having similar interests. It is usually a good idea to arrive well before the event's program is due to begin and to mix with others who are also early, and to do some relating with those who stick around after the event. Exchanging and comparing information on new equipment and techniques as well as job opportunities is a good use of this time together. Since scheduled gatherings are relatively infrequent and work schedules often conflict, it makes sense to seize the moment and make the most of each planned gathering—before, during and after the event. And it pays to participate in the event to the degree participation is provided for—panel discussions, question-and-answer sessions, assisting in demonstrations, helping set up and wrap.

The **right appearance** is crucial to making the most of the opportunities these meetings can afford. The initial impression of those who see or meet you for the first time is usually lasting. So present yourself to the best advantage when attending these gatherings. Dress and groom in a manner and style suitable to the type of meeting and the people you expect to interact with at that gathering.

It is well to attend these events with the **right attitude**. Attitude is an important aspect of appearance. It starts with a certain self-confident mindset which permeates the body. It translates into one's bearing which in turn communicates a certain feeling or mood to others. So a confident, upbeat attitude will provide more social mileage than a negative, uncertain, withdrawn or defeatist demeanor. A good way to achieve a positive attitude is to be totally prepared to follow up on any job opportunity at one's experiential level which may be offered.

With that in mind, it makes sense to dress in an acceptable style for the event and in a style that is also in current fashion. Fitting in is appropriate when togetherness is the keynote.

A gathering affords the opportunity of meeting at one place people with interests in common with whom you may not often, if ever, have worked. It enables public relations promotion to take place as well as an idea exchange with working colleagues and new acquaintances.

The purpose of a given gathering gives a pretty good idea of who will be in attendance and how that composition can be mutually beneficial. For example, a union-sponsored event will have union members in attendance; an industry-sponsored event will have people present who work in or run various key operations in the industry; a workshop will have people who are serious about learning more about that particular discipline.

There are union and societal membership meetings, committee meetings, seminars, workshops and screenings; industry-sponsored equipment demonstrations and expositions. Each type of meeting draws people with common interests and with particular reasons for attending that gathering.

Consider all gatherings collaborative events. The success of meeting, mixing and sharing with other attendees depends largely upon the amount and quality of give-and-take which takes place during each interchange. Come to gatherings prepared to give as well as receive useful quality-grade information and experiences.

Putting valued information and experience to use soon after the meeting can make the time spent at the gathering worthwhile. So look at gatherings as an opportunity to meet others and share and exchange information which can be helpful in furthering career opportunities for yourself—and for others.

NETWORKING—OR NOT WORKING

Ever since most of the major studios closed their Camera Departments, it has been necessary to contact individual production companies, each with its own show to produce, in order to advise the Producer, Production Manager, Production Coordinator, Director and/or Director of Photography of one's interest in and availability for their show(s).

Today there are more people vying for each available position than ever before (and this applies to productions both within and outside of union contractual jurisdiction). This search is a time-consuming but necessary process. Very often, by the time the contact is made, the show has been fully staffed. What's to be done?

Several steps should be considered: Keeping updated on the start date of productions, the name, address and phone number of the producing company, production site for the show, the name and phone number of the Producer, Unit Production Manager, Production Coordinator, Director and Director of Photography (or Category Head for your craft specialty).

This can be done by keeping current with the production schedule presented weekly in the trade magazines, or the Production Report in your union magazine or newsletter. Quite frequently this information appears after the fact; however, production companies, studio location and key personnel are listed. It is a good idea to develop and maintain a "book of names," with titles (or classifications) and phone numbers listed therein for ready reference when needed.

Features, TV Commercials and MOWs. Features, commercials and movies-of-the-week (as well as specials) can crank up at any time of the year. Bear in mind that single camera shows are "camera family" affairs where the Director of Photography, Camera Operator and Camera Assistants (as well as Dolly Grip, Gaffer and Key Grip) move as a body from picture to picture, occasionally inviting an extra Camera Operator and Camera Assistant aboard when needed.

TV Programming. The pilot shooting season generally goes from February through mid-May each year. By late May, the TV networks have announced which pilot series they intend to pick up and which series will continue. These series include episodic (single camera) and sitcoms (multiple cameras). Obviously, sitcoms offer more positions so far as camera and dolly work is concerned.

Notice of Availability. Even if all production positions are currently filled, it pays to inform (and periodically remind) the Production Manager and Production Coordinator of each show of your interest and availability for fill-in or replacement work in the event one of the regulars on the show is incapacitated or leaves the show for any reason.

Listing your special skills and availability with the union is a further means to expose yourself to work opportunities. Letting your fellow craftspeople know your availability and interest can help. Preparing and sending out updated résumés to potential employers is effective. Advertising in the trade publications can also pay off.

Importance of Follow-up. Following the initial contact (in person if possible and prior to the camera crew being set), it is important to send by mail, e-mail or fax, a current, updated résumé and a sample reel (if relevant to the prospective position). Follow that up by further phone and/or personal contact with the Production Company until all positions have been filled. In order to insure your prompt response to a job offer, it is well to consider acquiring a pager, a cellular phone, an answering machine or service, a personal fax machine and a computer with modem. Prospective employers expect a prompt response. Just one job can more than pay for the expense of these important communication tools.

Need for Networking. Even with all due diligence, it is difficult to get a handle on all that may be happening in production. It is therefore prudent to contact and keep in touch with others in order to **share** what information has been gleaned by each other. Sharing this information is essential, for when it is not shared, the network has lost its effectiveness. We have all had our experiences with those who don't do their homework and who continually call for information, but who seldom, if ever, return the favor. Each person in the unemployment boat should help row.

Networking means helping each other by sharing—giving and receiving—information, advice, and encouragement in not only the continuing freelance job hunt, but also regarding newly developed methods and techniques which will affect our job performance.

Networking can be facilitated not only through one-on-one contact in person, by phone, or at union meetings and gatherings, but also by means of seminars, workshops, courses of study, books and articles. The purpose is to stay informed and current.

The reality today is that Directors of Photography either select, set or approve each individual on their camera crews, so DPs are certainly people to get to know—soon and well.

The Camera Operator is also often in a position to recommend the First Assistant he or she would prefer working with, so if you're a First Assistant keep in touch with Camera Operators as well.

Today, there is ever-increasing competition for the available production positions from both union and non-union personnel. Add to that a disproportionate number of people in certain of the camera crafts and it becomes a real scramble for those limited available production positions.

Bear in mind that there is a considerable degree of insecurity at virtually all levels of the motion picture-making process. The saying, "You're no better than your last show," applies, in the minds of many in the business, to everyone (in all categories) associated with the show. Unfortunately stereotyped (so-called "safe" or "risk-free") thinking still prevails in the industry—at all levels.

Because of the many new people involved with creating and producing shows today, as well as new people entering the crafts, the preparation and presentation of a résumé makes good sense. A well-prepared résumé, along with letters of recommendation from Producers, Production Managers, Directors and Directors of Photography and/or a demo reel when applicable can go a long way toward securing the sought-after position.

Networking can help locate work opportunities, but the follow-up process of contacting and convincing the hiring source of your sincere interest and proven abilities are key to securing the assignment.

DEVELOPING AN EFFECTIVE NETWORK AND RÉSUMÉ

The well-known saying, *"Who you know gets you in. What you know keeps you there!"* indicates an important aspect of networking: Knowing someone who is in a position to hire, or someone who can recommend hiring, or someone who can tell you about or introduce you to either of these key people. Barring those possibilities, the acquisition of an agent and/or the preparation of a comprehensive résumé can be effective substitutes.

The Résumé. A résumé is an important tool to use in conjunction with networking. It gives the potential employer an opportunity to review the applicant's experience and to evaluate it with respect to the position being applied for.

The résumé should include: The show **title**, its **type** (feature, TV commercial, episodic, sitcom, etc), the **year**, the **Production Company**, the **Producer** and/or **Unit Production Manager**, the **Director**, the **Director of Photography** (for camera personnel) or **Category Head** (for other classifications). The "**credits**" may be arranged by type, but in any case should be listed chronologically in order to offer the reader a progressive perspective of your work.

Blocking the credits by type/genre has the advantage of providing the hiring source a convenient format for efficiently checking the experience of the applicant in any specific type of production, be it sitcoms, episodics, features, documentaries, commercials, sporting events or other genres.

The names of key personnel listed on your résumé are important in order to facilitate follow-up personal contact of these references by the hiring source in checking out you and your work. The importance of maintaining a good relationship with people in your reference network is of prime concern for anyone in the freelance job market.

To further convenience the hiring source, it can pay to extract and present on a separate sheet of paper just those credits which apply to the type of show which the hiring source is considering you for. Your complete and comprehensive résumé can serve as a backup reference for the total job experience perspective.

It is wise to update your résumé(s) regularly, adding credits as they occur. The "**Call Sheet**" contains most of the information needed for the résumé. This information can be easily extracted and placed on the résumé or in the computer for subsequent print-out.

An "Information Age" Résumé. Some enterprising individuals are currently presenting their job experience résumé in the form of a video tape (with sound) or CD-ROM disc presentation. This is certainly an effective attention-grabbing ploy. Others have placed their résumé(s) in trade magazine advertisements and/or on a web page in the internet for even wider exposure.

Developing and Maintaining a Network. As important as the résumé is in networking, the person-to-person touch is basic and on-going. Developing an effective network of contacts is a skill of secondary importance only to the skills required in the performance of one's job classification. This is especially the case when the job market is thin and jobs are few.

As we know, production volume oscillates during the year. The shooting season for **television programming** (where most of the work is for most of us) generally goes approximately eight to nine months, commencing during July or August and concluding in March or April with hiatuses during off-production weeks and holidays. **Sitcoms** (blocking and/or shooting two days per show per week) generally are three weeks on and one week off throughout the production season. **Episodics** shoot full time (five or six days per week per show) and may crank up a month or so before the sitcoms do and finish a month or so after the sitcom season ends. The principal **pilot season** begins after the first of the year and concludes by the middle of May (shooting one week per half-hour pilot).

Features, **MOWs**, **mini-series**, **specials**, **documentaries**, **industrials** and **commercials** may start any time of year. Each genre has its own pre-production and production time frame. In general, features are in the planning stages for a lengthy period of time. Major studios and independents usually have a schedule of projects listed for production. The television and cable networks also have scheduled MOWs, specials, episodics, sitcoms, game shows, sports events, news gathering and other programming fare well in advance of actual production. For industrial, documentary, commercial and music video (often shot on film) production, one must be in constant contact with companies specializing in these production genres.

Your network should be maintained and nurtured consistently year-round so that it will be effective when you need it to find and secure work for yourself or a friend. That window of opportunity is during pre-production, several weeks before production is to start. It is then that the phone calls should be made, the résumés and demo reels sent out and interview appointments set up.

Networks are a personal composition, composed of your fellow craftsmen and women holding classification in your category, in addition to Directors, Producers, Unit Production Managers and Production Coordinators with whom you have worked. Your most effective network is composed of those people with whom you have worked and who personally know you and your work, and those people whom you have helped get work and who have helped you get work.

A network, like any precision machinery, needs care and attention—the lubrication which keeps it functioning effectively. This nurturing maintenance includes fairly regular (preferably, social) contacts with your craft peers and hiring sources (i.e., DPs, Directors, Producers, Unit Production Managers, Production Coordinators, departmental Category Heads—and Production Secretaries). And whenever one of your brother or sister classification mates offers you a hot job lead when you need it, be sure to return the favor when he or she needs it.

Summing Up. Remember, a well-developed properly maintained and efficiently used network of contacts nets you work, provided you follow up and follow through.

ON MOVING UP

Many of us, at one time or another during our career, have moved up to a more advanced classification of work. Used to be, any union upgrade in classification came only after five years spent in classification. Some of us were moved up by edict of a Producer or Director with the collaborative approval of our immediate category superior and/or the Director of Photography which automatically assured ample work opportunity in the new classification. In recent years, others have decided for themselves when the time was right and made the move entirely on their own initiative (wangling the necessary signatory employer letter in order to satisfy union requirements) with no work guarantee.

The first process takes longer, but because of the experience factor generally offers a much more secure start in the new classification of work. Others higher in the production echelon have observed your performance in your previous work classification and having made a decision to move you up, are now rooting for you to succeed, thereby vindicating their judgment in the matter.

The alternative method puts one almost entirely on one's own—often before one is really ready for an upgrade and generally without work guarantees (or offers, for that matter). This requires actively and persistently seeking work, informing previous and prospective employers of one's new classification and hoping to get that first job in the new classification. Not a very comforting picture—a desired classification achieved, but no work to utilize it.

Of the two methods of reclassifying, the time-honored process of being moved up by the powers-that-be is far more preferable and productive than moving oneself up.

How does one get considered for upgrading? Most important is consistently performing one's classification responsibilities and duties in an efficient, responsible and exemplary fashion. Getting along well with one's category associates is nearly as important, for that is also an essential part of job performance. Demonstrating mutual respect, cooperation, loyalty, flexibility and a vital interest in and growing knowledge of the responsibilities and duties of the higher classification are elements that are considered in appraising a person for upgrading.

Producers have been heard to say that if an individual performs consistently well in his or her present classification that person would be a safe bet to perform well in a higher classification. Key to this is having worked in a given classification with/for the same Producer, Director and/or Director of Photography for an extended period of time. Working on a television series presents a favorable environment to work toward upgrading. Being a regular member of a Director of Photography's feature camera crew is another effective vehicle.

Learning is a continual growth process. One never knows it all. I feel that if I have not learned something each day that I am at work, I have not been paying attention to what's been going on.

Anyone who has been in this business any length of time knows that there is no substitute for experience; trial and error by experience is what counts. Observing how the individual crew members perform under all sorts of environmental conditions and pressures contributed to by the weather, the shooting schedule, and the varied personalities of those co-workers on the staff, cast and crew is of overriding importance in evaluating the progress of those crew people being considered for upgrading. For more lasting results, hasten slowly and build that solid experiential base.

Working at one's highest capability is perhaps the most important reason for moving up or being moved up. The tendency when moving up is to make the move too early and for the wrong reasons (more prestige, more control over people, more money, etc) before the experiential base has been solidly established.

For those interested in moving up, it would be well to consider the following:

- Perform your own craft responsibilities and duties at your very best capability at all times;
- Work with as many top craftspeople (holding the classification you aspire to) as possible, learning from their expertise—their trials and errors, and why they succeeded or failed as a result of each craft decision;
- Observe how highly rated craftspeople deal with coworkers—their superiors, peers and subordinates—the Producers, Directors, actors, Directors of photography and crew members;
- Listen carefully and heed the procedural instruction/advice given by superiors;
- Ask questions to clarify any instruction, procedure or technique that is not clear;
- Stay current with the latest advances in equipment, accessories, expendables and production techniques;
- Become knowledgeable about the specifics of various production types—features, specials, episodics, sitcoms, commercials, documentaries, industrials, educationals, etc.

- Then, after a reasonable length of time served in a classification, let people know that you want to be considered for upgrading.

Once a person has demonstrated a high degree of proficiency in his/her craftwork, that individual is often encouraged to extend his or her abilities into the responsibilities and duties of the next higher classification—i.e., Second Assistant Camera Operators are generally groomed for 1st Assistant work by setting up and working focus and zoom controls on an extra camera; a First Assistant Camera Operator is prepared for camera operation by being invited to operate on a take now and then (there is still no substitute for time on the geared head between setups when the camera is idle); a Camera Operator is given insert assignments and otherwise encouraged to profit from the lighting experience of the Director of Photography, sometimes being moved up to share a shooting assignment on the first or second unit.

There is a constant degree of attrition attributed to retirement, withdrawal, relocating, illness, injury or death. In addition, increase in production creates ample opportunity for upgrading. It is therefore important always to be prepared to work at one's highest capability and then, when the opportunity is presented, to perform the upgrade responsibilities and duties to the best of one's ability. Do this and the upgrading will take care of itself.

HANDLING TRANSITIONS

Among the most difficult, trying and challenging of times is during the period of transition: Into a new field of endeavor (school to production), from non-union to union, from video to film or film to video, to a higher classification (First Assistant Camera Operator to Camera Operator, or Operator to Director of·Photography) and from one type of production to another (single camera style to multiple-camera sitcoms). Most of us have gone through one or more of these transitions with varying signs of physical and emotional wear and tear. One thing was made clear: The better prepared we were for the change, the easier and more manageable the experience.

First-timers. For anyone coming into the field of motion picture production for the first time, either from some other occupation or from film school, the transition (or learning) period can be difficult to handle. The novice may have trouble determining the essentials of what is going on. If fortunate enough to have a mentor, the newcomer may learn to ask the right questions and be guided toward becoming competent in one of the production crafts.

There are well over 150 production classifications in the film and video crafts, each with its own set of responsibilities and duties, each with an important, if not integral, part to play in the collaborative production effort.

It is a good idea for first-timers to spend as much time as possible observing their craft in action during various types of production. Seek help from experienced personnel in the craft category of interest. More often than not, help is just a question away.

Watch, listen, absorb, and do. And in the doing, pay special attention to the details, and to the style in which the craftspeople practice and apply the details of their craft to their specialized work. Find your niche, then do your job at every opportunity and with your very best effort.

Non-union to Union. The move from non-union production work to that of union-organized work is another transition which can be troublesome. In non-union work, one often wears several hats while doing more than one job, some nearly simultaneously. This is often the result of flawed thinking on the part of the non-union producer who may have a low and very tight budget and has everyone working interminable hours at a flat rate, while eating on the run and catching sleep during short turn-arounds. Nevertheless, it is a learning place where heavy dues in kind are paid and craft experience is dearly bought.

On entering the union environment, especially that of the major studios, the transition may be dramatic. True, the practiced entrant may already know and perform his or her crafts quite well, but now, under union rules and the studio system, only **one** craft may be practiced at a time by an individual during a production. The union local by-laws allow a qualified individual only one working classification.

The potential problem for the new member is to limit him or herself to concentrating on and performing just those duties which apply to his or her assigned job function on that specific production. Get to know the particulars of the union basic agreement which was negotiated with the signatory producers. Whereas deals were made between and among non-union personnel by and with the non-union producers, the union is now the fronting entity for its production personnel in negotiating with producers. You are now free of having to continually negotiate for your wages and working conditions while attempting to perform your work. If a problem of contractual interpretation arises with management, step aside and have the union business representative handle the matter (with your input, of course). That is a basic union service and protection for freelance employees.

Video to Film/Film to Video. The transition from video to film and from film to video has been managed successfully by numerous individuals with a will to do so. Insofar as camera operation is concerned, the film camera, when it is mounted on a geared head, requires a high degree of hand-eye coordination, a sure and light touch, and getting used to having zoom sizing and focus position supplied by another individual and camera platform movement applied by yet another person.

The video camera, with two pan handles (one with a focus control and the other with a zoom control) and mounted on a mobile pedestal, is operated by one person who frames, pans, tilts, focuses, zooms and moves the camera ped and its riser as necessary. This requires considerable concentration, dexterity, eye-hand-feet (and sometimes knee) coordination and a sure and light touch.

As with most tools of the trade, concentrated practice time on the equipment can help make a competent Camera Operator comfortable with either a video or film camera.

Be aware that the chain-of-command is somewhat different for a video Camera Operator coming from network television operations. There, the Technical Director is crew chief. The Director and Associate Director are in direct communications with each Camera Operator, who "sells" shots to the Director visually via control booth monitors. In the major studio environment, however, whether film or video, the Director of Photography is the immediate head of all personnel in the camera category (and supervisorial head of production procedures done by electrical and grip category personnel). And unless the DP encourages anyone in the camera crew to originate direct communication with the Director, any communication should go through the Director of Photography.

To a Higher Classification. Upgrading to a higher classification is a transition which requires a good deal of preparation plus cooperation from the powers-that-be (peers, superiors, and higher authority). A thorough knowledge of the craft involved and smooth management of the politics required can make this transition smooth and relatively painless.

Episodic to Film Sitcom Style. Moving from single-camera episodics to multiple-camera sitcom production is probably more difficult for the **operative film camera crew (Camera Operator, First Assistant Camera Operator and Dolly Grip)** than the reverse simply because there are more things to be continually concerned with in the episodic filming procedures. In addition to operating the camera (framing, panning, tilting), the **Camera Operator** must make a series of long, continuous takes which require detailed notes on the subject matter to be held in frame at each stopping point, both during the take and during its multiple dolly moves. The **First Assistant Camera Operator** must also make detailed focus/sizing notations which reflect both the tape-measured distance from subject to camera and designated frame size for each stopping point during the take and the variable sizing which may be required during its several moves. The **Dolly Grip** makes a detailed list of notations regarding varied camera heights, actor moves which motivate dolly moves, and floor marks relating to the stopping points for the dolly chassis during the blocking of each scene.

The Camera Operator and Dolly Grip are on RF headset communication with the Technical Coordinator who feeds information to the Dolly Grip for each dolly move during each camera rehearsal and take. The Camera Operator must coordinate as necessary the efforts of the First Assistant and Dolly Grip in order to maintain a synchronized and harmonious flow of camera movement with actor movement.

Summing Up. Transitions need not be difficult to deal with. Having sufficient desire and perseverance in applying oneself to learning the craft, and understanding and adhering to the "rules" can help ease the way to a successful career repositioning.

KEEPING YOUR COOL

Every Camera Operator who has been in the business any length of time has a bag full of useful shortcuts to save either time or energy, to minimize emotional stress, and to give peace of mind during the often fitful production process. If one is prepared, informed and ready, then staying composed and poised becomes a breeze, even under sometimes challenging production conditions.

Relax. Chief among these aids is the ability to relax and stay loose while on the job. This doesn't mean goofing off, slowing down, or losing interest in what is going on. Quite the contrary. One can only stay relatively relaxed while on the job when he or she is completely aware of what is going on and what will be required in the application of one's skills to the production process—and then being prepared and able to adroitly apply that know-how to the production.

Stay Alert. This awareness is the key to using off-camera time to physically and mentally relax by visiting the craft service "bounty," socializing with co-workers (networking) and taking care of necessary phone business.

The First Assistant Director is the on-set expediter of the production, controls the production pace and determines work breaks during the production day. Check with the 1st AD when time away from the camera is required. Then, of course, let your Category Head know that you will be away from your post. Be aware of what is happening (and not happening) on the set and your needs can be met at no cost to the production process (or to yourself).

Know and Do Your Stuff. Thoroughly knowing and understanding job duties and responsibilities is basic. Being capable of skillfully and appropriately applying that knowledge on a day-to-day basis in the workplace, is the very basis for our being employed in the motion picture-making process in the first place. Keeping informed about new technological developments and taking (or making) opportunities to get hands-on experience with that technology can give us the assurance that we can adapt to whatever new system comes down the pike.

Know Your Co-Workers. It pays energy-saving dividends to invest time and attention to get to know your crew and other co-workers on a production. Short-term productions don't afford much opportunity to do this, but productions with longer shooting schedules do. Getting to know one's working associates removes another unknown from the energy-consuming worry bag. Developing mutual respect encourages cooperation, team effort and a more pleasant working environment.

Stay Flexible. Because the production process involves both technology (which doesn't always work) and people (who don't always get along), it may be best to keep expectations about both of these elements at a reasonable level. Nothing and no one works perfectly all the time. And that goes for each of us, individually and collectively.

Being patient with our tools, our colleagues and ourselves has the added benefit of reducing wasted energy on things and events often beyond our control anyway.

Ultimate Cool. Since we spend a major portion of our lives in the workplace, what helps determine our individual comfort level is how we feel about and deal with ourselves and our work—the people, technology and environment we experience—on a day by day basis. To the degree we can help make our workplace an arena of collaborative challenge and satisfaction, we can reach and maintain a level of fulfillment and poise which can help transform that workplace for everyone there. That's when expectations become **preferences**, problems become **challenges**, and the work and workplace become worthwhile experiences, not to be just tolerated, but rather to be thoroughly participated in and enjoyed.

THE UNION CONNECTION

As important as is the technical aspect of our work, which has been the subject matter of nearly every one of these columns since inception, this time around we will consider the collaborative part the union plays in the work we do.

How often do we consider, when we are operating on a production, the connection between what we do and how we got there? Of course, education, experience and luck play their part. But how often have we considered the part the union played, and plays, directly and indirectly, in what we do and where and under what working conditions we do our work?

For those of us who belong and understand its purpose, the union is of, by and for **us**. It certainly is not of, by and for **them**, them being those who "run" the union, or those outside our particular coterie of working associates.

We pretty much take for granted the wages and working conditions we experience when we work under a union signatory contract. Many of these were established when unions were formed by craftspeople who were tired of being exploited by uncaring, self-serving employers. A few of the essential changes brought about by union-leveraged negotiations were: The eight-hour day with time-and-a-half for the next four hours and golden (double) time for additional continuous working hours; appropriate staffing for productions; adequate turn-around for rest between work shifts; vacation and holiday pay; penalties for not calling meal breaks by the sixth hour of work; hazard pay; safety procedures to protect production personnel; screen credits; grievance procedure for settling employer-employee disputes; and, far from least, pension, and health and welfare benefits. The essence of the change in labor-management relations was that the principle of collective bargaining to determine wages and working rules was established between the parties and that process continues to this day.

And so, there comes a time in the working experience of every person employed in the cinematic media when the decision is made to either join or decline affiliation with a labor union.

Unless one grew up in a union-affiliated family environment, there might not be enough experience or information from which to make an informed decision. For those without that background, the choice, when the time comes, can often be a dilemma of major magnitude. The questions: "What is the union all about?" and "What can the union do for me?" then come to mind.

For those without that union-related advantage, those just coming out of film or video school, those who have been working in the non-union field of film and video production, the need to join a union often comes after numerous negative experiences—working virtually unlimited hours at flat rates at well under union minimums; with or without monetary deferments and/or points of participation in any profits; not being fed on time, if at all; getting enough rest time between shifts and functioning under marginally safe or outright hazardous conditions—conditions which are not negotiable on an individual basis, conditions which a union would not tolerate for its members to experience.

For example, today, a person graduating from film/video school and intending to pursue a career in a below-the-line technical craft has nowhere to go but into the non-union job market, or start a production company. Not that these options are bad. Since there is no substitute for experience, the early objective of every neophyte should be to gain that experience as soon and as extensively as possible. Non-union production work of all generic types can satisfy that need. Such work can usually be found in the industrial sector, educational and religious film/tape production companies and organizations, music-video enterprises, TV commercial companies, cable networks and the low-low-budget feature market.

All current union members came from one or the other of these backgrounds. Each had to make the decision at some point in time whether or not to join the union. Some had always wanted to be union members because they had learned that in unity there is strength and that the union would represent them in disputes with management and negotiate their wage rates and working conditions, thereby freeing them from that chore and permitting them to focus their energy and talent on making a living while practicing and honing their craft skills.

They know now, as they knew then, that the union represents to producers an extensive and reliable labor pool and that the union represents to its members employment opportunities with a substantial list of signatory companies. That translates into more work with quality product over an extensive time period, but only so long as the superior quality of the craftwork by union personnel is maintained.

Obviously, consistent and superior quality of work is one of the principal attractions for producers of quality product. These producers will go where they have to, foreign or domestic, paying what they have to and dealing with whomever they have to—union or non-union—to assure this result. Because of the extensive quality control and training, both on the job and off, union personnel invariably assure this result.

Budget control is another prime concern of producers, particularly when the product has a tight and/or low-budget. The bottom line here is limited dollars and cutting every corner possible. Here is where the opportunity for the non-union film or video technician to work often presents itself along with the inevitable economic, technical and logistical problems attendant therewith.

The maxim "In unity there is strength" is particularly appropriate when applied to unions. Organizing and collective bargaining with employers in order to establish fair wage rates and working conditions in the best interests of the membership are central to the purpose of a union. And this collective bargaining process requires the interest and support of an informed and caring membership. The responsibility of the union leadership is to be alert to economic, social, political and technical developments which can affect union labor and to keep the membership currently informed while being receptive to any input from the membership. The responsibility of the membership is to be informed and give informed feedback and input, direction and support to the efforts of the union leadership.

As we muse over the collaborative union connection to our work, we should be cognizant of what the union has already done to help make our jobs secure, safe, well-paying and properly staffed. It is in our best interests to participate in union affairs in order to help maintain the benefits we now enjoy. A secure union experience makes it possible to concentrate fully on sharpening and applying the cinematic skills and to go with the flow of the job at hand. Knowing the union is strong and effective and helping to keep it that way is one of the most effective forms of job security ever devised.

EMPLOYEE OR INDEPENDENT CONTRACTOR?

Sometime during your career you may be propositioned to accept employment on a picture project as an "independent contractor," which generally bottom-lines as a flat rate, no deductions (for Worker's Compensation Insurance, Social Security and other fringe benefits) and often no medical coverage. In accepting such an offer, unless you are acting as a consultant, or unless you will deliver a self-supervised finished product to the other party (you having supplied the matériel, work place and work force), you enter into a charade which benefits neither you nor the employer and can, in fact, be detrimental to both parties, particularly if you are injured on the job.

Employer-employee criteria have been established by several governmental agencies, including the Internal Revenue Service, the National Labor Relations Board, the California Labor Commission, the California Board of Equalization and the Worker's Compensation Commission. No matter what the agreement may be between you and the other (hiring/contracting) party, when one or more of the following conditions prevail, **you are an employee**:

1. If you work under the supervision and direction of the other party (the owner, entrepreneur or producer) or his/her representative (i.e., the Director, Production Manager, Assistant Director, Category Head);

2. If you are told **what** to photograph, **where** it is to be photographed and/or **how** it is to be photographed—i.e., where the camera is to be placed, whether and how it is to be moved during the shot; what film stock, T-stop and/or filter pack to be used; when to roll and when to cut the camera;

3. If you are supplied the matériel (camera equipment and raw stock) with which, and/or work place in which, to do your work;

4. If you are told where and when to report for work;

5. If you are transported at the expense of the other party;

6. If you need permission to leave the work site;

7. If you are told when and for how long to break to eat and when to wrap;

8. If you can be discharged at any time;

9. If there is a history of a long-term, continuing relationship, with services performed relatively frequently;

10. If written or oral reports are required;

11. If you are required to fill out and/or punch a time card in and out; and

12. If the other party causes deductions to be withheld from your paycheck(s).

In summary, if you are "subject to the will and control of [the other party] **both** as to what shall be done and how it shall be done," irrespective of whether or not you have the **legal right** to control both the method and result of your services, **you are an employee**.

"If an employer-employee relationship exists, describing the relationship as anything other than that of employer and employee is immaterial . . . ." (Quotes are from the **IRS Employers Tax Guide**.)

So, before entering into any working arrangement that is not clearly that of employer-employee, consult with an attorney who specializes in labor law to give you guidance in the matter.

PRODUCTION PRACTICES

Professionally executed production practices are what keep a craftsperson employed—whether a freelancer or staffer. Production management is constantly looking for competent, reliable self-starters with a cooperative and collaborative attitude, who keep abreast of innovations in production procedures, and who are also highly skilled and congenial.

Being well aware of the chain-of-command (to whom you are directly responsible) and the lines-of-communication (with whom you need to keep communication channels open) and adhering to that reality will go a long way to keeping you employed.

Knowing what you are responsible for, then delivering it, is absolutely essential to assure an adequate performance level. In order to deliver, it is imperative to understand all the duties and protocol involved in achieving and delivering work that is not only acceptable but skillfully crafted.

SAFETY FIRST AND FOREMOST

Personal safety, for ourselves and our coworkers, is something we tend to take for granted. After all, we are working with other caring, careful and skilled colleagues who take pride in their work, ever alert to minimize risk factors. Nevertheless, it pays to be aware of situations during which mishaps and accidents can and do occur.

As film and video craftspeople, we practice our craft in the studio, under hanging lamps and light control devices, and on location, in various weather conditions, on varying terrain, domestically and in foreign lands.

We photograph Special Effects, Stunts and vehicular run-bys from exposed positions or from various mobile platforms on land, sea and air.

We operate at our highest efficiency, within the constraints of budget, shooting schedule and logistics, in order to help make a production successful, with as much quality and care as we can contribute.

We, more often than not, concentrate on crafting our shots to such an extent that we become oblivious of potential danger to our persons during those most vulnerable moments while the take is in progress.

While looking through the reflex viewfinder, during the effort to keep the action properly placed in frame, we tend to lose our sense of proximity to danger, because the lens may distort perspective, distances and relative approach velocity of the subject matter we happen to be shooting.

We become candidates for danger under any of the above conditions and must take certain steps to protect ourselves and our colleagues on the staff, cast and crew from potential harm.

In the Studio. Much of our work is done in the production studio and on the studio lot. In the studio, heavy lamps and light control devices are hanging overhead, clamped to sets, greenbeds and/or pipe grids, beneath which cast and crew perform their duties without benefit of hard hats. Nails, debris and other solid material frequently fall from the greenbeds to the stage floor. Lamps and light control devices have come loose and/or been dropped, hitting the deck and sometimes falling on unaware company personnel.

REMEDY: Lamps and light control devices should not be installed when anyone is on the floor immediately below. At the time lamps and control devices are installed, safety lines should be securely attached to each installed item overhead in order to restrain those items from falling and injuring someone.

On Location. Location shooting brings a number of safety concerns to bear. Varying topography, terrain and wind conditions require care in placing and securing light and grip stands to prevent their falling over and injuring personnel.

Unfamiliar surroundings, with its flora and fauna, can result in physical danger to those working in that environment. Poisonous plants and insects, dangerous animals, hostile natives and treacherous terrain can be serious concerns during location shoots in certain countries.

REMEDY: Have adequate operating personnel setting up and securing light, grip and reflector stands, particularly on steep terrain and during windy weather. Wear clothing appropriate to the climate and topography; be alert and follow the guidance of a qualified person who is well acquainted with the culture, the indigenous peoples, the terrain, and the weather patterns for the area.

Special Effects, Stunts and Run-bys. Shooting Special Effects, Stunts and run-bys requires particular attention and care on the part of all personnel involved throughout every moment of the shoot from preparation and rehearsal up to and including the actual take.

Special Effects include explosives, wire gags, firearms, water and smoke effects. Each kind of effects work requires a thorough briefing of all concerned, and selection of safe camera positions by the Key Special Effects Technician, followed by a rehearsal or test shot, **and then without any modifications,** the real thing.

Stunts include falls, fights, vehicular manipulation and/or mayhem and battle scenes. Again, careful selection of safe camera positions, a thorough briefing of all participants and a rehearsal prior to the take tends to minimize guess work and maximize safety.

Run-bys include passes by autos, boats, airplanes, animals, skiers and cyclists, and often require the camera crew to be in close proximity to the action as it passes by at high speed. Should anything go amiss, the camera position stands a fair chance of being wiped out.

REMEDY: First, thoroughly understand the elements of the effect(s) or stunt(s). Then, if it is potentially dangerous or unsafe, insist that a remotely controlled camera be used to frame and follow the action. The control mechanism, the Camera Operator and Assistant can be placed a safe distance from any explosions, stunt crashes and run-bys, thereby placing only the camera in harm's way.

Mobile Camera Platforms. Mobile Camera Platforms include dollies, cranes, cherry-pickers, forklifts, insert cars and trailers, boats, submersibles and aircraft. Riding a mobile platform, with one eye in the viewfinder, while concentrating on getting the shot, puts one at risk.

REMEDY: With careful and thorough briefing and preparation, the potential for injury can be minimized. Strapping oneself to the mobile platform is always a good idea. Seeing that guard rails are installed on the camera car, or posts, rails and/or cable restraints around the perimeter of the flatbed trailer, are good preventive procedures.

Budget, Shooting Schedule, and Logistics. You might not think these three items could present potential for injury, but they can, and do. A tight budget may restrict the size and expertise of the technical crew as well as the type and quantity of equipment needed on the production. For example, you may be working with inexperienced people and/or there may not be money for a remotely controlled camera setup.

A tight shooting schedule can also raise the potential for injury, by requiring undue haste in setting up and getting the shot done within a minimal time frame.

Logistics can also require an extra measure of care and attention to the details of moving crew and equipment from one location site to another, off-loading and on-loading, time after time. The more moves, the faster the moves, the greater the potential for injury.

REMEDY: Compensate for tight budgets and shooting schedules and multiple logistical moves, by planning setups well in advance to accommodate the shortages in personnel and matériel and to help make the many moves go as safely and smoothly as possible. Be particularly aware of inexperienced and/or fatigued crew personnel. They can contribute to a potentially hazardous event.

Summary. "Better safe than sorry," as the maxim goes. And it's particularly true in the work we do. We are under various pressures to get the work out. Often we are not as aware as we should be of the potential for physical harm which surrounds our work at various times.

If we want to continue in this very demanding business, we must always have our antenna out and focused on potential hazardous situations. We must listen and understand the parameters of every potentially hazardous operational setup, and if we do not feel secure in manning the proposed camera position, we must let the powers-that-be know and find a solution which will assure the safety of all concerned.

We must not let the possibility of losing a job offset the potential of risking life or limb. We owe our family, our friends, our coworkers and ourselves an obligation to practice safety at all times.

CHECK & DOUBLE-CHECK

If ever there was an activity which requires a mix of technical detail and a functional, if not creative, application of technique it is our vocation—the moving-image-making, image-capturing process, whether on film or video tape.

During Pre-Production. Not all of this myriad detail is going on behind the camera. Much of it is taking place in front of the camera. Even *before* the camera finally rolls film, considerable image-enhancing detailing has gone into all aspects of the production project: The script; the selection of key creative personnel (Producer, Writer, Director, Production Designer, Director of Photography and cast); creation and updating of the production plan; selection of key technical personnel (Category Heads and their Assistants).

The purpose of this effort is to carefully build a combination of elements which will orchestrate into cost-effective and emotionally affective audience programming. This takes considerable creation of, and attention to, details. In fact, on a quality product, it may be said that the details have details (and then some!).

Details, large and small, comprise all items to be photographed (settings, set dressing, props, costumes), mode of display of the items, the grooming and blocking of the actors, the lighting, exposure and camera/dolly/lens work. For example: Each setting contains numerous component details (walls, windows, doors, decoration, dressings, texture, coloring, etc); each costume has its distinct material, color, and accessories; each dressed set has its combination of distinctive items, selectively placed on or about the setting; each actor is appropriately and consistently groomed for each take of the scene in process; and the lighting and camera procedures are duly set and consistently executed.

It is up to the Art Director and Assistants to check for the inclusion and proper execution of planned details (set construction and set dressing) before photography takes place. It is the responsibility of the Costume Designer and Costume Supervisor to make certain that the appropriate costume, with all its accessories properly placed, is on the assigned actor's person. The Director of Photography is responsible for the placement of lighting units, the control of the direction, quantity, intensity and quality of the overall lighting, and setting camera movement, lens configuration and filtration, and exposure. Again, each step in each categorical process requires close attention to detail by all those involved.

During Production. It often falls to the Camera Operator to have set dressing items reset and/or actor positions adjusted for compositional purposes, noticing that hairdressing and makeup may need touching up before the camera rolls film. During the take, the Camera Operator must constantly be aware that camera, lens and dolly moves are coordinated with the action being framed and followed. He or she is also expected to have instant recall of the position of every element in frame at any given moment during a take, to be able to cite when and for how long the mic or its shadow dipped into frame, when focus buzzed, when and who looked into the lens, which actor was moving/looking left or right at any given time.

Of course, it is the prime responsibility of the Script Supervisor to keep track of all this and more: actor business, positions and facings; makeup, hairdressing, wardrobe and hand prop appearance (and condition by the end of each take—liquid levels in glasses and ash length of cigarettes); what was moved, and where; the focal length of the taking lens; actors or objects included in frame, and how tightly framed; dropped or added dialogue; scenes shot, and yet to be shot; wild lines recorded, or to be recorded; etc, ad infinitum (nearly).

During Post-Production. All this attention to the quality and consistency of detail, augmented by check and double-check procedures by all craft personnel, continues and culminates with the work of the Picture Editor in the editing bay. The Editor, mindful of the content of each shot and post-recorded element, selects and juxtaposes the shots and ancillary elements into logical, meaningful and rhythmic arrangements to best present the material for its optimum affect on an audience.

Summing Up. At each step of the production process—pre-production, production and post-production; conception, execution, photography and editing—details must be checked and double-checked for accuracy, consistency and appropriateness. Attention to detail is an essential part of our job. It is what we are trained, paid for and expected to do. It is our attention to this check and double-check detailing procedure that helps keep the camera category consistently delivering the good stuff. It is this attention to detail by *everyone* in *every craft* involved, from beginning to end of the moving-image-making process, that can help transform a good project into a great one.

PERILS & PITFALLS

There are many more ways to spoil a shot than there are to make it a thing of beauty. Even though there are several people intimately involved in making the shot, it still falls to the judgment of the Camera Operator to say, immediately upon completion, whether or not the take appeared acceptable (insofar as framing, focus, and coordination of lens sizing and camera moves with the action are concerned). Even the video assist, monitored by the Director and Producers, does not show soft focus, or even always reliable framing (and as for color consistency—FORGET IT!).

The resolution of the video floor monitor is much less than that of film, and if the monitor is not properly adjusted, the framing and color can be significantly askew or distorted. It is the image appearing on the ground glass in the viewfinder which displays the true quality of the captured image (assuming there have been no internal mechanical or exposure problems). It is this image which the Camera Operator sees as it is being recorded.

The responsibilities of the Camera Operator go beyond the technical duties he or she is expected to perform. How to manage interpersonal relationships with superiors, peers and subordinates is not written in the job description, but is essential to achieving optimal job performance and the job security that goes with it. It is especially important to keep the operating camera crew working as a team, supporting and protecting each other as they perform their job functions.

That said, what are some of the perils and pitfalls which await the otherwise careful but vulnerable Camera Operator? And when, where and under what circumstances are they most likely to occur?

Potential Problems. A problem occurs when there is an error of commission or omission, or a failure to function, or assuming functions outside of one's classification, and/or a misunderstanding. There are plenty of potential problems lurking about, ready to ensnare the camera crew. These problems can be either internally or externally caused, affecting those both in and outside of the camera crew.

Internal problems are those which occur among members of and within the confines of the camera crew. External problems are those which originate with and/or affect those apart from the camera crew. Internal problems can be handled discreetly within the camera group. External problems which affect or involve other crafts can go beyond the possibility of discreet control or containment.

Lack of technical knowledge on the part of Directors, Producers, Unit Production Managers and Technical Coordinators can create problems for members of the camera crew. Examples, directing blame at the Camera Operator and/or Assistant Camera Operator, would include: Not knowing that performers are missing marks, thereby blocking other performers or resulting in incorrect or unplanned sizing; a performer swaying from side to side in closeups, requiring corrective panning action ("fishing") to keep the actor in frame; seated performers rising too abruptly; not getting adequate rehearsal time to perfect complex moves. Continuing and un-resolved problems, either technical or personal, can result in job termination of those in subordinate positions among technical craft personnel.

REMEDY: Neither create, nor contribute to, any problem. Make the Director of Photography aware of any problem that does surface. As Category Head, one of the DP's prime responsibilities is personnel management—protecting and supporting the camera crew.

Personality conflict, one of the most common problems, can be internal or external in nature. It can take the form of being too talkative, too argumentative, too uncommunicative, or inarticulate, uncooperative, insubordinate or disruptive. These problems can also lead to ongoing friction and can undermine job performance, resulting in job termination and lasting enmity.

REMEDY: Keep your cool, show respect for other craftspeople, allow everyone their space, or leave the production.

Lack of experience sets the stage for many potential internal and external problems. Errors in execution—those of commission or omission—are among the most common glitches, followed by assuming and performing duties normally assigned to other categories and classifications.

REMEDY: Know your job and its responsibilities and duties, perform them consistently well, and stay within your job parameters.

Assembling, setting up and checking the camera and its accessories are critical to achieving reliable image capture. An internally dirty, damaged or faulty camera or film magazines; a principal lens missing, damaged or out of alignment; an incomplete or damaged set of filters; a malfunctioning control head; faulty batteries: any one of these can result in missed or unusable shots.

REMEDY: Make certain all camera equipment ordered is accounted for, compatible, and in reliable working condition **before** rolling film.

The time it takes in **setting up a shot** is often of significant importance when working on a tight shooting schedule, such as episodics and movies-of-the-week. Placing the camera, planning and rehearsing moves, take expertise, efficiency and Teamwork. When this collaboration fails or falters, it reflects directly upon members of the camera crew.

REMEDY: Stay alert, follow directions, anticipate when appropriate, and execute flawlessly and efficiently.

Camera settings, accurately set and/or ridden, are critical in maintaining optimum image capture quality. A mistake by any member of the camera crew can reflect negatively on the entire camera crew. Errors in exposure, focus, sizing, frame rate or shutter angle, and also mistakes in loading, threading, framing or moving the camera can reflect negatively on the operative camera crew.

Uncorrected/unreshot takes with problems reflect on the work we do and, if not caught during dailies screenings are most likely to surface during post-production processes. Errors in exposure, focus, sizing and framing are among the most common. It is during post-production examination that these anomalies are noticed, either by the Director of Photography, Colorist or Post Production Supervisor during telecine transfer, or by the Director or Producer while screening the printed footage, or by the

Editor while assembling and editing the produced material.

REMEDY: Check and double-check film threading and drive movement in addition to all lens and camera settings; pull and inspect the film gate for residue in the aperture following each print take and correct any camera movement miscues during the rehearsals. Help make each take a moment of perfection.

The Memory Factor. It is well to keep in mind that not all we do as Camera Operators has to do with our dexterity with the geared head, pan head or remote controls. What we see in frame during the take is at least as important. We must be ready immediately following each take, at the Director's request to recount our exact framing (what was included in frame) at any given moment during the take. Even with video assist, we see it first and we see it most clearly and accurately through the reflex viewfinder. Our visual comprehension is relied upon and often called upon to help determine whether or not certain elements in frame were properly positioned at critical moments during the take. For example: Was the belt buckle in frame at any time? Did the performer look at the camera at any time? Did the performer have the prop in her left or right hand during the exchange? If we fail repeatedly to accurately recall key elements in frame during takes, we are falling short of our responsibilities as Camera Operators.

REMEDY: During setup and rehearsal time, study the performers, their action, gestures, costumes, makeup, hairdressing and hand props, as well as foreground and background props and set dressing, in addition to the lighting illuminating the set and players, being ever aware of the mic, its boom and their shadows. Should anything go amiss with any of the foregoing elements, the Camera Operator should be prepared to recall the take in detail.

Personal Relations. As we are well aware, filmmaking is a highly collaborative medium. It is well to keep in mind that: Many people with various specialized skills and of various personality types are involved in the production process; each is protective of his or her turf—role, responsibilities and duties—and does not want anyone else to encroach thereon. It is where the seams meet in job functions that misunderstandings and friction can result.

By not being aware of the job functions of others both within and outside one's category, their job performance could be inadvertently interfered with, resulting in confrontation, hard feelings and delay. It is equally stressful when others exceed the bounds of their job parameters and encroach on the job functions of others. Respecting the role each production team member plays, and knowing **what** each member is responsible **for** and **who** each member is responsible **to**, along with a pretty complete idea of what their specialized duties may be, will go a long way toward avoiding inadvertent conflict through misunderstandings. It is when the line is crossed, advertently or inadvertently, that trouble occurs.

When this "job blur" happens, it is well to determine promptly the intent of the interloper. The act could have been entirely accidental or done without realizing that the line has been crossed. There are a lot of new kids on the block coming into the business who have been used to wearing many hats on student, non-union and low-low or no budget productions on which job blur is the rule rather than the exception. Recognizing the need to cooperate in executing job duties, several of the crafts have reached some agreement on the need to cross over and help each other at certain times during production. This is particularly so when heavy property or set dressing items need moving.

On the other hand, there are those who would like to write or re-write their own job description to suit their own purposes. This can result in serious disruption of the production process. When one allows this to happen by not protecting one's own job description, then the line-crosser has prevailed and one's job role has been compromised.

REMEDY: As new equipment and techniques are introduced to the business, the staffing requirements need to be fully described and adhered to in order to assure that the additional personnel will fit into an efficient collaborative mode with a minimum likelihood of problems.

The Deal Memo. The deal memo is an important document which states the understanding reached between the employee and management with regard to the wage rate; hourly, daily and/or weekly guarantees; hiatus carries; box rentals; screen credit; and the like. Carefully make the agreement, then stick by it. A misunderstanding here can result in serious problems. The deal memo should not abrogate any provision of the union basic agreement with the signatory company. A deal memo with a non-union Producer may require legal action to achieve an equitable solution.

REMEDY: Think out the conditions you desire prior to drafting or signing the deal memo. Have the deal memo checked by a union representative to assure conformance with the basic agreement or, if the work is non-union, have the memo checked by an attorney.

Negotiating Hazard Pay. Hazard pay, a potential external problem, is a negotiable item. Whether or not a position, participation or environment places one in jeopardy of injury or death is quite subjective. A camera position in proximity to a stunt or Special Effects may be considered hazardous to the people manning the camera, but considered safe by the UPM negotiating the deal. In general, each and every run-by, stunt or special effect which places the camera position in close proximity to the action, or places the camera on rigs other than a camera crane above 20´ from the ground, requires a Hazard Pay adjustment for each take. Knowledgeable Camera Operators required to ride with the stunt ask for and get the pay rate the Stunt Driver is receiving. With the remotely controlled, radio-activated camera heads available, there is seldom an absolute need to place camera personnel in harm's way to get a shot.

REMEDY: Refuse to man a camera in potentially unsafe conditions. Confer with your Director of Photography and/or call for union intervention, if necessary.

Protecting the Camera Crew. It must be remembered, the camera becomes the center of activity and attention during the filming process. By focusing on job responsibilities and duties during each take, and by working cooperatively and collaboratively as a team, the camera crew can protect its personnel and its interests while reducing tension and potential internal and external conflict.

Every Camera Operator demonstrates a certain level of skill based on practical experience, technical knowledge, physical and mental dexterity and handling interpersonal relationships. Every Camera Operator, serious about the craft, makes a point of knowing where his or her strengths and weaknesses lie and makes a continuing effort to correct deficiencies while sharpening and maintaining the reliable skills.

Not Knowing One's Skill Limitations. As Camera Operators we are (or ought to be) in a continual learning mode. Our skills need continual sharpening, and that means practice, practice, practice, not only on the job but on our own time. Knowing which skills to work on and then working on them is the key to progress and success. The non-caring alternative can put one on the road to ruin in the present-day highly competitive environment.

Included in our job skills are the non-technical aspects—following instructions, adhering to the chain-of-command and interpersonal on-the-job relationships—and the technical functions of framing and following the action. Lack of attention to any of these areas of responsibility can be job threatening.

Each of us is at a different level on the learning tree. Some of us are good with the friction head. Others are whizzes with the geared head or remote controls or handheld shots. Some of us favor feature work; others, television programming, TV commercials or documentaries. Often the choice of which productions to take and which tools to use is ours to make.

Employers are interested in the skill and dependability of their employees. This skill level evaluation is made on a continuing basis by those who employ, as well as by superiors, peers and subordinates. The peril is in not understanding the importance of always "putting the best foot forward" when it comes down to job performance.

REMEDY: It is well to be prepared to function with confidence on a variety of productions with a variety of techniques so that opportunities will not be lost. However, it is better to turn down a job than jeopardize a production and future employment by unskilled performance. There is no substitute for experience. There are no shortcuts to excellence.

Violating the Collaborative Process. Situation comedy is the production genre which requires multiple cameras to work collaboratively in choreographed effort in order to capture the action on film or tape. In this form, both lighting and camera positioning are procedures frequently flawed by the necessity for compromise. Nonetheless, now and then, "the territorial animal" in us raises its fur to protect its camera position (even though the angle could be maintained by readjusting the dolly to one side or by moving back and taking more on the lens), resulting in less than optimal shot angles for the other camera(s). This sort of non-cooperative, thoughtless and ego-driven behavior is not tolerated by knowledgeable Directors, Producers or Directors of Photography.

REMEDY: In order to avoid or minimize this "territorial problem" on multiple-camera sitcoms, the two master cameras which occupy and move in the central portion of the camera floor should be positioned far enough back from the downstage line to afford the wing cameras sufficient space to get assigned closeups and cross-master shots. The two wing cameras should stay outside the downstage wings of the set, making their shots with the long end of the lens, in order to allow the master cameras room to move in order to hold unobstructed wide angle shots of the moving action. When positioning conflict occurs, consult the Director and/or Director of Photography for guidance in resolving the problem.

Lack of Physical and Mental Conditioning. Staying physically and mentally fit and alert is essential for the requirements of camera operation. Operating a film or video camera places sometimes severe demands on both the physique and the mind. Physical conditioning and mental preparation are important. Durability and concentration are essential. The Camera Operator is expected to position him/herself to be able to effectively operate, frame and capture any planned set of images which present themselves to his or her camera. The bodily position may be contorted, compressed and contrived; weather conditions may be hot and humid or cold and clammy; the Operator may have to maintain the position for an inordinate length of time. In these circumstances, only a well-conditioned body and mind can be expected to prevail. Production executives expect the Camera Operator to make the assigned shot on each take, but especially on a one-time opportunity, such as during a stunt or a set-destruction scene. There is no substitute for concentrated attention on the many details of the job at hand. Should the body or mind fail to deliver the shot, another body/mind will be found who can consistently deliver the desired results.

REMEDY: A wholesome and well-balanced diet along with a good exercise regimen will go a long way to assuring proper physical conditioning. Meditation and visualization can help clear the mental cobwebs and encourage non-stressful concentration. A number of studies have shown that visualized practice is as effective as actual physical practice when it comes to improving skill levels. Finally, rest and relaxation are necessary for giving the body/mind the time to recover, recharge, file and retain the learning experience.

Operating Under Pressure. Time is not only money but is of the essence during production procedures. You may be waiting while other crafts adjust the lighting and prepare the set dressing, or while the performers are getting into makeup and wardrobe, but the moment the Director is ready to rehearse and shoot on-camera, the operative camera crew had better be at their posts and ready to roll. Any delay at this point will not be in the best interests of the camera crew.

REMEDY: Always be aware of what is going on on the set. Check with the DP and First Assistant Director before absenting yourself from the shooting site. Let the AD know where you will be, and return within the time frame the AD gives you. During rehearsals and takes, communicate as necessary with your Camera Assistant and Dolly Grip, but keep it subdued and concise. While in the pressure cooker during rehearsals and takes, and especially for difficult complex shots, never let dissension raise its ugly head. Maintain control of oneself and operative camera crew members.

Communication Errors. Because of the ever-present time factor, it is important that we communicate effectively and economically. All the Dolly or Crane Grip needs to know is where and when a move was faulty. All the Camera Assistant needs to know is when the lens sizing is incorrect, the zoom movement rough, or the focus soft. And what the Director needs to know is whether these technical aspects of the shot were within visually acceptable limits. Immediately following a take, it is essential for the Camera Assistant to advise the Camera Operator of a possible focus error, for the Dolly Grip to advise the Operator and First Assistant of a missed floor mark, and for the Operator to advise the Director of a possibly faulty take.

REMEDY: Be concise and precise in instructions and comments to operative colleagues regarding shot production. Advise the Director immediately following the take if the take is not satisfactory. Be concise and precise in responding to the Director's inquiry regarding your acceptance of the shot. A simple response of "good" or "no good" will usually suffice. Never equivocate or ramble. Besides consuming valuable time, it creates uncertainty in the Director's mind, not only about the take but also about the Camera Operator.

The Learning Curve. Keep moving up the learning curve—technically, interpersonally and creatively. Failure to do so will invite perils and pitfalls during production. Stay curious. Stay interested. Stay involved. To repeat, there are no short-cuts to excellence and there is no substitute for experience. Which means, there is no substitute for practice. So above all, practice, practice, practice, on and off the set—and in your operating visualizations.

Summing Up. Internal and external problems are perils of our business and become pitfalls when we fail to recognize and promptly address them. Understanding the cause of a problem goes a long way toward its solution. Helping each other to understand and avoid these perils and pitfalls is an important part of a caring and effective collaborative process.

OPERATIONAL TECHNIQUES

As in any other activity, there are techniques that can be employed in order to save time and/or to protect against unforeseen exigencies.

Allowing for Unplanned Camera Movement. When faced with space con-strictions for moving the camera, it is well to leave the Dolly Grip with at least a foot of space between the dolly and the wall or other impediment in order to allow for an unplanned pull-back to maintain coverage. Allowing similar space latitude also applies to the video camera on its mobile pedestal.

On multiple camera film or video sitcoms, sufficient space should be main-tained between cameras at their static positioning points, in order to allow slight correctional moves to improve framing when performers are, or move, off their marks.

Allowing for Unplanned Subject Movement. At the same time, it is well to reserve at least 2mm to work with on the wide angle end of the zoom lens and at least 10mm on the long end of that lens to allow appropriate sizing corrections during unplanned or unexpected subject movement and/or positioning.

For Rapid Panning in Any Gear. No matter which of the two or three gear ratios (depending upon the geared head in use), smooth and rapid panning moves may be made by starting the head in motion, with the left hand turning the pan wheel and at the same time pulling or pushing the head with the right hand which is holding the tilt wheel. At the end of the pan, the left hand helps the right hand slow the panning movement by riding the rim of the spinning pan control wheel, then taking control and easing the geared head into a stop and hold at the conclusion of the rapid panning movement.

For Extremely Extensive Pans. When camera pans have to be made which exceed 100°, it is well to consider having the Dolly Grip put the dolly into the two-wheel guidance mode, with the rear wheels set to pivot around the front wheels, and have the Dolly Grip fishtail the dolly in coordination with the movement to be followed, while panning and backpanning to maintain optimum framing as necessary.

Technique for Controlled Fast Panning. When using a friction head with pan stick control while following fast moving action and/or close, quick movement, use an iris rod on the side of the lens matte box. By holding onto the front end of the iris rod with the left hand, pans to the right or left can be more quickly and surely controlled from start to stop.

Adjusting the Tension and Locking the Control Head. Every manually controlled head, whether friction, fluid, spring-loaded or geared, has at least one tension setting for panning action and at least one for tilting movement. Tension, or drag, should be checked by the Camera Operator at the start of the shooting day and adjustments to the desired pan and tilt tension should be set at that time. Every control head should be locked off in pan and tilt positions when not in use in order to preclude the possibility of damage to the equipment and possible injury to those around it.

The Importance of a Balanced Head. With any bi-axial film magazine, and particularly with the larger 2,000´ 35mm magazines, it is important to rebalance the camera on its control head after each take. As the film moves from the front compartment of the magazine through the camera and into the rear chamber, the camera becomes progressively tail heavy. If this unbalance is not periodically corrected, this additional weight makes it more difficult to appropriately handle tilt shots. Cameras carrying the 1,200´ 16mm film magazines require similar periodic attention.

The Self-Leveling Viewfinder. The self-leveling viewfinder capability offered on several cameras helps make operating on extremely low or high angle shots from a dolly or tripod much more comfortable and effective. When a shot is designed to go both extremely high and low, set the eyepiece for the high position and crouch for the low portion, or have the First Assistant reset the viewfinder to an appropriate level at a designated moment during the shot.

Use of the Illuminated Ground Glass. The ground glass is a key element in composing the action and in visually determining focus. The engraved scribing thereon provides the format template within which the action is framed. More often than not the dark scribe lines against a well lighted setting clearly indicate the aspect ratio which must be used to frame the action. However, against a dark set or setting or a set with many strong vertical and horizontal lines, the illuminated ground glass can be of significant help in placing clearly readable aspect ratio lines over the action.

Use of the Swingover Viewfinder. The swingover viewfinder makes it possible and more convenient to use a camera in an otherwise difficult or impossible camera position. It makes it possible, with a camera having this ocular, to use the right or left eye as necessary. Further, although the image may be inverted, the viewfinder can be placed across the camera body when in a confined space (such as in a corner or on the passenger side of a vehicle, framing the driver). This finder can be placed in virtually any position—directed forward, upward, downward, rearward and across the camera from either side—to achieve the camera angle required.

Background Check. It is a good idea during rehearsals to carefully examine the background of the impending take in order to determine if there are any correctable problems which should be dealt with. Chief among these are: Reflections of lights, equipment and personnel in set windows, mirrors and picture frames; scenic and translight backings which do not fully cover the window area from the planned camera angle(s); flares from set lighting instruments; reflective flares from set dressing pieces; set dressing which conflicts with the position of the performers. Problems of this nature should be brought to the attention of the Director of Photography.

Foreground Check. A foreground check of set dressing is important in order to avoid set dressing items obscuring the performance. These pieces can be moved or eliminated to avoid masking important action, or pieces can be added to enhance the action or to purposely block the camera view of certain areas or action. Again, the Director of Photography should be made aware of any potential problems in this area.

STAGE AREA DESIGNATIONS

Each day that we report for work we are dealing with myriad details, not the least of which are those which concern the staging area—the setting, set dressing, props and, not least of which, the performers.

Behind the camera, cinematographically, we designate relative position or direction as camera right and camera left as we move the camera and compose objects and performers in frame, because that is the way these elements will appear on film or tape for viewers, including the Camera Operator.

On the other hand, the dramaturgy of stagecraft, which preceded the cinema by many centuries, has always designated relative direction and position based on the performer's position, movement and direction of look as he or she faces the audience during a performance. In fact, in early days, performing stages, often flatbed wagons, were sloped so that rear stage areas were significantly higher than the frontal stage areas in order that the standing groundlings could see all the action occurring on the entire stage area. Hence the terms, "up stage" and "downstage."

A good rule of thumb is to use the appropriate **staging position/direction designations** for everything that appears for presentation to the camera and to use the appropriate **camera position/direction designations** when referring to camera movement and to the position and direction of look or movement of all elements as they appear in frame.

It matters not the size of the area we may be photographing, whether landscape or table top, for purposes of prop, set dressing and/or actor positioning. It helps to visualize the shooting area as nine discrete areas. It is particularly important to refer to the stage areas when communicating with the Director or performers with regard to adjusting their position, movement or look with respect to the camera. The following graph will serve to illustrate the stage areas within which the performers are blocked, positioned and move, and with which they are familiar. (See Figure 2, above.)

As you can see, the camera and/or audience area is located across the proscenium from the staging area. In general, the staging area is divided into three

FIGURE 2

STAGE AREA DESIGNATIONS
WITH RELATIVE VISUAL IMPORTANCE

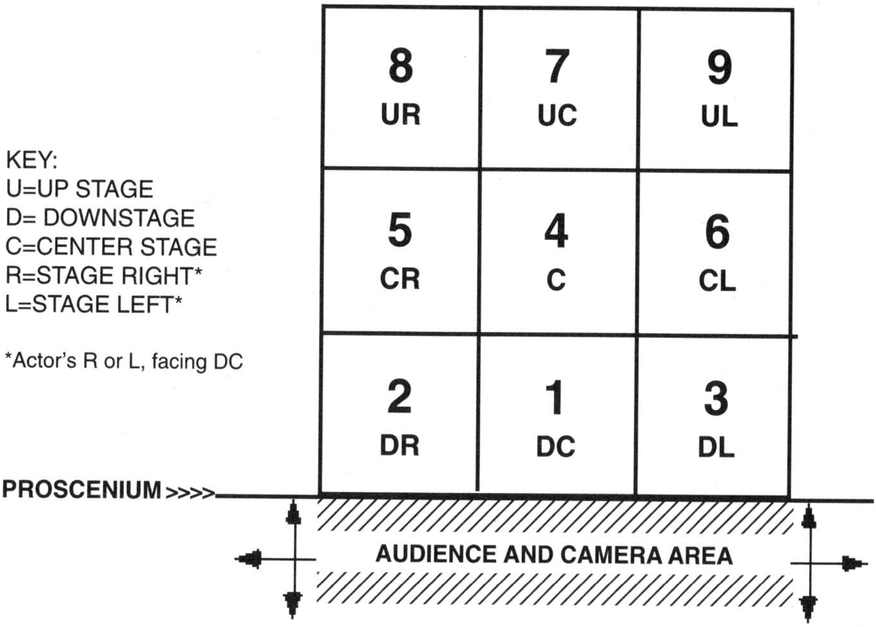

KEY:
U=UP STAGE
D= DOWNSTAGE
C=CENTER STAGE
R=STAGE RIGHT*
L=STAGE LEFT*

*Actor's R or L, facing DC

8	7	9
UR	UC	UL
5	4	6
CR	C	CL
2	1	3
DR	DC	DL

PROSCENIUM >>>>

AUDIENCE AND CAMERA AREA

cross-sections, each of which is divided vertically into three sections, resulting in nine stage area sections. Each resulting individual one-ninth stage section is accorded a designation of importance based on distance from the audience and on the left-to-right reading/scanning direction of eye movement used in the Latin-based writing.

Although the relative importance of the various stage areas is principally the concern of the Director, it is well to be aware of this aspect of stage positioning.

The down stage third of the staging area is the most important stage area in gaining eye attention of the three lateral cross-sections because it is closest to the audience/camera position which is the approximate equivalent of the cinematic closeup.

The center stage third is next in relative importance because it is also relatively close to the audience/camera, probably equivalent to the medium shot view.

Least in relative importance in stage positioning is **the up stage third** of the stage, the area farthest from audience/camera view, roughly equivalent to the long shot.

Further dividing each staging area cross section into thirds results in nine discrete areas, each with its own designation and position of relative importance insofar as eye attention is concerned. Referring to Figure 2 on page 43, we can see that stage right is to camera left and stage left is to camera right. In each third lateral section, the stage center third is the most important from an eye attention factor; in rank of visual attention importance are down stage center, center stage center, and up stage center, in that order. Next in importance is the stage right third (to camera left) and least in importance is the stage left third (to camera right).

Summary. It adds to our operating tool kit to understand and be able to efficiently communicate with those who are responsible for placing performers, props and items of set dressing for presentation to the camera. "Camera left" and "camera right" may not be understood by set dressers, prop people and performers who are more accustomed to hearing and following staging direction terms like "up stage left" and "down stage right." Learn and use the terms most familiar to the performers. In the long run, this will serve you well.

THE SCRIPT—TO READ, OR NOT TO READ?

The importance of the script to a production cannot be over-emphasized. Production of a motion picture is a very complex process from concept to finished product. The script is the blue print for the construction of a cinematic project. It describes the action and the progress of plot and character development. It specifies the place, period, season and time-of-day in and during which the action occurs. It calls for a continuity of varying moods and ever-changing rhythm and pace of scene movement and performance in support of the action. It describes each setting, its decorative style and set dressing. It may call for particular music and sound effect cues to comple-ment the continuity, and Special Effects (optical/digital, liquid, smoke, mechanical, or pyrotechnic) to punctuate or augment the action.

The script is like a road map, with the planned route highlighted. It tells any-one interested enough to read *and analyze* the route and direction the production vehicle will take, the terrain to expect along the way, the destination, and the time it will take to get there.

In another sense, the script (as represented by the shooting schedule) is the "game plan" for the production process. Specified and implied in its pages (and storyboard and production strips) are the contributions required and expected of the staff, cast and crew. Although it is the Director's objective and prerogative to inter-pret the script, to establish and orchestrate the interrelationships and interplay among the actors and to emphasize certain aspects of plot and action, it is important for key players to fully comprehend the role they will play in assisting the Director achieve this objective. The Camera Operator is (or can be) one of those key players.

It takes approximately as long to read the script as it takes to view the final cut version—24 minutes for a half-hour sitcom, 46 minutes for an hour-long episodic and whatever the full running time for a feature. Analyzing the script or breaking it down obviously will take much longer. Speed-reading will take a much shorter time. By not reading the script, in effect you declare yourself out of or on the outer edge of the creative collaborative team-effort loop.

The script is must-reading for: The **Producer**, who puts the entire project together (financing, staff, cast and crew) when reasonably certain that the script is right and ready to go; the **Director**, who prepares a shooting and character-orchestration plan which conforms to his or her understanding of the intent of the Writer; the **actors**, who study their roles in relation to other cast characters and to the scenario as a whole; the **Production Manager**, who breaks down the script into its production elements and prepares a shooting schedule and a budget breakdown for the project; the **Production Designer/Art Director**, who designs and plans the settings in accordance with the period, place, time and mood; the **Costume Designer/Costumer**, who designs and/or selects wardrobe and accessories for the actors; the **Set Decorator**, who selects items with which to dress the sets and production sites; the **Property Master**, who determines the hand and set props to be utilized; the **Makeup Artist**, who prepares a makeup plot conforming to the characters to be portrayed by cast members; the **Director of Photography**, who plans the lighting design for each scene and sequence of the production in order to help bring the Director's vision to life; and every other departmental **Category Head** involved with the production.

Why do these people read and rely on the script? Because nearly everything they need to know to do their specialized work is contained in the script. Knowing and understanding the script provides them the opportunity to apply their expertise and to add personal artistic/aesthetic touches to their contributions.

Why then should a Camera Operator (or First Assistant, for that matter) take the time to read the script? For the same reasons that others with a need-to-know do: To make a necessary, significant and efficient contribution to the production; to be a pro-active part of the creative, collaborative team effort. The alternative is to be supervised and directed in all aspects of one's job function—relegated to being a mere functionary—a switch-flipper or a button-pusher type.

By knowing and understanding the script elements, it becomes more convenient to make knowledgeable contributions to camera movement and framing. Being aware of the relationships among the characters, the twists and turns and development of the plot and action lines, keeps one alert and able to suggest and/or employ ways and means of emphasizing these key dramaturgical elements as they occur.

Of course, if you have a Director (or departmental Category Head) who does not want to hear or accept input or suggestions, or wants everything to be done one way—*his/hers*—then it is well to button the lip and comply.

The scripts are available for anyone with a need-to-know to read and to study. Remember: We can do our job better by having a thorough knowledge and clear understanding of the script. If you aren't already regularly reading the script you will be shooting, try it. The script is an important tool which can help us do our work better—with more heart, understanding, and effect.

ANALYZE, VISUALIZE, EMPATHIZE, MAXIMIZE

Whether you are a Director of Photography, Camera Operator, Camera Assistant or Head or Assistant in any of the other production or post-production categories, doing everything possible to help the Director achieve his or her visualization of each shot, scene and sequence of the production, that is what professionalism—skilled attitude and performance—is all about.

For artists, performers and technicians involved in the cinematic process, the first step is to analyze the elements of the script, particularly those which most directly involve the functions of one's working category. The second step is to visualize how each shot, scene and sequence can be integrated to achieve the intended result. The third step is to involve the emotions and empathize with every changing mood of the piece, determining where, when and how the mood levels can best be captured and enhanced by one's specialized contribution. The final creative step is to maximize the desired visual effect by employing all applicable techniques during image capture and design, sound capture and design, and the editing process.

A motion picture begins with a vision in its creator's mind and continues through each stage and phase of its realization, from concept through pre-production, production, post-production and marketing. First, the concept—a visualization in the mind of the Producer and/or Writer as the story is originated, developed and finalized into the word—scene, action and character descriptions, and the dialogue.

Analysis. Before analysis can occur, there must be a plan or guide to examine. That plan is the script, to which all step-by-step preparation and execution of production elements by personnel in each production category must conform. The shooting script is an on-going, often evolving, record of the production process as it progresses day-by-day from shot-to-shot. The script is thoroughly analyzed by each Category Head and those Assistants most directly involved in the specialized work of that category. At this stage, the idea is not to miss any item or detail which directly affects departmental responsibilities, its contribution to the production effort and the final result.

Visualization. With script in hand, the Director, guided by the intent of the Writer, as evidenced in the script, decides on an approach which best accommodates his or her vision of the final product. The Production Designer must follow the intent of the Producer and Writer, implicit in the scenario, in visualizing the detailing of the production design, but within budgetary constraints. Each actor must have a clear, internalized mental and emotional picture of the character he or she is to portray and its relationship and interplay with the other characters.

The Director of Photography, in close collaboration with the Director, endeavors to internalize the Director's vision and then with the understanding and cooperation of camera, electrical and grip personnel, to translate that co-vision into visual images which conform in all aspects to that mutual intent.

The Camera Operator, too, must be able to visualize the effect of his or her framing and following of the action. The Camera Assistant and Dolly/Crane Grip(s) must also be tuned in. Those visualizations must agree with that of the Director and Cinematographer, otherwise visual inconsistency and/or chaos can ensue. After all, creation occurs by selecting and organizing elements which have been in a state of chaos; when that organizational chain is broken, chaos can result.

Empathy. The emotional content—its level and movement—of each scene and sequence must be imaged and internalized as well as the physical visual content and movement in order to help flesh out and close in on the overall desired effect. The Director and cast must be particularly aware of the interactive emotional level and movement within each shot, scene and sequence since it is the emotional level that involves audience sensibilities and response.

Because color, form and design also have an emotional effect on the viewer, the overall production design, including its settings and dressings, costuming, makeup, propping and location selection, are production elements which require thoughtful consideration and execution in order to maintain optimum visual impact within the parameters set by the scenario, the Producer, and the Director.

Maximizing. Refining and maximizing the performances, settings and visual imagery requires evaluating the overall desired effect of staging, performance, and image and sound capture.

Performance can be enhanced during readings, rehearsals and between retakes by careful attention to character interpretation, by orchestrating character interaction to maintain appropriate and consistent interrelationships, and by purposefully refining blocking and stage business in order to fully utilize the settings and lighting.

Although by shooting time it is often too late for major modifications in the sets, locations and set dressings, wall surfaces can be "aged" by the Standby Painter, ceiling pieces can be flown in for low-angle shots, and backings, drapes, wall hangings and furnishings can be moved, replaced, or toned down or up to maximize the desired effect.

It is following the dry-run prior to set lighting, when the Director blocks and runs the scene with the performers, that the Director of Photography is given the time to determine, set and refine the lighting and camera movement. Stand-ins sub for the performers while the camera position and lighting are established for each move and static position of each actor in the scene.

When the "realies" return to the fully lighted set, a dry-run is made in full costume and makeup to check performance, blocking, makeup, costuming, props, lighting and camera moves, any of which may be modified or refined by the Director or Director of Photography prior to a take.

Refinements in order to maximize results can be made during image capture and design by modifications in lighting, lens selection, filtration, framing, camera positioning and its movement, and later by adding digital/optical effects and/or image manipulation. During audial capture, the sound elements can be designed to fit and enhance the effect of the action; composed and arranged music can be tailored to the specifics of the action in order to influence and intensify the audience response. The final opportunity for maximizing the result is during the editing process, when the selecting, arranging and/or modifying of the visual and audial elements into a composite whole takes place, with each element placed and sized with an imposed internal rhythm and pace, and finally combined in the final mix which, if fully effective, will maximize the collaborative efforts of all that has gone before.

It is this refining process which tends to maximize and optimize the final image capture. It is this attention to detail and desire for excellence and perfection which raises craft to art and enhances the quality of the visual experience for the audience.

VARIOUS ROLES THE CAMERA PLAYS

Because we exist in a living, vibrating, constantly changing world environment, events of various natures are continually occurring. Most events are recorded only in the memories of those participating in a given event. Based on individual background and experience, each participant has his or her own view, or perspective, of an event. These perceptions may vary greatly and be so divergent that when reported by those individuals quite different events seem to have occurred.

When viewed by a non-participating observer, an event and its observed detail will be duly and selectively impressed on the mental screen and memory of that observer, based on his or her background and viewpoint. When the recollection of details of that event is reported by that observer, the reporting of those events come out of memory, through the twin biasing filters of experience and emotion, onto the mental screen, and are then reproduced and transmitted to others through oral (live or recorded speech) or visual (writing, drawing, acting-out, or photographic) output.

The Camera. The still camera was a device developed to capture images sequentially, one at a time; each shot taken at a given moment in time, at a certain place, captured on a chemical medium which would preserve those images for convenient reference by others. To adequately cover an event, the individual shots were made one at a time during the chronological sequence of actions, each shot from a varying angle of coverage of selected elements of the event.

The motion picture camera was developed to capture continuous action sequentially, a take at a time. With the ciné camera, an event could be covered capturing most or many of its occurring actions from one or more viewpoints.

The motion picture camera, whether film or video, can be used in varying modes, depending upon the purpose for which it is being applied. It can be used as an impersonal recorder, as an interested observer, as an active participant, or as an involved performer, but always with the Camera Operator at hand to manipulate, direct and control the mechanism.

The Camera Operator. The Camera Operator is an observer and preserver of the visual relationships taking place within the scope of view of the taking lens. The Camera Operator is a participant to the degree that he or she sees the subject matter occurring through the viewfinder and reacts to it by manipulating the camera in order to selectively frame, follow and focus on the action being captured.

The Camera as Recorder. When the camera is used as an impersonal observer of an entire event, it functions as a recording mechanism, reproducing nonselective coverage of images captured on a recording medium. To avoid the bias introduced by selected and varied angles of coverage, the camera should ideally operate from one camera angle covering the entire action area of the event, and turning without shutdown, during the entire event from beginning to end.

Examples would be: A single position, holding wide angle coverage of the entire proscenium stage area of a play from the audience level, while shooting each act in real time without a cut or any camera movement; or coverage of a football, soccer or baseball game from one camera with a wide angle prime lens located high above the action taking place on the playing field. In these examples, the Camera Operator, after placing the camera and setting the lens, acts as a switch-flipper, only monitoring the action through the viewfinder, since the camera will not be moved during the take.

The Camera as Observer. When the camera becomes an observer, the coverage angle is often varied, depending upon the nature of the subject matter being observed. In this mode, the camera is not an intruder, but rather an impersonal onlooker of selected elements in the overall milieu. Use of zooms, camera movement and varying camera placement in order to achieve the most appropriate angle of coverage are part of this technique, which is often used in documentary production.

Wild animal, nature, time lapse, surveillance and combat photography are other examples of using the camera as an observer. During this type of coverage, the Camera Operator must be ever observant and alert for photographic opportunity as well as being prepared to properly frame, follow and focus unrehearsed action.

The Camera as Participant. When the camera participates in the action, it becomes integrated with the action and is often subjective in the perspective it records. In this mode, the camera becomes an extension of the Camera Operator.

Examples of this use of the camera would be any event during which the camera is free to move freely in and out of the event elements while selectively framing and photographing those elements from various positions in order to capture the essence of the event and/or to evoke an intended viewer participative response to that event, such as agile handheld or body-cam work during demonstrations; or sporting events, with a camera mounted on a helmet, skis, skates, skateboard, race car, airplane, etc. In shooting demonstrations, the Camera Operator needs to be agile and alert to the centers of activity; covering sporting events—including hang-gliding, sky-diving, bungee-cord-jumping, surf boarding and wind surfing—the Camera Operator may be a participant in the event being photographed with the camera carried or mounted on the body during the activity.

The Camera as Actor/Performer. During staged cinematic productions, each camera position and angle is selected and each move is planned with the intent of capturing the essence of the action which has been blocked and/or prepared for presentation to the camera. The camera (and its Operator) then becomes an active participant, affecting and being affected by the staged action.

The camera becomes a performer when it is used to act and interact with the performer(s) whose actions it is recording. The subjective camera, during which the camera *becomes* the performer, moving, acting and reacting as the performer would, with the point of view of that performer, is a prime example of this use of the camera.

The camera is used as an actor primarily in cinematic feature and episodic dramatic productions in which the camera can be integrated with the staged action of the performers. Handheld and body-support systems such as the Steadicam™ are often utilized for this purpose.

A Camera Operator involved in this type of camera use must get into character and by skillful and empathetic manipulation move the camera in a manner designed to best elicit the intended emotional response to the captured imagery from the intended audience.

Summing Up. No matter to what type of use the motion picture camera is put, it becomes an extension of the Camera Operator. The manipulation of the camera by the Operator and of the lenticular settings by the First Assistant Camera Operator and movement of the mobile camera platform by the Dolly or Crane Grip require a very high degree of concentration, dedication and coordinated effort for optimum results to be obtained.

SHOT-MAKING

Shot-making is the basic procedure used in recording each and every segment, or shot, which comprises a link in the chain of shots from the beginning to the end of the production, whether on film or video tape.

In general, shot-making involves, for each shot setup: **1)** Analyzing the subject matter and the action to be composed and photographed, as well as the terrain and time of day, if applicable; **2)** determination of a camera position viewpoint; **3)** lighting the subject matter and area to be photographed; **4)** selection of the camera and camera support equipment, including the mounting platform or device—tripod, dolly, crane, plane, boat, or body support; **5)** specifying the taking lens, optical filters, shutter angle, frame rate, and exposure setting and any planned variations thereof during a shot; **6)** planning the direction and velocity of movement of the camera on its mobile camera platform in relation to the action to be covered; **7)** adjusting the direction and velocity of movement of the camera and subject matter, as necessary; and **8)** coordinating the movement of camera and zoom lens sizing with movement and positioning of the subject matter.

Analyzing the Subject Matter. It is important that the Director, Production Designer, Director of Photography and Camera Operator analyze the subject matter and its movement in the context of its setting in order to help determine the most efficient and effective plan for presenting the subject matter to the camera.

The Camera Position is usually determined by the Director in collaboration with the Director of Photography in order to cover the essential subject matter and action at an appropriate angle, although the Production Designer, through the selection and/or design of the locations and/or production settings, can have a marked influence on camera placement.

Lighting the subject matter and its environment is the responsibility of the Director of Photography who determines the type and amount of matériel needed to accomplish this task (within budgetary constraints). The DP then works through and supervises electrical and grip personnel in order to set in place the appropriate type, size, quantity and positioning of lighting units and to control the beam spread (coverage), intensity/key (exposure), quality (soft, hard and/or color), and balance/contrast ratio (mood) of each luminaire which has been set in place for each shot setup.

Camera Equipment, accessories and support equipment considered necessary and appropriate for the production (within budgetary constraints) is selected by, and put in place under the supervision of the Director of Photography.

Optical Selection and Settings are the province of the Director of Photography in order to provide and maintain the coverage and consistency of the overall visual effect desired by the Director.

Camera Movement. Blocking of the actors and the camera is the prerogative of the Director, often in collaboration with the Director of Photography, and frequently with requested input from the Camera Operator.

Adjusting and Coordinating Camera Movement. Once camera movement has been plotted and the mobile camera platform tracks are put in place, the Camera Operator has the responsibility of making minor adjustments during blocking and rehearsals as to direction, timing, velocity and placement of the mobile platform, thereby coordinating the work of the First Assistant (for zoom sizing and focus) and the Dolly/Crane Grip(s) (for camera platform movement) in order to perfectly blend with the action being presented to the camera.

Specifically, shot-making involves great care in selecting and composing elements through the camera viewfinder within the dynamic, moving, ever-changing proscenium—the cinematic frame—the transporter of audience presence.

The **frame** is the basic cinematic element of first concern to the camera operator. It is the frame which provides the physical parameters within which the elements to be photographed must appear and be arranged. During rehearsals, at every point during progression of the action—whether static or dynamic, whether the camera is stationary or moving—composition (sizing, position of elements in frame, and focus) is carefully checked and adjustments are made in order to maintain optimum composition and visual effect throughout the duration of the shot.

Each **shot**, a sequential progression of still pictures, or frames, must be composed and framed to clearly communicate the purpose and content of the shot in order to help accommodate a seamless juxtaposition and continuity in its placement between and/or among other shots.

The **take** is the total continuous running length of film or tape—from turn-on at the head start to the final frame, when the camera is cut and the film stops its movement through the camera.

The **transition points**—the head and tail point at which the shot will be cut and joined to (or visually combined with or superimposed over) another shot—of each shot are generally at or near the beginning and the end of the take. Subject matter, camera angle (perspective) and placement (high, normal or low), image size, direction of look, and direction, duration and velocity of movement are among the elements to carefully consider and control at the point during the shot for which the transition is being planned. Some of the options to consider are: **Matching** object sizes, shapes, textures, consistencies of substance, color(s) and/or action, type, mass, velocity, direction and duration; **contrasting** an object in movement with one at rest, a large group or object with a small one, a dark object with a light one, a smooth surface with a textured one, a fluid shape with a hard-surfaced object.

According to Webster's Dictionary, a **transition** is a change or passage from one place, state, stage of development, type, period, time of day, to another. Transitions are visually communicated by various mechanical linear techniques, such as the **cut**, the **dissolve**, the **wipe**, the **fade** and **racking** (in to out-of to in) **focus**.

Making the Shot. Making the shot means more than putting it on film or tape. Making the shot means making a take during which **all** the elements—performance of the actors, the movement of subject matter and camera, setting adjustments on the camera, sound recording, stunt and/or Special Effects execution—have, individually and collectively, been executed in a consistent, orchestrated and directorially acceptable manner.

Although shot-making is what we do and take pride in, it is how well we do our job that makes the shot fit seamlessly into the overall product. The better and more collaboratively we each do our individual job the better the final product is likely to be. And, ironically, the less obvious our specific contribution to the production effort is sure to be.

EVALUATING THE PRODUCTION PROCESS

It is often useful to evaluate the production process when the job is completed, pinpointing: What went right. What went wrong. At what point during production. In which departments. Under whose responsibility. To what effect on the production. And what can be done to correct the problem(s) and to encourage successful, productive endeavor.

When everyone is cooperating and collaborating in doing his or her job to perfection and treating each other with due respect for productively contributing to the project, then things are going right. The production is more likely to be completed well within the shooting schedule, under budget, and enjoy critical and monetary acclaim.

When there is lack of interest, lack of cooperative productive input, or dissention among the staff, cast or crew, damage to the production entity is imminent and certain. Under these circumstances, it pays to ferret out the causes—the department, the individuals, the circumstances—and set about correcting the problem before the ripple effect contaminates the entire production and its personnel. This task generally becomes the Producer's responsibility when the Director either cannot correct the problem, or is part of the problem. Problem productions generally go beyond the scheduled shooting period, go well over budget, and either fail to get released, fail to make production costs at the box office, or fail to get the mandatory television viewer ratings.

We have all been on productions which have been a joy to work on. The script was well written. The players were well cast. The Director had properly prepared. The Production Designer had provided exceptional sets and settings on stage and at locations. Set dressing and props had given a touch of reality to the settings. Makeup, hairdressing and wardrobe had given the performers comfort in their assumed characters. The technical crafts all had adequate production tools with which to do their jobs. Production management had carefully crafted a realistic shooting schedule. And everyone on the staff, cast and crew felt assured that they were significantly contributing to the production and regarded each other with compassion and respect.

And then again, we have all experienced productions on which whatever could go wrong did just that: Poor pre-production planning; badly written scripts; unrealistic budgets and/or shooting schedules; sets or location settings not adequately researched and/or not prepared and/or dressed properly or on time; fouled up logistics; inappropriate casting; indecisive and/or screaming Directors; feudal-acting ADs; devious UPMs; martinet-like Category Heads; competing, conniving, inexperienced and/or incompetent co-workers; lack of safety concerns; some personnel dosing on controlled substances; and more; each and all contributing to the debacle in process of occurring. Under such circumstances, particularly if the problems are not promptly solved, it might be well to consider abandoning ship. It is well to remember the Hollywood maxim, "You're no better than your last picture."

Most correctable problems seem to stem from personal interrelationships on the technical or creative level. Differences of opinion regarding procedure or performance are often at the root of a dispute. Personnel problems among staff, cast or crew can be managed by replacing recalcitrant, uncooperative, incompetent or substance-abusing individuals. The very bottom line is to be sure that you are not part of the problem.

On the other hand, problems concerning Production management—scheduling and inadequate notice of rescheduling; logistical foul-ups; less than adequate transportation, food and lodging; reneging on understandings, promises and/or deal memos; faulty interpretation of contractual provisions; timecard shenanigans; etc— may, if a union shoot, require intervention by union representatives to settle such disputes. Either that, or optioning to terminate your employment with the company.

The so-called post mortem process, that of dissecting and analyzing the production elements for quality control, has its roots in stage productions. Following each evening of out-of-town try-outs, it became the practice of examining each integral part of the play in relation to the whole entity, taking into consideration audience responses to help determine where weaknesses may have occurred during the performance and then doctoring the production to correct these perceived weaknesses. This procedure helped refine the quality of stage plays prior to committing to the financial burden of taking the production to Broadway.

Sitcoms, on the other hand, rely on "TV village," the array of floor monitors displaying what each of four cameras is framing, before which sit the Writer/Producer/Director team, reacting and rewriting at each run-through and rehearsal, commenting on dialogue, performance, framing and focus. Some sitcoms even bring an audience in to view and respond to a dress rehearsal (often filmed or taped) so last-minute modifications can be made before committing to the final filming or taping done in front of the showtime audience.

The purpose of personally taking the time to examine, analyze and evaluate the production process of a show or series you are working on is to learn from the experience. We probably learn more from determining what went wrong and why it went wrong than by what went right. As professionals, we all do our utmost to help make the production process go right. Like other professionals, we practice our craft regularly on a daily or show-by-show basis. We either learn from our experiences and improve in our craft, or we stagnate and atrophy. The choice is ours to make.

THE MIND'S EYE

As Camera Operators, we depend on making our living with our sight. But there is more; for it is not enough just to look, or even to see. It is vital to absorb and understand the purpose—the placement, mood and movement—of the visuals displayed on our viewfinders, which we are asked to include, frame and follow. Only by internalizing the purpose of the scene and the Director's blocking thereof can aesthetic justice be done to the captured imagery. In short, we form a mental template of the shot we are about to take. To do this, our mind, body and spirit must be set to work visualizing and identifying with the desired effect which the captured imagery is designed to evoke. In a word, we must activate the mind's eye.

We must assume that the visuals presented to the camera are purposefully selected, placed and moved in order to logically and effectively tell a story and involve an audience's emotions without drawing attention to the fact that a camera is at work, capturing and recording the images.

Placement. The Director selects and positions the principal subject matter for the camera in consideration of the requirements of the interaction among the actors, of the imperative dramaturgical processes occurring during the scene, and of the positioning at the end of the outgoing scene and at the beginning of the incoming scene.

Placement of actors concerns who talks to whom, which actor is most important in the scene, whether the scene is static or dynamic in whole or in part (do the camera and/or actors move?), how it will cut with the preceding or outgoing scene and with the following or incoming scene.

Props and set dressing are positioned according to their use and importance in the scene.

With each angle of coverage, "cheating" or other adjustments in the placement or positioning of actors, props and set dressing are standard operating procedures in order to reduce distractions and to refine compositional framing of the captured imagery.

It must be remembered that the design of the set, the selection of the shooting site and the placement of performers and objects is done for presentation to the camera. Each angle of coverage places a differing perspective on the subject matter, often requiring repositioning of the elements to be included in frame in order to feature or provide an unobstructed view of the essentials.

It is well to know the name of each performer so that efficient communication can take place with the Director and/or actors regarding positioning and the like. Memorizing actor positions and their relationship with each other can smooth the shooting process.

Movement. How, when and where the actors and/or camera move are important cinematic story-telling techniques.

The actors can move in various directions, at various velocity, by various means, with various intent, depending upon the objective and dramatic circumstances enabling and motivating their moves.

When the moves are made depends upon the timing of the blocking which the Director has put in place. The direction and velocity of moves and movement by actors depends upon the factual, emotional and motivational content of the scene.

The camera, in turn, may be called upon to follow that action by panning and, occasionally zooming from a static position, or by moving on a mobile mount in concert with the action.

It is well for the Camera Operator to internalize the movement of both subject matter and the camera during rehearsals. Each performer will have a rhythm and pace in keeping with the character he or she is portraying. This, in turn, will vary according to the emotional content of the scene being recorded. By placing this visual and visceral data into the mental imagery data bank, each take will be facilitated.

Mood. The mood, the emotional feeling which the Director wishes to evoke in the intended audience during a scene, is an important consideration for the Director of Photography in the selection of lenses and filters, plotting camera position and moves and planning the lighting. This understanding is also important for the Camera Operator in making and refining the camera moves.

Mood is a product of story content, blocking, performance, setting, set dressing, property, makeup, wardrobe, special effects, camera angle (placement/lens selection), camera movement, and lighting quality and balance. Each element in frame contributes in varying degree to the whole. Intent and consistency are key to an effective result.

The mood and emotional context of each scene should be thoroughly internalized by the Camera Operator in order to go with the flow in framing and following the action.

To Include. What to shoot and why are important Directorial considerations. To include certain elements in frame and exclude others is an essential part of the selection process established by the Director. It is an important function of camera operating to know and include the essentials and their surrounding elements and to exclude the extraneous and distracting non-essentials.

To Frame. The process of framing has the added responsibility of composing the elements which have been planned and arranged to appear in the shot. This is often done by the Director while he or she is setting up the shot with the performers and Director of Photography.

It is important that the Camera Operator keep the elements which have been designated by the Director and DP comfortably composed within frame during the take.

To Follow. Keeping all essential elements in frame while the elements and/or camera are in motion becomes the prime responsibility of the Camera Operator during rehearsals and takes. Maintaining both optimum static and dynamic composition during a shot depends, of course, upon actors, vehicles, and mobile camera platform moving in concert along a planned pathway, and hitting marks accurately.

As the seeing eye during this process, the only person with the clearest view of what the camera is capturing, the Camera Operator sees through the lens what is included in frame, whether or not the desired composition has been maintained during the shot, what's in or out of focus, and whether or not lens adjustments and camera moves have been without fault; in short, whether the shot is acceptable or not.

Nexus. With all the excellent tools with which we ply our craft, the ultimate tool is our mind's eye, the visualizing and truly *seeing* eye, the screen upon which the mental images play. Developing an eye with a sensitivity which sees with cinematic precision, appreciation and understanding and guides us as we operate the camera during our cinematic journeys is a challenging, fulfilling and never-ending endeavor for as long as we continue to practice our craft.

ART OR CRAFT?

There is craft in the least of art just as there is art in the best of craft. Which it is depends upon the experience and sensitivities of the artist or craftsperson who is producing or contributing to the end result, whether painting, sculpting, designing, writing, composing music, or performing for theatre, opera, motion pictures or television.

We are all involved in a truly collaborative effort—crafting and creating cinematic product for film and video. The cinematic media represent a combination and culmination of the arts, drawing artists and craftspeople from each of the arts, encouraging them to bring their best efforts to bear in creating both subtle and grand illusions for the wonder and entertainment of their audiences.

The Craft Aspect. The craft aspect of this process has to do with the mechanics of the work, the manual art or skill required to understand, manage and manipulate the matériel—the tools and materials of the trade. Bear in mind that the "tools and materials" can also be people.

More than 150 job classifications in up to 24 working categories can be called upon to properly service a major motion picture production from development through completion and display—during its pre-production, production, post-production and marketing/exhibition phases.

Each person working in a classification, whether an administrator, a technician or a laborer, has specific duties and responsibilities—the nitty-gritty of the job—which can be considered the craft skills required to accomplish that job's contribution to the production. How well that job is done—how complete the attention devoted to completing each specified detail—is a matter of craft skill. How innovatively, creatively and affectively the craft part is accomplished and how telling its effect is on an audience determines whether or not the craft effort deserves the appellation: *ART.*

Over all, the motion picture-making process requires several general categories of expertise from concept through completion. First is the producing aspect. And the first concern in this category is the recognition of the idea, the concept, and the logical and efficient development thereof. The second concern becomes production management: The organizing of a staff of overseers, a cast of performers and a crew of craftspeople to craft the cinematic mosaic piece by piece. To use basic generic terminology, these craftspeople are the builders, hunters, selectors, gatherers, distributors and sellers of elements needed to create an environment in which the performance will occur. Then the Director takes over with his or her materials: The performers; those who assist the performers in assuming their acting personas; the gatherers and placers who find and/or design and dress the sets and settings; the technicians who record (on film or video) the action of those performers; and the finishers who piece together selected portions of recordings, adding the ambience of sound effects and music, to create the final, finished and multidimensional sight-and-sound mosaic. Finally, there are those who market, distribute, and display this finished product to the public for its mass and/or financial response to the effort.

Conceptualizers, Developers, Designers, Overseers. Among the many skills required to get a production started and maintained are those of conceptualizing, funding, developing, designing and administering the overall production plan.

The chief conceptualizer, the Producer, is the one who makes it happen, but only after providing and applying a strong concept of how the finished product will look and how each part will fit in and contribute to the final result. This concept, as exemplified by the script, will be the guiding light for the Writer, Production Designer, Director, Director of Photography, Editor, and all other collaborators in the effort.

The craft part of these essential functions is dealing with the basic routine necessary to each. The art aspect is determined by how appropriately, creatively and harmoniously each of these functions fit into the overall production design.

Builders, Hunters, Selectors, Gatherers, Distributors. Each job classification utilized becomes responsible for crafting and producing a specialized element in the overall design of the production. Some classifications search, select, clean, prepare, construct, paint and detail sites and/or settings for the production. Other classifications hunt, select, gather, make and place items in the appropriate settings.

For each craftsperson, the *CRAFT* in all this is in knowing where, when and how to do his or her individual functions. The *ART* is in how well, appropriately, tastefully and meaningfully (emotionally moving to the viewer) the functions are carried out.

Directors, Performers, Recordists, Finishers. The crafters are those who take the developed concept and proceed to translate the scenario into visual images which follow the intent of the Writer and the vision of the Director. In order to reach the level of art, those fulfilling these functions raise their level of commitment and perception and execution, leading by example and encouraging or inspiring their collaborators to greater and more dedicated effort.

Marketers, Distributors, Displayers. And then there are those who take the product to market and sell to the public. Without their skills a product could sit on a shelf and never be seen, or never be seen by enough people to turn a profit. With their artful planning and execution of the marketing plan, a quality motion picture can gain the attention of the viewing public and go on to critical and financial success.

The Art Aspect. Art, too, requires skill—the skill of execution and/or performance of the finished product—along with the simultaneous application of consummate aesthetic taste by craftspeople and artists each step of the creative way, in order to achieve a purposeful and harmonious effect on audience sensibilities.

Art emerges when the consummate application of craft skill is subordinated by a harmony of those crafted elements which transcends the material aspects and leads the viewer onto an emotional plane. Art is in name only unless it effectively affects people emotionally—elicits in the viewer(s) feelings of sympathy, empathy, fear, rage, joy, humor, admiration, and other basic emotions.

Craft and Art. The routine of craft is in knowing when and to what degree to apply the appropriate technique. The skill of craft is in how appropriately, comprehensively and creatively those techniques are applied. Art takes craft to a spiritual level, where craft and content communicate with the self and soul of the viewer.

Consummate care and skill, in the crafting of each and every detail, from each person in the collaborative, contributory chain can create a critically acclaimed artistic result.

Summing Up. It takes many skilled and dedicated people on all levels in this highly collaborative motion picture-making process to craft, create and market a cinematic product. It is much like making a chain—each link made by a different craftsperson. A link can be strong but not perfectly formed, or strong but of divergent design. This is the craft aspect. But to be considered art, each link in the final structure of the chain must be structurally sound and of compatible and harmonious design—aesthetically pleasing to observe. Crafting and creating a mosaic, tile by tile, would be another appropriate analogy to the cinematic process and to the determination of whether the end result is craft or art.

Without craft, art cannot materialize. With consummate and creative craftsmanship and a clearly delineated and understood concept, art can be created.

"WHAT'S PAST IS PROLOGUE"

Shakespeare had it right. The events of the past do indeed portend the future. And those who have the inclination and interest to examine that past can get some sense of the direction which current and future events might take, and thereby ease the way to adapt to those changes as they occur. Those who don't or won't, who stick to the all-too-comfortable status quo, often find themselves out of sync with the reality of what's happening, what's emerging that is affecting (or will affect) the technology and techniques practiced in the workplace.

This is a particularly important consideration for those of us who work in film and video production. We work with a variety of equipment and material, using a variety of established techniques, all of which have evolved and been refined through the trial-and-error process of production—using and testing the limits of the matériel and the techniques of our crafts. Innovative ideas and concepts are developed in the laboratory and tested in the workplace. Because this is an ongoing research, development and implementation process, we can always expect innovation and change.

We can fight it, or we can cooperate and even collaborate with it. The choice is ours. As cooperative collaborative participants, we are exposed to and experience change whether positive or negative, subtle or overt. It is possible that we may actively contribute to or instigate change, ever seeking more efficient and effective tools and techniques to enhance the craft work we do. As unwilling or shortsighted participants, we tend to restrict our ability to adapt and grow in our chosen craft and may thereby make ourselves obsolete as changing conditions and technology pass us by.

Adapting to change is not always convenient or easy to do. It requires changing our work attitudes and habits. It requires the flexibility to adapt to the new or unfamiliar equipment and to learn the new techniques necessary to operate that equipment effectively and efficiently.

Signposts of Change. It pays dividends to be alert to what is in trend, new, or in development in the way of: Equipment, accessories, expendables and recording stock; production methods and techniques; electronic digitizing and manipulation of the visual image; TV programming show types and their content; feature films and commercials—types and content; exhibition facilities—broadcast (including satellite, laser and fiber optics), cable, theaters and home (includes interactive TV, video cassette, CD and film playback). Reading trade journals and new product reports and attending trade shows and in-house demonstrations are wise ways to keep abreast of what's new or forthcoming.

Matériel. The matériel—the equipment, accessories, expendables and recording stock—we use are in a continuing mode of innovative modification by manufacturers and suppliers who are continually striving to provide us ever more effective and efficient tools with which to craft our work. In order to accomplish this, they are open to and invite positive and/or negative critical input from potential users regarding design or modification of their products or services, followed by candid feedback after having tested or used the product/service. These procedures help assure "tailor-made" product development which in turn helps make our jobs more efficient and our craftsmanship more effective and satisfying.

Production Methods & Techniques. It is wise to specialize, but it is prudent to learn as much about other production techniques as possible. Things change, often for economic reasons. And the impact is felt in the workplace in the type and quantity of film and video product in demand at any given time.

When one specializes in a particular type of production—features, commercials, episodics, or sitcoms—one tends to become typecast by the hiring sources. One also may find it bothersome or difficult to quickly adapt craft techniques to another production method. For example, audience sitcoms are shot in a series of long takes, which require: A continual high degree of coordination among the operative camera crew (the Camera Operator, First Assistant Camera Operator and Dolly Grip) and with the other cameras moving on the floor; a penchant for making precise and concise notes regarding framing, movement and distances; a reliable memory; and being comfortable wearing a headset and working in front of a studio audience.

Film and video camera techniques vary, principally in the method of operating the equipment—for film: three collaborators; for video: one person. Each medium differs from the other in its interaction with the directing staff and the actors.

TV Programming. The programming balance between the hour-long episodic and the half-hour sitcom tends to change, sometimes dramatically. These shifts have to do with the success of the syndicators in selling their product to domestic and foreign exhibition sources. Presently, the half-hour format fits more conveniently and economically into the programming plans of syndication networks. Keeping current with upcoming trends and/or what is selling in the syndication market can give one lead time in preparing for work opportunities in each forthcoming production season.

Feature Films & Commercials. Feature filmmaking and TV commercial production have their own agendas. Whereas TV programming production has a more or less set yearly schedule, features and commercials continue throughout the year with few severe dips and peaks. What is important is to determine what areas of the country (and world for that matter) are getting the benefit of the production starts (it might be worth a move to where the action is). Also important is to analyze the content, style and treatment of both current features and commercials in order to determine any emerging trends. Once these have been determined, adaptation to those trends of content, style and treatment can be made. For example, if a specialty is being employed such as aerial, underwater or hand-held/body mount stabilizer shots, optical effects, process photography, second unit, inserts, etc, one might consider training, specializing in and presenting oneself for employment in one of these areas.

Exhibition Facilities. Exhibition facilities, whether in the theater or home, also have an effect on the work we are offered and do. Each purveyor of the visual image, whether by network, syndication, cable or cassette, requires product to display to its audience. So each is in the market to license or purchase rights to syndicated programming and/or to produce its own. Knowledge of this trend, and of who is doing what, when and where can result in substantially more work opportunities for those willing to ferret out and follow up on the information.

Summing Up. Trends have a direction and momentum of their own. A trend, irrespective of its velocity, tends to have a mass and inertia which carry it in a certain direction for a certain duration—similar to the action of a pendulum. The energy that drives trends in our industry is the variable consensus of the marketplace—supply and demand—the size of the viewing audiences as measured by research firms or by box office returns. We are on the demand side when we ask for better tools with which to ply our craft. We are on the supply side when we assist our employers in producing product for the demanding and varied appetites of the viewing audiences. The better we understand the dynamics of the marketplace for the product we help craft, the better able we are to put ourselves in a position of rewarding and ongoing employment.

ADAPTING TO NEW TECHNOLOGY

We've all heard the familiar truisms: *"Adapt or perish," "Survival of the fittest," "Nothing is certain but death and taxes"* (and, of course, *change*). Certainly change is constant—a process which is inevitable and ongoing in all areas of our lives and affecting all aspects of existence.

And yet most of us instinctively oppose change, particularly as it affects us in the workplace. Perhaps it is because we are creatures of habit, and modifying well-established ways of thinking and doing things is not the most convenient thing to do. It requires re-evaluating our thinking and then retraining ourselves to effectively utilize the particular methods and techniques required by the new technology in order to continue to be employable.

Fear of the unknown is one of the biggest limitations we place on ourselves. It can result in unfounded apprehension about all the potentially negative things the new technology could do to us while minimizing possible benefits. After settling into a comfortable status quo process of thinking and doing things in a certain way for a substantial length of time (some would call this a **rut**), it is difficult to realign our thinking and behavior with the reality of those events taking place which will directly effect us in our work place. In order to make a reasoned judgment, we need to acquire all pertinent information available. There is absolutely no substitute for time spent working with the equipment on any system with which we are not familiar. That there is no substitute for experience becomes demonstrably clear after you have had (and taken) the opportunity to get to work with and get to know the new technology.

The Economic Imperative. Although new technology is usually developed and put in place in order to be cost-effective (more and better-made units per unit of time) as well as improve the end product of its use, employers need and want trained employees to make the technology function as effectively and efficiently as possible. Therefore, most employers are ready to provide training opportunity to those persons who are interested and willing to put in the time and energy to learn and adapt to the new technology.

Technological Milestones. We and our predecessors have seen and adapted to a number of technological and related innovations which have had varying degrees of impact on how we as individuals or in collaborative groups perform job functions on a production. Not all technical innovations came to be accepted without fear and misunderstanding in the workplace at the time. In fact, our movie-making industry would not be where it is today without these technological advances. Major among some of these advances have been the introduction, development and implementation of: The motion picture camera and its perforated, emulsion-layered film stock; the film printer; the film projector; arc and incandescent lighting units; electric motors for cameras; camera registration pin(s); the major studio system; the camera dolly and crane; film unions; sound recording; lightweight, handholdable cameras; rear and then front projection systems; the self-blimped silent-running studio camera; reflex view cameras; the varifocal (zoom) lens; broadcasting networks; television and then video tape technology; video assist for film cameras and the RF application thereto; cable systems; satellite communications; integrated film camera systems; handheld and then CCD video cameras; portable sound mixing consoles; continuing improvement in granularity, color rendition and sensitivity of film emulsions; densitometric film timing; remotely controlled (hot-head) cameras; camera stabilizing and support systems; the personal computer with its graphics and number-crunching capabilities; electronic post-production; digital image manipulation; multi-phonic and digital sound delivery systems; fiber optics; the laser; holography; the programmable lighting console; compact, powerful and relatively cool lighting units; hypersensitive directional microphones; and the automation electronic controls applied to much of this technology.

To be sure, not all of these technological developments resulted in loss of work. In fact, more jobs were created than were lost. The ever-emerging technology brought with it the tools and techniques which made the production process more efficient and helped provide both products of superior quality and trained craftsmen and women of superior ability.

As Shakespeare wrote, *"What's past is prologue"* and prologue portends the future. So if Shakespeare was correct, and if change is immutable, we can expect a continuation in the direction of the process of technological advancement, a process we must continually adapt to or lose our value to the industry labor pool.

A Look Ahead. What technological advances are likely in the future? Application of the video multi-camera technique to the film camera; further film emulsion improvements; digital video recording and display; refined camera automation and remote and/or robotic programmed operation thereof; holographic motion pictures; even more compact film and video cameras; more effective camera stabilizing devices; more compact and powerful lighting units; refinement of fiber optic techniques for lighting and photographic applications; development of the digital domain as a production and exhibition mode; creating virtual reality programming settings, set dressing, props and even performers; and ongoing training programs for production personnel might well be a few of the innovative developments taking place in our future.

One thing seems certain. Finding ways and means of adapting to new technology (with its resultant organizational impact) as it surfaces may be a better, wiser course than the alternative. Remember, the development of new technology is a permanent and ongoing process which we avoid or oppose at our own peril.

OPERATING CINEMATOGRAPHY

Professional operating cinematography is about the skills required to manage and work with people, and to operate the equipment, in order to output quality cinematic product within the constraints of time and budget.

The camera, with the perspective it records, is in effect the eyes and ears of the viewing audience. The Camera Operator, the person manipulating the camera to capture the imagery within that perspective view, is responsible for seeing that all camera moves and adjustments are seamlessly coordinated with the action being captured during the shot. Which is to say, the compositional framing must hold all the elements required by the Director, while excluding any encroaching extraneous matter, at all times during the take. Either that, or a retake will be required.

The beginning apprentice will soon learn that there is much more to camera operating than pushing a button or flipping a switch. To approach and maintain the highest levels of operating competence requires total commitment of mind and body to the craft.

There is, of course, no substitute for hands-on experience. Printed matter such as this book can be helpful in calling attention to proven procedures and prospective perils, but like a map, until the journey is actually taken and experienced, the map is but a guide to that experience.

This section of the book will deal with the nitty-gritty of details essential to practicing the craft of operating cinematography in a responsible, efficient, effective and, hopefully, creative manner.

ON BECOMING A CAMERA OPERATOR

Many, if not most, First Assistant Camera Operators, upon moving up to Camera Operator, are somewhat surprised by the scope of the unfamiliar area of responsibilities suddenly thrust upon them.

As a new Camera Operator, he or she must get used to working much more closely with the Director of Photography and the Director than was the case as an Assistant Camera Operator working closely with the Camera Operator.

From the Abstract to the Aesthetic. Instead of dealing principally with numbers representing distances and zoom lens positions, the former First Assistant-turned-Camera Operator is now immersed in the visual result of the numerical settings and camera positions as these factors affect focus and compositional framing. From the left brain activity of abstract numbers, suddenly the emphasis has shifted to what is essentially the right brain activity of spatial perception, imagery and aesthetic judgment. In addition to this, the Camera Operator must be constantly coordinating the controls of the geared head with the work of the First Assistant and the Dolly or Crane Grips in order to properly frame and follow the action, while visually remembering any discrepancies in the framing, composition, and/or in the camera, dolly, crane, zoom or focus moves and/or whether extraneous elements, such as microphones, booms or their shadows, personnel or equipment have encroached into the framing, or if the framing has gone off the set at any time. All this takes some getting used to. And following each take, all that's been happening in frame bears on the inevitable question from the Director (or First Assistant Director): "**HOW WAS IT?!**"

Dealing with the BIG QUESTION. The answer to that question has been the bane of many would-be Camera Operators. It is the Camera Operator (barring video assist tie-in) who sees most immediately the result of the combination in frame of all the arranged production elements: The action and positioning of the actors; framing of that action; the settings; set dressing; relation of the camera, zoom, focus, dolly or crane movement to the movement of the actors or objects. Since it is much less expensive to retake a shot while in the same basic setup than to return later, it is essential that the Camera Operator give an accurate, precise and concise answer to the **BIG QUESTION**, preferably saying either: "*GOOD!*" or "*NO GOOD!*" But whatever is said, **don't equivocate**! If asked why the take was not good, the new Camera Operator must be prepared to specify any technical error and when it occurred, or when an actor may have missed his or her mark(s) and the focus or composition was affected, in order to enable the Director to decide whether or not to reshoot the scene or to do a pickup shot.

It is politically inappropriate to point a finger at an Assistant or Dolly/Crane Grip for a technical mistake, unless unrelentingly pressed for that information by higher authority. It is much better to say that there was "*a coordination problem*" or words to that effect. That way, whether an actor, Operator, Assistant and/or Dolly/Crane Grip error occurred, no one is singled out. The important thing is to get the reason for the error resolved (among the participants) so that it will not recur during the retake.

Budget and Scheduling Constraints. In general, the tighter the budget and shooting schedule, the less time is available for perfecting shots. For **episodics and sitcoms**, the budgets and schedules are quite tight and so shots are generally simplified and accepted if there is no critical miscue or intrusion, such as: Misframing, framing a wrong actor or object; principal subject matter out-of-focus; jerky, uneven and/or uncoordinated moves of the camera, zoom, or dolly/crane; flares into the lens; boom mics and their shadows; framing off the set—left, right, too high, too low; equipment and support personnel discovered in frame.

In **features**, the larger budgets and lengthy shooting schedules (at a pace of 1-3 pages per day) allow reasonable time to perfect setups and shots, which is unavailable to episodics or TV movies-of-the-week (at a schedule of 8-12 pages per day). Features allow the Camera Operator to apply a high degree of aesthetic judgment in evaluating a take, asking him/herself the question: "*Did all the elements of camera frame movement flow together with a smooth and unobtrusive visual result consistent with the action and mood of the scene?*" If not, another take may be in order.

Doing **commercials** is like watchmaking, with its attention to minute detail and the integrating thereof into the finalized product. Perfecting each shot to "committee" specifications is what commercial shooting is all about. The Director, Director of Photography, agency Art Director and account executive along with client reps, all may frequently converge on the camera to approve (each in his or her own way) each setup and shot, prior to and following each take.

Interpersonal Relations. Moving up also entails dealing with expanded interpersonal relations—the politics of the job. As one moves up, more people are there to assist, and therefore to be supervised to one degree or another. At the same time, one deals more directly with top authority. For the **First Assistant Camera Operator**, it is the Camera Operator and Director of Photography, while for the **Camera Operator**, it is the Director of Photography and the Director. Whereas for the **Director of Photography**, the politics of the job—dealing with subordinates (camera, electrical and grip personnel), with peers (the Production Designer or Art Director, Costume Designer or Supervisor, Key Makeup Artist, Production Sound Mixer and the Film Laboratory Rep), and with top authority (the Director, the Producer and the starring actors)—might require **75%** of his/her attention, for a Camera Operator it might be **50%**, and for a First Assistant **25%**.

The bottom line is to treat all associates with respect and to earn their respect by executing Camera Operator responsibilities and duties in a consistently professional manner at all times.

Summing Up. Moving up from First Assistant Camera Operator to Camera Operator requires learning or sharpening some technical, physical and social skills not generally required or practiced as a Camera Assistant. To the degree that these skills are applied and improved upon, the move to Camera Operator should prove to be less stressful and more successful.

OPERATOR RESPONSIBILITIES

If you've been operating a camera for any length of time, you know that your prime responsibility is to deliver shots which are smoothly executed, properly composed and free of extraneous elements, such as microphones, booms and their shadows showing within frame. But equally important, that delivery should reflect the expression of the Director of Photography's interpretation of the expressed intent of the Director.

As Camera Operators, we must be sensitive to this interplay and strive to efficiently and cooperatively deliver the desired result. This may require some degree of adjustment from our usual practice of shot delivery—more or less headroom, more or less space leading the direction of an actor's look or movement, tighter or looser singles and/or group shots, and higher or lower camera angles, among other considerations—but nevertheless delivering that result consistently. Thus, sensitivity, flexibility and consistency are desirable attributes of a Camera Operator.

Excluding a video assist tap on the camera, the Operator of a film camera is the sole on-the-spot authoritative word on whether or not the visual aspects of the take—those elements held within frame—went according to plan. That is: Did the composition hold throughout the take? (Did the actors hit their marks?) Did the coordination of camera and dolly moves with actor moves work smoothly and consistently? (Did the crane or dolly, zoom lens and camera head movement begin and end with actor movement?) Were the sound boom, microphone and their shadows out of the shot? (Did the Boom Operator exceed the minimum positioning limitations?) Was the shot in focus? (Did the First Assistant and/or the actor miss a mark?) Did one actor cover or shadow the face of another actor? (Were the actors and/or dolly on their respective marks?) Did the take have the quality and feel to it that the Director and/or Director of Photography communicated to you?

Just as it is true that the Camera Operator sees each take before others later see it in dailies, it is also essential that the Operator accurately and concisely convey what was wrong and right with a take, so that nothing unexpected or marginal should be seen as the *only* print takes in dailies.

There often is a fine line separating an "acceptable" (okay or good) take from an "unacceptable" (no good) take. This fine-line tuning is practiced more during the deliberate and more exacting production pace of feature film production than on the much faster-paced TV series shooting schedules. On the latter, as we well know, *compromise* (to some degree) is the key word in all aspects of production—the constant twin spectres of time and budget constraints allow little latitude for the process of refining shots. Nevertheless, the Camera Operator should specify to the Director those elements of the take which were faulty and let the powers-that-be decide whether a retake or pickup is feasible or will cure the problem.

The measure of the effectiveness of this response by the Camera Operator to the vision of the Director/Director of Photography liaison is a fully realized cinematic product in which the unity of purpose (style) is clearly apparent.

CAMERA OPERATOR FUNCTIONS

A Camera Operator is often asked by non-industry people just what it is that he or she does in the making of a motion picture, whether film or video. In lieu of mentioning the myriad details of the job, the following is presented as an overview for the reader who may not be familiar with the craft and contributions of the Camera Operator.

Nearly everything that is done, directly and indirectly, during the pre-production and production phases is done for presentation to the camera. The film or video camera is a passive piece of equipment which needs to be manipulated, directly or indirectly (by remote or pre-programmed robotic controls), by human thought and hands—in short, by the skill of a Camera Operator.

In addition to being able to operate film and/or video cameras of all makes, models and types, the Camera Operator:

1. May operate a camera which is mounted on a tripod, pedestal, dolly, boom, crane, a body-mounted stabilizing device, or hand-held;

2. May remotely control the camera which is mounted on a selsyn-driven-servo remotely activated control head, which in turn may be affixed to a tripod, turret, cable rig, or crane;

3. May operate a camera from a camera insert car or while on a motorcycle, bicycle, automobile, race car, or other vehicle or rolling stock, ship, speedboat, sailboat, surfboard, barge, submersible, skis, sled, skates, horse or other animal;

4. May operate a camera while aboard an airplane, helicopter, blimp, balloon, glider, kite or other airborne conveyance, or in skydiving or bungee jumping free-fall;

5. May operate a camera while underwater or underground in mines, caves, crevasses or excavations;

6. May operate from scaffolding, or while suspended in a rope halter from a structure, pole, cliff, pinnacle or tree;

7. May operate while on a construction crane, cherry-picker, forklift, hydraulic lift or any similar mechanism;

8. May operate a camera under extreme and severe climatic conditions or otherwise inclement weather on land, sea, or in the air.

Camera operation is frequently accomplished under hazardous conditions, that is, when a potential, if not substantial, threat to the physical safety of the Operator and camera crew is apparent and ongoing.

Camera Operators operate solo or with crew on single and multiple-camera productions, with or without an audience, on interior and exterior domestic or foreign locations, or at or in a studio site.

The Camera Operator is expected to follow the action by panning, tilting and in the case of video production, moving the camera (trucking or tracking in, out, left or right and pedding up or down), zooming (sizing) and focusing, keeping the essentials in frame and well composed and seeing that no take is accepted which is out of focus, misframed or which has microphone, boom shadows or other extraneous material in frame.

Of course, there's much more to camera operating than this brief and generalized outline presents, but perhaps now the reader will feel edified and satisfied that Camera Operators are doing an important, complex, demanding and specialized job.

OPERATING PROCEDURES FOR FILM

Proper preparation is essential at every level and phase of production. One of the most important is preparing to make a shot as Camera Operator.

First and foremost, at the start of the shooting day before a foot of film is rolled, is the process of checking and double-checking to make sure: That the equipment is properly assembled and in good working order; that the dolly, seat and arm are fluidly functional; that the camera is balanced and level on the control head; that the geared head is solidly seated on its mounting and fully operative in each of its gears, or, that the friction or fluid head is positively seated on its mounting and moves freely through its pan and tilt range; that the self-leveling viewfinder is set at the proper angle; that the diopter setting in the viewfinder is accurately adjusted to the eye; that the illuminated aspect ratio frame scribing on the ground glass is correctly configured and functional; that there is no vignetting from elements in the matte box; that the magnification adjustment is operative; that the shooting script has been carefully studied and its elements made clear.

When preparing for making a shot setup, the concern is to make certain that the rudiments of the shot are thoroughly understood by the operative camera crew and that the equipment is configured and set up appropriately: That the wishes of the Director and Director of Photography are clear and understood; that the essentials of the action to be followed are clear personally, as well as to the First Assistant and Dolly Grip; that the dolly riser arm is set at the proper height for the shot at hand; that the dolly seat is properly positioned in the correct port on the appropriate side of the riser arm and at a comfortable height; that the dolly is properly configured with sideboards, etc; that the taking lens and filters are in place; that T-stop, shutter angle and frame rate settings have been set in accordance with the directions of the Director of Photography; that the dolly track, or path, is free of debris, bumps and irregularities.

When rehearsing and making the shot, it is essential to report any variance in the take from that expected by the Director and Director of Photography. This has to do with anomalies in the framing, focus, sizing, camera movement or variation from the blocking of the actors and/or camera.

Setting Up the Equipment. To avoid undue delay during the shooting process, it is important that the **camera equipment** be properly assembled, in good working order and ready to go. Although this is the prime responsibility of the First Assistant Camera Operator, the Camera Operator should always visually and manually check the assembled equipment prior to putting it to use to insure that all elements are in place and functioning properly. All **cable** attached to the camera and lens—power, video assist, teleprompter, lighting and zoom sizing lines—should be carefully dressed to accommodate full rises without binding and to avoid interfering with camera, Camera Operator and/or dolly movement during the shot.

The **mobile camera platform**, in this case a dolly, must be fully operative—the hydraulic reservoir fully charged, the riser arm responsive through its vertical range, the drive operational in its several directional modes, the Camera Operator's seat fully fluidly functional and the dolly platform surface clear of extraneous material.

The **camera**, with a fully loaded film magazine, should be in balance and solidly aligned and mounted on the control head which in turn should be level on both axes, whether a geared, friction or fluid head. Each of the gear settings on the geared head should be checked for fluidity and range of movement as well as the functionality of the neutral setting. If a friction or fluid head is being used, the full range of pan and tilt movement should be tested as well as the amount of friction or opposable tension which can be applied to each mode of movement. In addition, the lock-offs for pan and tilt should be checked to insure against drift or movement of the control head.

If the camera has a **self-leveling viewfinder**, it should be checked and positioned for comfort. A clean eyepiece cover should be in place. The **diopter setting** on the viewfinder should be set for maximum image sharpness. And the **aspect ratio scribing**, which appears on the ground glass, should agree with the framing required by the production genre, whether it is for 1.33 TV, 1.78 hi-def TV, 1.85 theatrical, 2.35 anamorphic, or some combination of the aspect ratios—for example, 1.33 and 1.78 hi-def, or 1.33 TV and 1.85 theatrical. If the ground glass has an illuminating feature for night shooting, it should be checked out at this stage.

All **filters** should be in place, in front of and/or behind the lens. There should be no vignetting by elements placed in the matte box. If so, adjustments of the elements and/or matte box should be made to remove the problem.

The **image magnifier** in the viewfinder should be checked, functional and in the desired position—normally, non-magnification.

The **taking lens** should be tested for focus—eye focus on, compared with measured distance to, an object.

The **on-off switch** should be tested and the film should run without excessive noise emission. The **film magazine** should be feeding and taking up film without making excessive noise or buckling the film. The **footage counter** should be zeroed with each fresh load of film.

Taking great care in the selection and preparation of equipment, along with a clear understanding of the Director's and Director of Photography's desires for the framing and coverage essentials of each shot, is crucial to facilitating proper and/or acceptable execution of the shots to be taken.

Setting Up the Shot. The first step in shot preparation from the standpoint of the Camera Operator is to carefully observe the blocking and to receive and clearly understand the wishes of the Director and/or Director of Photography regarding the desired framing and camera movement during the shot. The next step is to be certain that the First Assistant Camera Operator and Dolly Grip understand the timing and essential elements of the shot and the coordination necessary in order to help make the shot work as well as planned.

Selecting the appropriate equipment and accessories to make the shot is an essential decision—whether a dolly, crane or static camera support; whether geared head or pan stick control; whether a prime or zoom lens—usually made well in advance by the Director of Photography.

Positioning of the physical body and the equipment is an important consideration. The decision to stand or sit during the shot should be made early on. The position of the dolly chassis in relation to the action needs to be determined. The dolly arm and operator's seat should be set at the proper starting height, and the seat post placed in the proper port on the appropriate side of the riser arm for the shot. Appropriate sideboards—high, low, riser platform, diving board or pork chop—should be installed to help implement any movement the Camera Operator may need to make while operating the shot.

Depending upon the characteristics of the action and the direction and velocity the dolly may be moving in relation to that action, the appropriate gear ratio setting for pan and tilt moves—slow, medium, fast, or neutral (free-wheeling) for each mode—should be selected. The **slow** setting for deliberate, smooth and/or precision moves usually involves macro lens shots or extensive pans and/or tilt shots, often used with extreme telephoto lenses; the **fast** setting for rapid and/or countering moves, where the dolly moves opposite to the direction of the action; and **medium** for everything in between. The **neutral**, or out-of-gear, setting is used to reset the control wheels or to manually whip-pan or whip-tilt the camera without gear restraints.

A quick visual check of **T-stop, frame rate, zoom lens sizing**, and **shutter angle** and **filter pack** will assure that these settings are in accord with the wishes of the DP.

Finally, it is important that the dolly track, or path, is free of debris and surface irregularities and is not out of level, any of which can affect the quality of the shot.

The Rehearsal. During the rehearsal phase is the time for the Camera Operator to report and/or suggest modifications of the shot.

- The Director should be made aware if the blocking is somehow not accommodating the framing.
- The DP should be informed of any lighting or camera equipment anomaly which surfaces.
- The First Assistant Camera Operator should be told of any instances of soft focus or improper zoom sizing.
- The First Assistant and Dolly Grip should be informed of any coordination problems which the Camera Operator observes during each rehearsal or run-through.

- The attention of the Key Grip should be directed to protect the camera from lights flaring the lens.
- The Boom Operator should be told of any appearance of the mic, boom or their shadows in frame.
- The Set Dresser and Prop Assistant should be asked to reposition set dressing and/or props which are distracting to the framing.
- Key Makeup or Key Hair should be called on if makeup or hair needs retouching.
- The Costumer should be notified when wardrobe requires attention or adjusting.
- The First Assistant Director should be told of any extraneous individuals or vehicular traffic appearing in frame so that appropriate controls can be set up.

The Take. Any problem experienced during the take which affects the framing, its content, or coordination of the camera movement with the action should be clearly, concisely and promptly reported by the Camera Operator to the Director and/or Director of Photography. Reportable incidents include: An actor missing his or her marks; any noticeable surface bump, misdirection or velocity change during the dolly move; a microphone, its boom or their shadows, as well as extraneous objects or persons, appearing in frame; plus any of the possible problem areas noted for the rehearsal stage which occur or recur during the taking phase.

The Camera Operator should make the First Assistant aware at what point in the take the focus went soft, or the sizing was off or out of sync with the movement.

The Dolly Grip should be told where the surface bump occurred and/or when the dolly move went out of coordination while following the action.

The Script Supervisor should be informed of any observed anomaly occurring during the take.

Summing Up. Proper and timely preparation is the key to a successful shoot. Going into a shoot knowing that the equipment complement is complete and operational saves time, trouble and concern, thereby affording more time and energy to properly plan, set up and make each shot.

Carefully preparing for each shot setup, checking that all adjustments have been made and all equipment appropriately modified, will help ensure that each take will go as well and efficiently as possible.

Because the Camera Operator is in the cat-bird seat, clearly seeing everything in frame, any anomaly he or she notices should be promptly brought to the attention of those whose responsibility it is to correct that problem.

ELEMENTS OF LIGHTING & EXPOSURE

For Camera Operators and Assistants who are looking to move up to Director of Photography one day, it is important to acquire an understanding of the elements and camera settings which must be considered by the DP when determining and setting the proper exposure necessary for a shot or scene. The artistry lies not only in the lighting balance but in the exposure setting, which places essential portions of the imagery within the effective latitude afforded by the particular film emulsion or video system being used. Consistency of both lighting balance—foreground, midground, background and action areas—and exposure are hallmarks of the master Cinematographer.

To begin with, there are currently nine variable or adjustable factors, involving the matériel used to make images for motion pictures, which can affect exposure. The first is selection of the raw/unexposed **FILM STOCK, ASA/EI** (exposure index) rating, which represents the sensitivity of a particular film emulsion to light. During the **SHOOTING PROCESS,** there are five adjustable elements: **f/c** (foot candles), a value which represents the intensity of light striking or reflected from the subject matter; **T-stop** (lens diaphragm/iris setting), which is set to the desired iris opening thereby allowing a given amount of light to pass through the lens to the film plane; **filter factor**, which has to do with the amount of light absorbed by the filter(s); **fps**, (frames per second/frame rate) which controls the duration of time during which light strikes a frame of film; **shutter angle**, which also controls the duration of time that light strikes a frame of film. The three **LABORATORY** variables include: **push/pull processing**, which equates to either more or less development time than normal of the negative; **printer light**, which determines the intensity of light passing through the negative to the print stock; and **flashing**, which lightly and evenly exposes the undeveloped negative or print film stock by post-flashing (when the film has a latent image) or pre-flashing (before the film has a latent image) in order to reduce overall contrast.

SELECTING THE FILM STOCK

The Film Stock. The selection of the film stock(s) to be used and exposed during a given project is the starting point on the journey of putting visual images on film. There are so-called slow and fast film stocks. The slow film stocks are less sensitive to light and require longer exposure times and/or more light to form acceptable imagery on the film emulsion. The faster film stocks are more sensitive to light and so require shorter exposure times and/or less light to form acceptable imagery on their emulsions. For example, a film stock with an ASA of 400 is twice as sensitive to light as one with an ASA of 200.

Exterior day shooting generally calls for a slower film—one with a relatively low ASA or EI number—because of the usually greater overall intensity of the light levels.

Exterior night shooting, with either available or planned lighting, nearly always requires a much faster film stock—one with a relatively high ASA or EI rating—because of the generally lower overall light levels.

Interior shooting, with planned and augmentative lighting, whether studio or location sites, usually means using a faster film to minimize lighting, lighting equipment and the heat (and discomfort) generated therefrom.

The latest emulsions have an image-detailing latitude approaching plus-or-minus 5 stops—a 10-stop range. It is well to know the exact latitude of the emulsion(s) being used in order to place the exposure precisely where optimum image capture, comprising the desired color saturation and contrast (which evoke the desired scenic mood) and ambient detail, will be attained.

FIGURE 3

EXPOSURE TABLES
(IN T-STOP EQUIVALENTS)

SHOOTING

FILM ASA/EI	F/C	T-STOP	FILTERS	FPS		SECS/FR	SHUTTER
12	0	1.0	0	1.5	=	1/3.8	1.16°
25	1	1.4	2	3	=	1/7.5	2.32°
50	2	2	4	6	=	1/15	5.63°
100	4	2.8	8	12	=	1/30	11.25°
200	8	4	16	24	=	1/60	22.50°
400	16	5.6	32	48	=	1/125	45°
800	32	8	64	96	=	1/250	90°
1600	64	11	128	192	=	1/500	180°
3200	128	16	256	384	=	1/1000	(230°=
	256	22		768	=	1/2000	1/3 stop)
	512	32		1,536	=	1/4000	
	1,024	45		3,072	=	1/8000	

LAB PROCESSING

PUSH	PULL	PRINTER LIGHT	FLASHING
0	0	0	10%=1/8 stop
+1X	-1X	8	20%=3/16 stop
+2X	-2X	16	30%=1/4 stop
+3X	—	24	
		32	
		40	
		48	

These numbers are in one-stop equivalents reading VERTICALLY (except where noted). The horizontal lines can be mixed and matched; there is not necessarily a relationship horizontally as pictured above.

LIGHTING ELEMENTS

The Lighting Sources. There are basically two sources of light—natural and artificial. Natural sources include the sun, moon and fire along with natural plant, animal and chemical luminescence. Artificial sources include candle, oil, gas, tungsten, fluorescent, arc, quartz halogen, mercury and sodium vapor discharge, HMI, UV (ultra-violet, or black light) and infrared lighting, laser, flash bulb and electronic flash.

Position/Direction of Sources. Position of the light sources is an important consideration. The vertical and horizontal angle of the lighting beam from each light source to the target area will have a determined effect on the illumination of subject matter (what is lighted and what is not) as well as the modeling thereof, and the display of shadow areas within the area covered by the light pattern.

For example, the varying angles of sunlight striking subject matter, from sunrise through midday to sunset provide differing looks. It requires careful planning, augmentation and execution to optimally utilize this prime lighting source.

Reflected light is that light from source lights which bounces off surfaces which absorb, spread and/or scatter light, along with the color, if any, of the reflecting surface, more or less randomly about the setting, depending upon the shape, curvature, texture, position and color value of the reflecting surface.

For example, a plane front surface mirror will reflect light without distortion or light loss, whereas a heavily textured surface will scatter light and a dark-colored surface will absorb light, reflecting very little. For maximum reflective effect, use a front surface mirror to reflect light. For minimal reflective effect, or to absorb a maximum amount of light, use a black, heavily textured surface material such as velvet or duvetyn.

Ambient light, often called **available light**, is natural or artificial light which is present in and illuminates an interior or exterior shooting site, or that emanating from a CRT, digital or liquid crystal display, before augmentative lighting is added.

Street and storefront lighting with illuminated signs are examples of ambient exterior nighttime "available" lighting. Stores, office buildings, bars and residences are examples where interior available ambient lighting can be used and/or augmented.

Quantity. The number, size and type of units and the spread or coverage of the lighting are important considerations which have to do with the size, configuration and location of the area(s) to be illuminated. After scouting and examining set designs and/or actual settings, figuring the size, power requirements, type, number and placement of lighting units is essential to determine in relation to the areas and subject matter to be lighted and the distance from them that lighting units must be placed.

In general, the larger and more extensive the area, the larger and more powerful the lighting units required, along with a substantial power source.

Intensity. Intensity, or lighting strength, is determined by the lighting sources used and whether the light is emanating from a powerful natural source, like the sun; or powerful artificial sources, like arcs, HMIs or PARs, and whether the light source is spotted or flecked; or from smaller, less powerful focusing or softlight units, like dinkies, peanuts, and peppers; or from low-intensity sources, like moonlight, candlelight, gaslight and firelight.

Distance of the lighting sources from the subject matter has a direct effect on the intensity of light hitting and reflected from the subject matter. In general, light falls off with the square of the distance from the lighting source to the subject matter. In other words, light from a given light source measured at 20 feet is approximately one-quarter as intense as a measurement made at 10 feet.

Quality. The degree of beam cohesion and its color temperature are the two qualities of light emission. Lighting quality can be related to the **degree of cohesion** of the light rays emitted from the source. For example, lasers and the sun emit nearly parallel light beams. A point source, such as an arc light, will cast sharp shadows with a diverging beam angle. Spotlights tend to emit a narrow, sharply defined beam of light. Plane front-surface mirrors used to reflect this light would maintain the beam integrity. On the other hand, flood lights and softlights emit, respectively, wide or diffused patterns of light. Depending upon the surfaces used, reflectors, bounce boards or silks could further diffuse any light beams striking their surfaces.

Color temperature is figured in degrees Kelvin. The higher the number, the bluer (cooler) the color quality of the light; and the lower, the redder (warmer). For example, the color temperature (not heat temperature) of sunlight may exceed 5,600° Kelvin (bluish) at midday and quite reddish at sunrise and sunset, while tungsten light ranges between 2,800° and 3,200° Kelvin (reddish-orange), candle or fire light may be in the mid- to low-2,000° Kelvin range.

Each lighting source emits a color (or colors) and therefore has a Kelvin rating. For example, sunlight is bluish and moonlight is also bluish (because the moon is neutral in color and reflects the bluish sunlight), tungsten light is reddish, the cool fluorescent light spectrum contains blue and green, mercury vapor is blue-green, and sodium vapor is red-orange.

Color correction gels can be used at the light source(s) or at the camera to accommodate the color quality of the predominant light source, or to augment the prevailing light source by adding other sources with varying spectral light.

Any colored surfaces near subject matter in a scene will reflect their color values onto that nearby subject matter, thereby affecting (sometimes adversely) the visual result to some degree.

Lighting the Scene. Lighting can strike the subject matter from the front, either side, back side, the top, and/or below, depending upon the source(s) of the illumination. A basic lighting setup comprises four functions: A **key** or principal modeling light; a **fill** light to illuminate the shadows created by the key light; **background** light to provide needed contrast to separate subjects and objects in the frontal action areas from the background; **effect or accent** lights to impart a distinctive highlight for separation from the background or for eye-grabbing attention. Accent lights include: Back or rim light, side light, hair light, eye light, item light, and projected pattern light. Of these accent lights, perhaps the most important is the **back light**, which should be subtle and set by eye.

A setting may have its own sources of illumination, that is, what's there and turned on. This **ambient**, or available, light may be used, augmented, or replaced. Ambient light levels include: Daylight in its various and varying intensities and qualities; evening street and shopfront lighting and illuminated signs; lighted interior locations; CRT screen emission level; digital and liquid crystal instrument displays.

Metering the Light. The intensity of the light may be determined and read by direct or reflected light meter readings. **Incident light** readings measure the light striking the subject at the point of measurement. **Reflected light** readings determine the intensity of the light being reflected to the camera from the surface of the subject matter being measured.

EXPOSURE MODIFIERS

The Lenses. Lenses are light valves which admit and pass a given amount of light through the camera aperture to the film plane. There are slow, standard and fast lenses, so-called because of the minimum amount of light they are designed and constructed to pass. Nearly every lens has an iris, or variable diaphragm, which may be adjusted/sized to control the amount of light passing through the lens to the film plane.

Professional lenses are calibrated in T-stops, settings which accurately reflect the actual amount of light transmitted through the lens diaphragm at each given iris setting. For example, a stop of T-4 passes twice the amount of light as a setting of T-5.6; T-8 allows half the amount of light to pass as will T-5.6.

Filtration. Filters are of several types. Some are **color modifiers**, others are **light absorbers**, and still others are **image modifiers**. Color modifying filters have a spectral color value which passes light of that spectral quality and withholds or limits light of other spectral values. For example, a reddish filter will pass reddish light but limit or withhold blue and green light. Both color modifying and light absorbing filters absorb light so, in effect, act to cut down on the intensity of light reaching the film plane. Filters, depending upon their density, may reduce the passage of light by up to several stops. Image modifiers—diffusion, star effect, diopters—pass light freely but act to modify the light rays passing through their surfaces.

Filters are often combined in a personalized filter pack by the Director of Photography to achieve a certain visual effect for a shot, scene, sequence or throughout a production. In order to reduce the light-scattering effect of multiple optical surfaces, certain color modifying and light absorbing filters are combined in manufacture and offered for more convenient use.

Frame Rate. The standard taking and projecting frame rate for the U.S. is 24 fps. The frame rate may be set for effect before, or varied during, a take. A shot that has been undercranked, exposed at fewer than 24 fps and projected at 24 fps, will appear to be in more rapid, if not erratic, motion than normal. A shot that has been overcranked, exposed at more than 24 fps and projected at 24 fps, will appear to be in relatively slow motion. Single frame, or stop-motion, shooting is used for time lapse shots of natural occurring but extremely slowly evolving events (plant growth, cloud movement or building construction) or for animating inanimate objects (ball rolling, plastic puppetry).

If the frame rate is doubled, light will have one-half the time to affect the film during the exposure interval. If the frame rate is halved, light will have twice the time to affect the film.

The Shutter. The shutter is a light control mechanism, set to stop all light from striking the film during film pull-down, and to allow a certain amount of time for light to strike the film while the film is immobile in the gate during the exposure interval.

The standard angle varies from camera to camera from 170° to 180°. A wider angle variable shutter can open to approximately 230°. A narrowed angle can close from 180° toward 0°. Each 50 percent decrease in shutter angle results in a loss of fifty percent of the light available to strike the film. Each 100 percent increase in shutter angle results in twice as much light striking the film during the exposure interval.

Determining the Exposure. In determining the optimum exposure for a setup, the Director of Photography must take into account a variety of considerations: The subject matter (including performers, objects, colors, shapes and textures in and of the foreground, midground and background areas); the film stock used; the lens selected; camera movement (in relation to the lighting); the frame rate; the shutter angle; the filter pack; the lighting level(s), balance and color temperature thereof; and finally, but not least, the visual effect desired for the audience-ready version.

First, the lighting is roughed in and refined to accommodate the action and mood. Then it is sweetened and finalized by eye to achieve the desired visual effect. Finally, when camera settings and filter packs have been established and factored, and everything and everybody is set and ready to shoot, the exposure is calculated and set, after averaging out the metered values and/or averaging out the visual values with the desired look of the film in mind as it passes from the image capture stage through processing until it finally arrives at the release print stage.

THE FILM LABORATORY PROCESS

Processing. Film processing can be normal, pushed, or pulled. When a film is **pushed**, it is kept in the developer a longer period of time, resulting in forced- or over-development. When the film is **pulled**, it is fed through the developer in a shorter period of time, resulting in under-development.

Printing. The full light range of the printer lighting scale is 52 lights of varying intensity. Every eight lights is equivalent to one stop of light.

Flashing. Pre-flashing occurs before image capture when unexposed the raw stock is exposed to a relatively small overall, even amount and intensity of light. **Post-flashing** occurs after image capture, but before the film is developed, when the exposed film is treated with a relatively small overall, even amount and intensity of light.

CORRELATION OF THE VARIABLES

Film Speed/Sensitivity Ratings. ASA or EI ratings are manufacturers' indicators of the sensitivity of their various film emulsions to exposure to light. Each doubling of a sensitivity rating indicates that an emulsion is twice as sensitive to light.

Light Intensity Readings. Light intensity is rated in **foot candles**. Each doubling in foot candle readings indicates that twice the intensity of light, incident or reflected, is present at the metered position.

T-stops. T-stops are the light-controlling incremental settings of the diaphragm in the taking lens. Each T-stop transmits a quantity of light which is twice the amount transmitted by a stop which is one T-stop higher, that is, with a one stop smaller iris opening. Each time the iris setting for any T-stop is increased by a one stop larger iris opening, twice the amount of light is transmitted through the lens to the film plane than at the one stop smaller opening size.

Filter Factors. Optical filters which are placed in front of or behind the taking lens can have an effect on the amount (and quality) of light reaching the film plane, depending upon the amount of light absorbed by their density. A doubling of the filter factor assigned a particular filter indicates that the amount of light absorbed by that filter will also double.

Frame Rates. Any change in the frame rate will affect the time that light has to play on the film as it rests in the gate during the exposure interval. Doubling the frame rate halves the time light has to play on the film emulsion, thereby requiring either twice as much light passing through the lenticular system, or doubling the light intensity reaching the film plane.

Shutter Angles. A variable shutter may have an opening angle range up to 230°. Normal shutter angle is 180°. Any change in shutter angle will have an effect on the time that light has to play on the film as it rests in the gate. Halving the shutter angle will cut in half the time that light has to play on the film emulsion, thereby requiring either twice as much light passing through the lenticular lineup, or doubling the light intensity reaching the film plane.

Push/Pull Ratings. Film processing procedures also can have an effect on the film image. A given film emulsion can be effectively increased or decreased in its normal sensitivity rating by varying the time that the film is in the development bath. Effective film sensitivity can be increased by a slower pass through the development stage. Film sensitivity can be decreased by less time in the soup. For example, a one-stop push doubles the effective sensitivity of the exposed film stock, thereby bringing out the detail in the underexposed areas.

Printer Light Settings. The 50-light printer scale translates to a range of approximately six stops—plus or minus three stops from its center point. This allows modification of the color and density of the camera negative during the timing/printing process.

Flashing Ratings. Pre-flashing and post-flashing have minimal effect on exposure. Each 10% intensity flashing is equivalent to approximately one-eighth of a stop increase. Flashing can also be applied during the shooting process by applying a light wash of white or colored ambient light obliquely across the surface of the taking lens.

SUMMARY

A number of elements are involved in considering the optimum exposure for a shot: The film stock; the amount, quality and position of light striking the subject matter; the taking lens; lenticular filtration; frame rate; shutter angle; T-stop setting; and film processing, flashing and printing.

The elements of exposure are interrelated. A manipulation of any one or more of the elements can have an effect on the sharpness and movement of the captured image and certainly will affect the amount and/or intensity of light striking the film plane but, in so doing, each modification will require a reciprocal adjustment of one of the other elements in order to maintain a consistency in exposure. For example, slowing the frame rate from normal requires proportionately decreasing the amount of light striking the film plane by any one of the following adjustments: Decreasing the amount of light on the subject, decreasing the size of the lens T-stop opening, increasing the filter factor (by adding neutral density), decreasing the shutter angle.

Understanding the function of each element of exposure and the effect any alteration of that element will have on image capture, quality and exposure is essential to the art and craft of cinematography.

CAMERA SETTINGS, COMPONENTS AND QUALITY

It is not only the Director of Photography who is concerned with lens and filter selection and with determining settings on the motion picture camera and lens which can affect exposure and image quality. The Camera Operator and, especially, the First Assistant Camera Operator must both be aware of the visual effect resulting from the use of each component and setting which the DP selects and of the potential limitations these components and settings can place on their work.

The film camera settings to be considered are: Shutter angle and frame rate.

The lenticular considerations are: Lens focal length, T-stop setting, and lenticular filtration.

It is important to understand the effect each of these components and settings can have on the quality of the recorded image and then consider how the First Assistant and Camera Operator can utilize that understanding to make adjustments as necessary, in order to deliver the best results possible.

The Shutter Angle. Changing the shutter angle has an effect on both exposure and image sharpness. Trimming the angle from, let's say, 180° to 90° cuts the light striking the film plane during exposure by 50% (one T-stop) and, because of the decreased exposure time, increases image sharpness by reducing image blur caused by movement of the subject matter and/or camera relative to each other during the exposure interval.

On the other hand, expanding the shutter angle from 180° to, say, 230°, increases the amount of light striking the film plane by about 33% (1/3 T-stop). This increased exposure time increases moving image blur.

To maintain consistent exposure, the shutter angle is inversely proportional to the lens diaphragm opening—the narrower the shutter angle, the larger the lens diaphragm (T-stop) required—a 50% (equivalent to a one stop of light loss) narrowing of the shutter angle requires a 100% (one stop) increase in the lens aperture setting. The First Assistant should be aware of these relationships and be in a position of understanding and support and to know whether to remind the Director of Photography, when necessary, about exposure adjustment to compensate for a non-standard shutter angle setting.

The Camera Operator must be aware that a decreased shutter angle can have a marked effect on the rate at which the camera can be panned without strobing the recorded image. This is particularly noticeable in panning scenics and otherwise static subject matter, not panning with action. The focal length of the taking lens is also a factor in the panning rate. In addition, the longer the taking lens, the slower the pan and/or tilt movement required in order to avoid the strobing effect.

The Frame Rate. Altering the frame rate also has an effect on exposure and the look of the recorded action. The slower the fps, the more rapid-looking the action when projected at the normal rate of 24 fps. The faster the fps camera setting, the more deliberate and/or dreamlike the projected action appears. Frame rate is inversely proportional to the movement of the action being recorded. To maintain consistent exposure, it should be remembered that the slower the frame rate, the higher the compensating T-stop setting. In order to maintain consistent exposure, consider frame rate as being directly proportional to T-stop. For example, at T-5.6, a 50% (one stop) decrease in fps requires a 100% or one stop lens diaphragm size decrease, to T-8.

First Assistants must be aware that, in order to maintain a consistent exposure, any variation of frame rate during a shot must be compensated for by a coordinated variation in the T-stop (and/or shutter angle) setting.

The Camera Operator, particularly on undercranked shots, must be careful to smoothly follow the action in order to minimize any uneven camera movement which will be accentuated when the scene is projected at the standard frame rate.

Lens Focal Length. Whether a prime or zoom lens, the selection, or position, of focal length has a marked effect on the image, the subject matter framed, and the visual perspective. The depth of field, or area wherein the subject matter appears in acceptable focus, is always a principal concern for the First Assistant, particularly when longer focal length lenses and lower exposures come into play. Depth of field is inversely proportional to the focal length of the lens being used—the longer the lens, the shallower the depth of field. Wide angle lenses have great depth of field. Longer lenses, because of their relative narrow depth of field, require careful and extremely accurate focus pulling, especially in low-light level situations and when the subject in sharpest focus is relatively close to camera.

The Camera Operator must be more concerned with panning/tilting speeds when longer lenses are up on the camera in order to avoid the strobing effect on the recorded images.

Exposure Setting. The T-stop or exposure setting sizes the lens diaphragm aperture to allow a specific amount of light through the lens elements to strike the film plane. The higher the T-stop number, the smaller the opening in the diaphragm and the greater the depth of field. Improperly set exposure can degrade or damage the recorded image.

First Assistants must be aware that in order to maintain consistent exposure during a shot, say, from a bright scene to a more subdued surrounding (from an exterior to an interior on a continuous move), optimal exposure may be maintained during the transitional point—from the brightly lit area to the area in shadow or subdued light—or by increasing the size of the lens aperture and/or widening the shutter angle and/or pulling graduated neutral density filtration.

The Camera Operator must be visually alert during takes involving exposure manipulation to be sure the adjustments provide a seamless visual look.

Lenticular Filtration. What is placed in lenticular alignment—inside of, in front of, or behind the lens—may affect exposure and/or have a marked effect on the quality of the recorded image.

Each filter has a filter-factor which ranges from zero for an optical flat plain diffusion, or diopters to much higher numbers for the varied density range of neutral density, colored and polarizing filters. The higher the factor, the more light the filter absorbs. In order to compensate for light loss, a filter with a factor of 2 requires opening the lens aperture one stop, a 4 factor needs two stops, 8 three stops; each doubling of the filter factor requires an additional full stop of exposure, or 100% more light applied to the subject.

The First Assistant must be careful to check that all lens and filter surfaces are immaculately clean before being placed in the lenticular lineup. Any foreign substance on lenticular surfaces can affect exposure and damage image quality. And the First Assistant must be sure to take into account the fact that a pellicle reflex camera will direct 30% of the light coming through the lens to the viewfinder ocular, requiring a 1/3rd stop increase in exposure.

The Camera Operator must ascertain that the filters placed in the lenticular lineup are properly positioned so that edges will not encroach in the visual frame, or, in the case of split diopters and graduated filters, that these add-ons are accurately aligned with specific foreground or background elements.

Summing Up. It is essential that both the Camera Operator and First Assistant Camera Operator be aware of the implications inherent in the determination by the Director of Photography of each adjustable setting on the camera and taking lens as well as of each component placed in the lenticular lineup. Understanding the effect that each setting and lenticular component can have on exposure, perspective and image quality can help the Operator and First Assistant make the necessary adjustments and will go a long way toward insuring that the best result will be obtained.

FACETS OF FOCUS

An important facet of our work is focus. Focus has two important functional aspects: One is compositional—to artfully direct viewer attention toward a specific area or areas and/or an image or images in frame; the other is a refining process—to selectively create sharply defined images in frame.

COMPOSITIONAL FOCUS

Viewer attention can be focused on—directed toward—any area of the frame by a number of functional compositional techniques. These elements include: The type and familiarity of subject matter—story, cast of performers, vehicles, objects; relative size, facing and positioning in frame; direction, velocity, duration and mass of that movement in frame; velocity of zoom lens sizing variations; the attention-directed positioning of subjects; intensity and quality of the lighting; the attention-directed design elements of settings and set dressing; the type of makeup applied; elements of costume design; continuity and coverage of the story elements; mood and emotion; contrast of elements.

In planned and structured productions, most of these options have been put in place before the camera turns, by the Producer, the Production Designer, the Casting Director, the Director, the Director of Photography, the Costume Designer and the Key Makeup Artist. Nevertheless, the Camera Operator, with an understanding of these compositional elements, their relative importance, and how they interrelate and impact a scene, can make an important contribution to the production by appropriately framing the elements, or, if the compositional elements are not optimal in frame, by tactfully calling this to the attention of the Director or Director of Photography.

The following elements are related to composition and are given as a starting point in the consideration of the part they play in focusing viewer attention on the displayed images.

The Target Audience. The viewing audience for whom a given production is being made is important for all collaborating personnel to keep constantly in mind during all phases of pre-production, production and post-production. This audience will have its own set of defining demographics, of its likes and dislikes, of its preferences and displeasures. Although this is an area where the principal elements—subject matter, cast, location, period––have been determined prior to production, it is well for the Camera Operator to be tuned in in order to keep the framing consistent with subject matter and the Director's interpretation thereof.

Subject Matter. The story and visual subject matter have marked influence on a viewer's sensibilities. The viewer will relate more readily to a story and visual subject matter he or she can identify with—for example, a performer of the same gender and age as the viewer(s) being tried and tested. On the other hand, if there are visuals comprising horrifying monsters and activities, because of the implicitly implied threat of this imagery, the viewer is likely to focus even more attention thereon.

Familiarity. Familiarity with the subject matter—cast, story, setting, period—plays an important role in focusing viewer attention as the production unfolds. So long as these elements are developed logically and smoothly, audience attention will be maintained.

Continuity. To maintain viewer attention, it is important that the story progression and character development be logical, consistent and efficient.

Coverage. Without adequate coverage of the action by the Director, the Editor will be hampered in assembling a product with the rhythm, pace and flow necessary to maintain viewer interest and attention.

Composition. The visual elements, properly arranged in frame, can draw the eye and interest of the viewer to the screen like a nail to a magnet. Use of the "golden section" principal in setting static framing and/or astute use, or placement, of foreground elements in helping frame the midground-background areas will result in pleasing and attention-arresting compositions. For static subjects with the subject matter at rest, lead framing in the direction of the look makes for a satisfying viewer response; a look across frame will require more lead space in the direction of the look than will a look directed toward the lens axis. For dynamic framing with subject matter in motion, adequate lead framing consistent with the direction and rate of movement of the subject(s) is essential to maintain audience comfort and attention.

Facing Position. Subjects facing the lens draw more attention than those in profile or facing away from the camera. Not only does the face identify the person or character, facial features convey to the viewer a host of emotions and intentions needed to develop character, action and story.

Relative Actual Size. At the same distance from the lens, a larger subject will receive more viewer attention than a smaller subject of the same genre. Larger is more imposing and generally accepted as more important than smaller. In addition, larger may be considered as potentially more threatening.

Relative Size: Positioning in Depth—Near to Far. The actual or apparent distance of the subject from the lens is an important function of the focus of attention. The closer the subject is to the lens, the larger the subject is in the viewfinder, the greater the viewer attention factor.

Relative Size: By Choice of Lens. By selecting a longer lens, the subject, though some distance from the lens, can be brought into apparently close proximity, thereby appearing quite large in frame, resulting in focusing audience attention on the prominent image in frame to the exclusion of any concern for the minimal, and often undefined, background and foreground areas included in frame. The closeup view of a person or object is akin to utilizing a magnifying glass to more thoroughly examine every aspect of the subject appearing in frame.

Lens Sizing—Dynamic Variations. When the variable focal length lens is used in zoom mode, re-sizing the subject matter during a shot, viewer attention is focused on the event. Zooming in—making the subject image larger in frame— is more attention-getting than zooming out—making the subject image smaller in frame. Again, larger is more attention-demanding than smaller.

Positioning in Frame—Left, Center, Right; High, Low. The position a subject occupies in frame has a pronounced effect on focusing viewer attention. Size and all other variables being constant, a centered subject is the most prominent, or attention-gathering, image in frame. In those cultures accustomed to reading from left to right and from high to low, a subject positioned in the left side of frame is accorded first look and more prominence (viewer attention) than a subject positioned in the right side, while a subject positioned higher in frame receives more viewer attention than a subject positioned lower in frame.

Attention-Directed Grouping of Subjects. During the action blocking process, subjects can be arranged in such a manner as to focus viewer attention on a certain individual in that group. This is done by having all players in the group face, look, point and/or lean toward the principal player of the moment. This Directorial technique, in turn, focuses viewer attention on that player.

Screen Direction: Static. The relative direction in which the subject is facing (the staging or action line) should be maintained from shot to shot in a scene or sequence which includes that subject in frame in order to avoid a disruption of viewer attention.

Screen Direction: Dynamic. The relative direction of movement of the subject should be maintained from shot to ensuing shot for the same reasons. An inexplicable crossing of that action line will result in viewer disorientation and disruption of attention.

Direction of Subject Movement. Subject movement can be directed to, from, across—left to right and right to left, up or down—and always draws viewer attention. The direction of movement will determine the extent of that attention focus. In a static frame, for example, action moving toward the lens has more impact than action moving across or moving away from camera. Depending upon the subject matter in motion, generally right to left movement (action opposing the left to right eye movement of western cultures) is more arresting than left to right movement and ascending movement has more impact than descending movement.

Velocity of Movement. The velocity of movement of a subject has a direct effect on viewer attention. The faster the action, the greater the attention factor.

Duration of Movement. A short-lived action has less effect on viewer attention than does a movement of longer duration. A short quick action will have more effect than a short slow movement.

Mass of Movement. The more mass to a movement, the stronger the effect on audience attention. When movement takes the form of waves of humanity moving relentlessly in battle attack or exodus, a massive cattle stampede, an avalanche, a rock or mud slide, a tidal wave, volcanic eruption or nuclear explosion, galvanized viewer attention is sure to follow.

Follow-Action Framing. Following and properly framing the action by panning and tilting from a static position or mobile camera platform have built-in attention dynamics, because the audience is being virtually transported by these camera moves.

Lenticular Focus. Subjects which are in sharpest optical focus tend to draw more audience attention than subjects which are out of focus.

Lighting. The direction, intensity and quality of light have a measured effect on directing viewer attention. In general, the more brightly lit subject or area in frame will attract more viewer attention than less brightly lit subjects and/or areas. More often, frontal key lighting is more attention-getting than side or back lighting. Unusual lighting angles—for example, low-angle-key "Lugosi lighting"—can rivet audience attention. Undiffused and unfiltered white light is more striking than diffused or filtered light. As to color diffusion on lights, the advancing colors along the warm area of the color spectrum will generally attract more attention than the cooler receding colors.

Attention-Directed Design of Settings/Set Dressing/Props. Just as sets can be designed to draw viewer attention to a player or action taking place, settings can be dressed to accomplish the same goal. For example, the horizontal and/or vertical lines of a set can be designed to draw viewer attention to a specific area in which the action will take place. Set dressing can be arranged to lead viewer attention toward a certain area of the set. Special props can be constructed that will absorb audience interest in the way these objects look or work.

Makeup. The appearance of character and special effects makeup on a subject or subjects can be riveting for an audience. The creative application of rubberized skin over prosthetics can create terrifying images for audience gratification.

Costume Design: Style/Texture/Color. The style, texture and color of costumes, along with their accessories, can be attention-arresting for the viewer. In general, fully saturated colors are more attention-demanding than unsaturated, pastel colors.

Morphing. The digital metamorphosing—recomposing—of an image into something else has reached a nearly seamless state of the art. It is the visual result that focuses audience attention so completely. In so doing, digital morphing has taken its place among the sure-fire viewer attention-grabbers.

Mood and Emotion. Mood and emotion have an effect on viewer attention. Mood, solidly developed and consistently maintained will attract viewer interest. emotion, logically developed, will elicit viewer interest and response.

Contrast. This brings us to the important part contrast plays in focusing viewer attention by using striking differences in the application of the production elements. For example, contrasting: The familiar with the unfamiliar; large elements with small; subjects facing with those facing away; near subjects or objects with those far away; subjects and areas brightly lit with subjects and areas in darkness or shadow; saturated colors with de-saturated colors; advancing colors with receding colors; fast action with slow action; massive movement with individual movement; sustained movement with staccato movement; dynamic framing with static framing; zooming in with zooming out; hard focus with soft focus; heavy visual mood with light visual mood; heavy dramatic moments with light, comedic ones.

SELECTIVE OPERATIVE FOCUS

It should be remembered that depth of focus is happening behind the lens at the focal plane; whereas, depth of field is that near-to-more-distant area in front of the lens wherein subjects are in acceptably sharp focus.

In general, the most sharply defined images in frame are the ones drawing audience attention. The sharpest focus is normally set for the most important subject matter appearing in frame. When more than one element in frame is of equal importance, the focus can be split between the elements, provided each is positioned within a defined depth of field so that all are in acceptably sharp focus; or the focus can be alternated between (or among) equally important subjects in turn as each becomes the most important element in frame. In addition, when subjects in frame are separated beyond the acceptable limits of the field of acceptable focus, the focus can be racked (radically adjusted) from subject to subject, bringing each into sharp focus at selected moments while causing the other subject to be in relatively soft focus. Change of focus can also be used for transitional purposes, at the ending or beginning of scenes or sequences.

Principal Focus. Principal focus is the sharpest focus and is usually placed with, and follows, the most important subject matter appearing in frame. During the days of the parallax viewfinder, it was important to assist the Camera Operator in maintaining accurate framing so that the principal focus was always placed precisely on the principal performer.

Split Focus. Where important elements are appearing in frame at varying distances from the lens, the principal focus is set at an intermediate distance between the closest and farthest of the subjects in order to place all selected elements within a range of acceptable focus. To achieve an acceptable result, there must be enough light intensity and/or an appropriate wide angle lens in order to afford an adequate depth of field within which the subject matter resides.

Alternating Focus. During a shot, the focus can stay with one subject throughout, or shift from one subject to another as each subject becomes, for the moment—because of action, dialogue or positioning—the most important element in frame.

Rack Focus. Rack focusing is a radical form of alternating focus between, or among, two or more subjects whose positions in frame are widely separated in depth and well beyond the limits of acceptable focus in the available depth of field.

Transitional Focus. Selective focus can be used as a transitional device to end and begin a scene or sequence, going out of focus at the conclusion thereof and/or coming into focus at the beginning.

Summing Up. Of the two facets of focus discussed above, we of the operative camera crew are most concerned with selective operative focus—maintaining our subject matter in sharp to acceptable image sharpness. Of equal importance is the manipulation of compositional elements to focus viewer attention in an optimum manner on composed subject matter. And not least, the focused attention of the Camera Operator to all the above aspects of focus is essential in the process of optimizing image capture and its effect on the final product. In these applications, it is **focus is as focus does**.

CLUES & CUES:
READING BODY LANGUAGE

Body language is a form of non-verbal communication which, consciously or unconsciously, we all "speak," and about which we, as Camera Operators, need to be sufficiently knowledgeable in order to become proficient in applying this know-how to our craft.

Understanding body language as it applies to movement, the preparation therefor and the execution thereof, can be very helpful in framing and following performers during the shooting process. Knowing when, how rapidly and in which direction a subject will move can capture the moment on documentary or news assignments, or save time, film and money in retakes on planned productions.

Expressive Body Parts. Every one of us produce some degree of bodily reaction or movement in response to various stimuli. Depending upon the particular stimulus, the physical response can vary from slight to extreme. Various parts of the anatomy may respond individually or in concert.

The most expressive parts of the human anatomy are the head and face, perhaps because most of the primary sense organs are located there along with the master receptor/computer/manipulator—the brain. The eyes, brow and mouth, in that order, are the most emotionally expressive facial elements. Eye movement usually leads head movement and head movement generally leads body and limb movement. So head and facial cues are important indicators of imminent movement and the likely direction such movement will take. The likely velocity of the impending move can be determined by the physical signs of the initiating energy exhibited by the subject as he or she prepares to move.

Because of the importance of the face in conveying emotion and intent, a majority of shots, up to 80% of the total composed for dramatic programming, are in the closeup category—shots holding subjects from waist-to-head to head-only. Studying, and careful attention to, eye movement of the subject can give adequate notice of impending movement, especially head turns, by that subject.

Of the physical limbs, the arms and hands are the most expressive. The hands are especially so because they can be articulated in so many expressive configurations, exceeded only by facial expressiveness. Movement of the arms usually immediately precedes body turns.

The legs, being the principal means of moving the body from place to place, generally deal with gross movement, but can be expressive in their positioning and movement while the body is at rest. More often than not, the body will move in the direction the feet are pointing.

The body, with its neck, shoulders, chest, back and abdomen also sends non-verbal signals with its varying positions, postures and degrees of relative movement of its parts.

The Quest for Visual Cues. Where (upon which part of the anatomy) and when does the Camera Operator focus his or her attention to access the often subtle physical signals given by the subject? In short, this depends upon the nature of the shoot—the type of production, whether rehearsals and retakes are possible, the experience level of the photographic subjects involved—and the sensitive perception of the Camera Operator.

Maintaining Framing. At this point it should be emphasized that in static shots, with the subject at rest, the subject should be framed in a shot size which allows a minimal amount of subject movement without having to continually adjust the framing in order to accommodate that movement. Excessive framing adjustments during a take call attention to the camera and detract from the subject matter.

For the Closeup View. The upper body, including the head, is the subject matter of the closeup for the human figure. The **medium closeup** view, from the waist to the top of the head, includes the shoulders and the arms, to the elbows. Thus, the face, head, neck, shoulders, upper torso and upper arms are in frame and can be observed and relied upon to give signals which the Camera Operator can tune in to in order to make minor continuing adjustments in framing or to prepare for sudden and/ or major moves by the subject. The **closeup** includes the upper chest, shoulders, neck and head. The **extreme closeup** frames the face, or portions thereof, only. It is apparent that as the framing tightens, there are fewer body parts in frame to observe for the often subtle signals of intended movement; however, with each closer view, the parts in frame become progressively larger, with the result that subtle movement becomes ever more evident in signaling an intent to move.

For the Medium Shot View. The medium shot of a human figure includes the knees to top of head. With more of the subject in frame, and smaller in frame than closer views, there are more bodily parts to observe for cues leading to motion and movement.

For the Long Shot View. Because long shots hold the human figure full size to infinitely small in frame, visual cues are not as critical framing considerations. Gross movement of the figure in frame can be conveniently followed without need for anticipation of the move. The **medium long shot** includes the entire human form, from head to toe. In the **long shot**, the human figure is approximately half the height of the frame. In the **extreme long shot**, the human figure is further reduced in vertical size. Because the subjects are relatively small to insignificant in frame compared with more intimate medium or closeup views, movement of body parts are not as critical in giving lead time to the Camera Operator to get ready to pan or tilt the camera in order to properly frame and follow the developing action.

For the Group or Full Shot. When the frame is filled from edge to edge with subjects, whether closeup, medium shot or long shot views, any lateral movement by those on either end of the group can disrupt the framing composition. This movement generally takes the form of upper body leaning, and shifting the weight from one foot to another. The Camera Operator and First Assistant Camera Operator must be alert to any tendency of subjects on either end of a group to lean out toward, thereby pressing against, either frame edge. In this case, in order to keep all elements of the group in frame, enlarging the zoom lens sizing while making a panning correction is in order.

For Planned Production. During a production wherein action is planned and blocked, there are rehearsals so that camera movement can become synchronized with the action of the performers. And if there are misses in coordination, misframing and the like, then there are retakes until the problem is corrected and the shot perfected. Nevertheless, from the camera standpoint, and to be able to recognize and follow visual clues and cues, it pays to apply the care necessary to get to know the experience level as well as the physical idiosyncracies of the performers—whether the person is nervous or calm, athletic or sedentary, facially or bodily expressive. In general, the more experienced the performer, the more knowledgeable that performer is going to be regarding the need for synchronized camera/actor movement and the clearer the physical signals given by that person to the Camera Operator will be. For example, in a closeup shot, an experienced actor in turning 90° from full face to profile will subtly reposition his or her body during the move to maintain proper framing without the Camera Operator having to make a framing adjustment; or the veteran performer will lean forward as a move is made to rise from a sitting position, thereby cueing the Operator and smoothing the rising action. In short, it is left to the alert Camera Operator to pick up the physical signals and properly frame and follow the subject matter during each take in order to ensure that the camera crew is not at fault for a blown shot.

For Documentary Shooting. This style of shooting usually deals with untrained subjects, doing what they do naturally in their familiar environment. To a certain extent, coverage can be planned; however, this is more likely to be opportunity shooting. Framing is often not as precise, but can be helped by careful attention to visual body cues unconsciously given by the subjects.

For News Gathering. Time plays an important part in news gathering. News is not news if not new. Quick capture and rapid delivery to the public are essential aspects of this specialized form of shooting; visual finesse is seldom a concern. During static subject interviews, framing can be refined by attention to body cues. During moving interviews or coverage, however, the hand-held camera does not provide a stable base for consistently proper framing of the subject.

For Sporting Events. Sports shooting requires Camera Operators familiar with the basic parameters of the activity and of all the physical aspects of the event—the ebb and flow of the action, the physical cues leading to the essential action and reaction. With a thorough knowledge of the sport, the Camera Operator will go with the flow of the movement of the participants as they engage in their action and interaction, and will be able to accurately read and anticipate movement and thereby be able to appropriately frame and follow the action.

For Grab Shots. This is true opportunity shooting, taking what is available, sometimes called "shot-gunning." Framing is often relatively imprecise because of the nature of this type of rapid-fire image capture, frequently done while subject matter is in some degree of activity, agitation or movement. Crowd reaction shots, wild animal shooting, and singling out athletes as they participate in events are some aspects of grab shooting.

Some Signals to Watch For. Nearly always some area or part of the body will signal a move shortly before the move takes place; each individual will provide some sign of intended and impending movement, often giving the same signal before each move: A subtle tensing of the muscles in the face, neck, shoulders, arms or legs; eyes moved toward or looking in the direction of the next move; head turning in the direction the eyes have taken; head/body leaning back and/or bending forward before rising from a sitting position; hands moved forward on an armchair, or toward the knees, preceding a rise therefrom; unclasping the hands prior to a position change; hands/arms raised toward a person or thing, or to point; uncrossing the arms prior to changing position; body leaning in the direction of a move; crossing or uncrossing the feet prior to changing position or rising; feet moving—lifting or stepping—pointing in the direction in which the body will move; allowing the impetus of a move to lead the framing of a moving subject in the direction of that movement.

Summary. In order to maintain appropriate composition of the subject in frame, the tighter the framing, the more alert the Camera Operator must be to the often subtle signals of intended movement given by various body parts of the framed portion of the subject. Each subject often has individualized physical responses that can be relied upon to indicate the probability of imminent movement. Studying subject movement prior to shooting, or during blocking and rehearsals, can greatly assist the Camera Operator in maintaining appropriate framing at all times. Body language is a non-verbal form of communication constantly, and usually consciously and rather obviously, emanating from skilled performers accompanied by their spoken lines. On the other hand, the usually unconsciously given body signals by subjects who are untrained in the performing arts may not be as obvious or reliable. Like any other skill, practice and application will help the observing and persevering Camera Operator add this ability to his or her bag of skills.

SUGGESTED
FRAMING CRITERIA

As Camera Operators, we are continually framing shots. In fact, framing is our thing. As controllers of the moving proscenium, we frame individuals, objects and groupings thereof in a manner which provides a pleasing balance—an harmonious whole.

We are often asked for a specific sizing, such as a "choker," "head-and- shoulders," "T's," "elbows," "waist," a "cowboy closeup," "knees," "full figure," and so forth. We frame and deliver the requested sizing, often more by-guess-and-by-god than by specific parameters. The sure test is in reproducing the exact size in the reverse, or opposing, angle of the other actor in a tête-a-tête setup. A sure way to reproduce exact size of both actors in closeup and reversal is to place the camera(s) the exact distance from each actor, at, or near, the same camera elevation and with the same focal length lens (and T-stop) used for both angles.

In multi-camera sitcoms, matching closeups is especially important. In the days before zoom lenses, the wing cameras had 100mm primes. To match sizes for closeup singles, the Dolly Grips would move the wing cameras to 15 feet from the actors. For two-shots or over-shoulder shots, the distance was 17 feet from the actors. Since development of the zoom lens, the subject-to-camera distance is not often a factor in sizing the frame contents. The size matching between wing cameras is designated by each framing their respective image in one of the following sizes, from tight to loose closeup, which includes the top of the subject's head: A choker (from the throat up); or head-and-shoulders (from the second shirt button up); or including: the T's (breasts), elbows, or waist; or a cowboy (including the guns); or the knees; or full figure; etc. (See Figure 4, previous page.)

Short of exact matching of shots, it is convenient to refer to sizing categorically as **long shot, medium shot** and **closeup. Figure 4** suggests the maximum and minimum vertical framing designations for shot sizes relating to the human figure and based on generally applicable criteria as practiced in the industry. **Long shot** size designations are broken down into three perspectives—**extreme long shot** (with subject at infinity to filling about 1/3 of the frame); **long shot** (subject height fills 1/3 to full frame); **medium long shot** (frame includes full figure to cutting the figure at the knees); the **medium shot** (from top of head, cutting between the knees to waist); and four closeup perspectives—**medium closeup** (from waist to head and shoulders); **closeup** (head and shoulders to full head); **extreme closeup** (full head to eyes and mouth); and **doubly extreme closeup** (eyes or mouth only).

A designation such as **cowboy closeup**, which includes the upper body as well as the holstered gun(s), tends to cross over into the **medium shot** parameters.

Nevertheless, these shot description designations are useful in communicating

FIGURE 4

SHOT VALUE CLASSIFICATIONS
RELATING TO THE HUMAN SUBJECT
WITH MAXIMUM AND MINIMUM
VERTICAL FRAMING DESIGNATIONS

<- MOTION PICTURE—1.85 ASPECT RATIO ->   <- TV—1.33 ASPECT RATIO ->

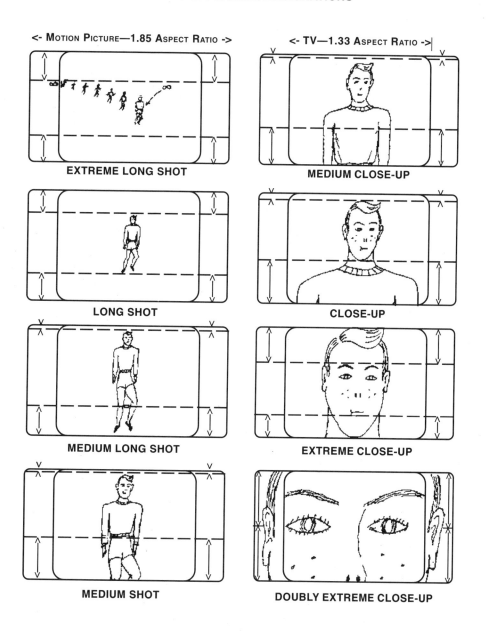

EXTREME LONG SHOT   MEDIUM CLOSE-UP

LONG SHOT   CLOSE-UP

MEDIUM LONG SHOT   EXTREME CLOSE-UP

MEDIUM SHOT   DOUBLY EXTREME CLOSE-UP

in a more precise way about shot sizing. Where exact figure sizing replication is required, there is still no substitute for setting focal length and positioning the camera at a measured distance and height relative to the person or object to be photographed.

FRAMING THE ACTION

Framing the action is what camera operating is all about. *Static framing* (when the action is at rest) and *dynamic framing* (when the action and/or camera is moving) are two of the several aspects of framing which concerns the film or video Camera Operator.

Compositional elements held within the frame—whether static or dynamic—are the third aspect of framing. And the final aspect is to exclude extraneous elements from the frame, such as: The microphone, its boom and their shadows; electrical and grip equipment; technical personnel and visitors; plus all of the off-set, non-dressed perimeter.

The Action Line. In order to properly consider framing, it is necessary to take into account the so-called *action line* (AKA, *stage line*). The action line is that imaginary line which bisects any two people engaged in an interaction; it is also that imaginary line which continues the direction of movement of a person or object (and/or the camera). So, the *static action line* is that imaginary line (like a rope) which "connects" two individuals who are at rest and engaged in face-to-face conversation or interaction, while the *dynamic action line* is that imaginary line (like a pointer) which projects through the object in the direction the movement is taking relative to the camera position. In addition, the direction (and velocity) of the movement of the camera platform in relation to the framed subject matter (at rest or moving) is yet another aspect to consider in framing.

Camera Angles. Camera angles are those positions at which the camera is placed in order to frame and record the staged action. Camera angles can be *static* (non-moving) or *dynamic* (moving). The **static camera angle** is when the camera does not move from its setup position except to pan and tilt to carry the action. The **dynamic camera angle** is when the camera is placed on a mobile mount (i.e, dolly, crane, hand-held, vehicle, boat, plane, balloon, horse, etc) and is maneuvered laterally and/or vertically during the shot in order to follow and properly frame the staged action. The camera can be positioned high or low relative to the action. This can be done because of practical constraints (lack of space, or to exclude unwanted backgrounds or foregrounds, or to achieve an appropriate POV perspective) or for aesthetic reasons (a *high angle* to demean or diminish, or a *low angle* to ennoble or enhance, a character or action).

There are three categories of frame content and perspective, having to do with relative object proximity to or apparent distancing from the camera—the **long shot**, the **medium shot** and the **closeup**. In general, the **long shot** is made with a wide angle lens in order to establish the environment in which the action takes place and to include any broad action; the **medium shot** is used to introduce characters and their attire and to cover smaller group shots and relatively confined action; the **closeup** is used to concentrate the audience's attention on the most expressive part of an actor—the face (the most important and expressive of which are the eyes and the brow)—at the exclusion of all else.

PERSPECTIVE

Lenses. In general there are three categories of camera lenses, each with distinct characteristics of perspective and depth of field with respect to the captured imagery.

Wide angle lenses deliver great depth of field which means that nearly everything in frame can be in acceptable focus—foreground to background. The wider the angle of acceptance of this lens, the more that action which moves toward or away from the camera is accentuated (or distorted) and the more that any vertical lines in frame are distorted.

Mid-range/angle-of-sight lenses are those so-called "*normal*" lenses which have an angle of acceptance similar to that of the eye (a 40mm-50mm lens for the 35mm format). This range of lenses is often used predominantly during production for most of the midrange to close action and general stage business.

Telephoto lenses are lenses with a narrow angle of image acceptance relative to the midrange lenses. Telephoto lenses deliver a relatively shallow depth of field which, in effect, isolates images on the focused-upon plane from both foreground and background information. In addition, these lenses also deliver a flattening effect, visually compressing elements which overlap one another in frame. Because of these characteristics, telephoto lenses are often used for closeups in order to soften background detail and to draw the viewer's attention to the actor.

These three categories of lenses can be, and are, used interchangeably to record establishing shots, traveling shots and closeups, respectively, in order to achieve an effect which the characteristic limitation of that lens may provide (i.e, distortion caused by a fish-eye wide angle lens closeup; or a broad desert-like landscape with approaching, galloping horsemen making little apparent progress in the distance and shimmering heat waves rising through the scene distorting the action which is being framed by an extreme telephoto lens).

CAMERA PLACEMENT

The camera is placed and/or blocked (moved) according, and in relation, to the staged action. The broader the action the further away the camera is placed and/or the wider the lens to be used in order to properly frame that action.

The *apparent proximity* of the camera to the action (*psychical-distancing*) is another aspect which helps determine both camera placement and lens selection.

During sitcom camera blocking, each mobile camera is positioned and moved on the audience side of the action (or stage) line for show shots and for pickup shots.

During episodic or single camera positioning and blocking, the camera is positioned on one side of the action line for all angles made of that staged action unless, of course, the camera is intentionally moved across that action line during a take and all subsequent juxtaposed angles are then developed on that side of the action line.

Bottom Line. Whether working closely with the Director (and occasionally the

DP) in setting shots for a sitcom, or having the shots set by the Director or Director of Photography on an episodic or feature, the Camera Operator is expected to expeditiously and appropriately frame the shot and to always keep it pristine, containing the essentials, free of any extraneous elements, and compositionally pleasing.

FRAMING FOR HI-DEF TV

Now that we have the new high-definition framing requirement for television programming production of the 16x9 (1.78) aspect ratio to protect, while framing prime coverage for the standard 4x3 (1.33) aspect ratio, several problems have become obvious and need concerted attention of those responsible for set design, for action and camera blocking, and for framing the action occurring on the sets and shooting sites. So, Directors, Art Directors and Camera Operators, your attention, please.

Granted, it will take several years before we will see widespread display of the wider 1.78 TV screen format; nevertheless, we, as Camera Operators, have been given the responsibility of protecting the additional areas (16.7%) on each side of the established 1.33 TV framing area. This means keeping the entire framing area clear of undesired content such as microphones, booms and their shadows, equipment, and personnel, while not framing beyond the confines of the set or setting.

Figure 5

HI-DEFINITION TV

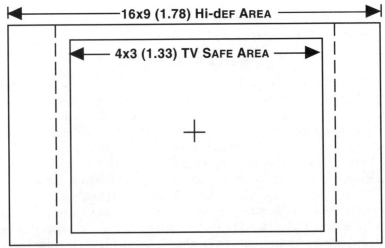

GROUND GLASS SCRIBING FOR 3-PERF HI-DEF FRAMING

To help us do this, a ground glass scribed with both aspect ratios has been placed in the viewing system of our film cameras, whether we are shooting 35mm four- or three-perf pull-down, or 16mm stock. (See Figure 5, below.)

While this additional format will apply to all product displayed on TV, the following discussion applies to all product especially produced for TV—episodics, movies-of-the-week and mini-series—but most especially to the multiple camera film sitcom. With four cameras trained on the action—two wing cameras for closeups and two master cameras for wider shots—often exchanging master shots, Directors of the sitcom genre are being forced to limit the use of raking and cross masters until sets are designed specifically to accommodate this expanded framing format. This often limits the options open to a Director to more fully exploit the creative possibilities of expanded action.

Less Room for Error. Incidentally, the three-perf pull-down format leaves very little latitude for up- and down-reframing/repositioning during telecine transfer. This means that for this format, the Camera Operator must pay close attention to vertical framing margins and limits while composing shots.

Set Design. Production Designers and Art Directors need to be made aware of, and design sets for, these current framing requirements. In order to frame 1.33 while protecting the 50% wider letterbox-shaped 1.78 scribing, entrances need to be placed upstage, at least six feet from the downstage edge of the set in order to provide a decently wide shot of action entering or exiting a set. Exterior settings may require even more expanse in order to avoid shooting off the setting.

The downstage areas of sets, particularly the floor or ground area, should be extended two to three feet more than before, in order to allow angled or cross-master "letterbox" framing to remain fully within the setting.

While we are on the subject of set design, it would be well to consider adding a couple feet to the set headers on very wide sets in order to better accommodate wide master angles of groups of performers which some Directors tend to spread out during action blocking.

Set Lighting. Directors of Photography and Gaffers should be aware that additional header space will go for naught unless back lights are mounted above, or well up on, the headers.

Set Dressing. For the present, important set dressing and prop items should be placed in areas, from one wing of the set to the other, which are sure to fall within the 1.33 aspect ratio, placing less important items on and within the 2 to 3 feet of the far right and left downstage set areas.

Actor & Camera Blocking. Directors also need to be aware of the new framing parameters. Action blocking needs to take into consideration the wider area which is now included in frame. Action therefore needs to be kept further upstage, particularly when approaching the vicinity of either wing of the set, in order to allow cameras with raked, angled or cross master shots to frame 1.78 fully within the set .

As sets are presently designed and dressed, all the Camera Operator can do, when proper framing within the 1.33 scribe puts a portion of the 1.78 letterbox off the set, is to inform the Director during camera blocking or rehearsal, who may then redesign the blocking in order to avoid the problem. When framing off the set during a take, it's a good idea to inform both the Director and the Script Supervisor (so the problem is properly noted in the shooting script). At present, most Directors are more concerned with the 1.33 being protected and right than with the added frame width being pristine. Nevertheless, make sure. Each Director and Producer will have a position on this question. Remember, each Director is usually there on a per show basis, while the Producer puts each show together right through editing and is along for the duration of the series.

Summing Up. The additional framing area included in the wide-screen format for the planned high-definition TV display requires the immediate attention of Producers, Art Directors, Set Designers and set dressers to plan and prepare sets and settings specially designed to accommodate the extra width of the hi-def TV screen of the future.

Until these steps are taken, Camera Operators, for filmed television production, will have to frame all essentials within the 1.33 aspect scribe while protecting the additional areas mandated by the 1.78 aspect ratio, extending on either side of the 1.33 scribe lines—e.g., keeping these areas framed on, and within the confines of, the set or settings.

PLANNING THE CAMERA ANGLE

Positioning the camera in relation to the planned action is a major consideration in putting a cinematic product on film or tape. The positioning of the camera(s) can affect, and be affected by, the staged action, the setting, the set dressing and the lighting. The choice of lens and the height of the camera lens in relation to the action (and/or actors) can have a marked subjective effect on viewer sensibilities.

Normally within the province of Director responsibilities, the choice of camera angle may be determined by the Director's collaboration with the Director of Photography, or with the Camera Operator, depending upon the type of production, the shooting schedule, and most importantly, the preference of the Director.

Nevertheless, for Camera Operators contemplating the move up to Director of Photography, it is prudent to absorb as much as possible of the technical expertise aspects practiced by the DP. The key is to observe procedures practiced by each Director of Photography you work with, analyzing and understanding the reasons for, and logic behind, each decision related to DP responsibilities and duties, particularly those decisions related to lighting, to selecting and preparation of camera setups, the choice and use of the camera, its accessories and operative camera personnel, and the ways in which the DP relates to superiors, peers and subordinates during the production process, in particular, the Director and the cast.

Elements of a Camera Setup. The elements of a camera setup include the following: The type and size of the setting or location site; the type and scope of the action to be staged therein or thereon; the particulars and sequential coverage of that action; the number of camera angles required to provide the Editor with sufficient coverage of the action to be able to manipulate time and space and enhance the rhythm, flow and pacing of each scene; whether a day or night shoot; whether interior or exterior; whether studio or location; the desired mood and emotional level of the scene to be shot; the sense of perspective appropriate to the scene; the degree of difficulty in establishing a desired camera angle; etc.

Types of Camera Positioning. There are two types of camera positioning: **Static positioning**—where the camera does not move its base, although it may be panned and/or tilted to follow the action and/or the zoom lens, varied in its focal length to suit that action. The other is **dynamic positioning**—where the camera is mounted on a mobile platform and is moved from position to position during a take with the flow of the essential blocked action being photographed.

The Moving Camera. The principal reason for moving the camera is to keep the essential action appropriately faced and in frame at all times during a take. Camera movement should never call attention to itself, but should blend into the movement of the action in frame.

Camera movement, while framing static subject matter, calls attention to itself as a purely mechanical device unless, of course, such movement represents a POV (a subjective point of view) of another actor (who *is* the camera).

In general, camera movement should be used with discretion, to provide some variety to the choice of angles used in the overall production, and only used when a static camera position cannot appropriately cover the planned action.

Use of the Zoom Lens. Use of the zoom lens to simulate camera movement should be carefully planned and executed. For example, when foreground material is included in frame, in order to maintain proper perspective, the zoom move should be used with a dolly move in direct relationship to the zoom move—zoom in **with a dolly in**; zoom out **with a dolly out**. A zoom move without a coordinated dolly move under such circumstances will result in a rather mechanical-looking size change (much like manipulating a cropping template on a still photo). The best use of a move toward an actor or object is of course to physically move the camera all the way along the required distance without zoom assistance. When there are no foreground pieces, or when the subject is moving laterally, the zoom move alone can work well and without distraction.

Selecting the Lens. The choice of lens is a crucial aspect of the camera angle, having to do with the perspective in frame of the subject matter. A telephoto (narrow angle) lens will compress the focused-upon subject matter in frame as well as reducing the depth of field, thereby being very selective in the plane in which the subject matter is in sharp focus. On the other hand, a wide angle lens will provide a broader view and extensive depth of field, resulting in overall sharp (acceptable) focus. Choice of lens is also a function of actual (*physical*) or apparent subjective (*psychical*) distancing from the subject matter.

Determining the Height Placement of the Lens. The height at which the lens is placed, relative to the subject matter, may be a result of several considerations. The physical positioning of the subject matter in relation to the available camera position—i.e, the camera on a structure, mountain, or in the air, shooting downward toward the ground; the camera on a lower level, shooting upward to tall structures, mountains, or objects in the air; the confines of the space available to shoot in; the actual height of the actor(s); the relative height of the actors when shooting over-shoulder shots or opposing closeups.

In shooting over-shoulder shots or opposing closeups involving two actors of differing height, the general practice is to place the lens very close to the line of eye contact between the two actors—utilize a higher angle (shooting down) at the shorter person and place the camera lower when shooting toward the taller person.

The Direction of the Action. The direction in which the action moves requires another crucial decision in placing the camera. **Static action** (as in face-to-face encounters) should maintain the direction of look and/or positioning of the subject matter in frame. **Dynamic action** (when the subject matter is moving) should maintain its relative direction and momentum in frame from camera angle to camera angle. In each type of action, the goal is to keep the audience properly oriented and comfortable with the geography presented in frame.

Of course, rules are made to be broken under the proper set of circumstances, so if the purpose at any given moment is to disorient and disturb an audience, this is one of the first rules to break.

Type of Camera Equipment. The type and amount of camera equipment has an impact on camera positioning. For example, if a production is using 65mm camera equipment, there may be some restriction in the placement of that camera. The lightweight production cameras with their rotating and swinging extension viewfinder oculars have made it possible to place the camera(s) in the most propitious place(s) in order to appropriately capture the action—whether broad, fast and violent or intimate and endearing.

Remotely controlled cameras have made possible shot angles from camera positions in close proximity to special effects, stunts and drive-bys which would be too physically dangerous to place a Camera Operator and First Assistant, or in a setup with severe space limitations, or in an environment with hazardous atmospheric conditions.

Setting Considerations. One of the primary concerns of the principal creative team—the Producer, Director, Production Designer and Director of Photography—is to provide settings appropriate to the action which can be performed therein, lighted efficiently and properly, and photographed within budgetary, logistical and scheduling constraints. The sets may be designed to afford one or more optimum master camera angles. Closeup positioning for the camera(s) is seldom the problem.

Production Theme. The production theme has a lot to do with the placement of the camera(s). Productions featuring multitudes of people, panoramic views of scenics or cities or space, battle/riot scenes, and/or period costumes in profusion may be better served by shooting with an anamorphic or other wide-screen system. Productions featuring a more intimate or passive theme or style may be handled very effectively with spherical lens systems, framing for aspect ratios from 1.33 to 1.85.

Type of Production. The type or form of production—whether commercial; documentary; TV episodic, sitcom, miniseries or movie-of-the-week; film test; insert; industrial; or theatrical feature—each has its own allowable latitude for perfecting shots. This perfecting process is limited by budgetary and shooting schedule constraints as well as the efficiency of the Director of Photography and the technical personnel.

For example, film tests, inserts shooting, TV commercials and large budget theatrical features operate at a rather deliberate pace thereby affording an approach to excellence, if not perfection, in the execution of takes from absolutely appropriate camera angles.

Film tests, insert shooting, documentaries, industrials and commercials generally have smaller, more compact crews which cost less per production hour than feature length films (although there is much more negative cost per frame of a national, prime time TV commercial than of any other cinematic product). Low-budget features, movies for TV and miniseries generally require small crews but must move efficiently because the budgets are relatively modest—and tight.

TV episodics have a fast-moving production pace, leaving little time for perfecting setups, camera angles and shots.

The multiple-camera TV sitcom, whether film or video, is an unique production form. Utilizing three to four cameras which cover an angle of up to 160° from one wing camera to the other does not make for lighting perfection. Therefore a compromise is reached in the lighting balance. By very soft front fill across the set and cross back keys, positioned high and well upstage, covering the principal action areas, very acceptable results are obtained by the angle afforded each camera.

Shooting multi-camera sitcoms is essentially a series of relatively long takes with considerable camera movement in order to coincide with the staging of the actors' blocking. Each camera (on a dolly for film or on a mobile pedestal for video) may be moved in, out and laterally, raised or lowered, and further varying the size of the objects in frame with a zoom lens.

In multi-camera film sitcoms, the Camera Operators work directly with the Director in establishing position and angles. In multi-camera video sitcoms, the Camera Operators may be somewhat more constrained in modifying camera angles. But since positions of the cameras and actors are seldom marked, the video Camera Operator often has to improvise both camera positioning and lens sizing in order to cover the action and get the planned-for shot angle.

The Budget. The amount of "production value" packed in a frame is a pretty good indicator of approximately how much a picture has cost to make—whether a picture had a high, medium or low budget. In short, the more production values, the higher the budget. The shooting schedule, of course, is directly related to budgetary parameters.

Interpersonal Relationships. How the Director of Photography relates to the Director, cast and crew is an important aspect of moving the production process along. Good rapport gets it done efficiently and effectively. Poor rapport subverts the effort, making it difficult and inefficient for everyone concerned.

Other Considerations. Some other considerations in determining camera angles (particularly closeups) are the facial characteristics of the actor(s). The facial features, particularly the eyes, brows and forehead, are the most expressive parts of an actor's anatomy. As a rule, one side of an actor's face is visually more "photogenic" (photographically pleasing) than the other side. So it behooves the Director of Photography, by means of appropriate camera angles and lighting (and diffusion), to help the actor present as effective an appearance as is consistent with the mood and intent of the scene.

Moving shots take longer to set up, light, and shoot than static shots. So if there are budgetary or shooting schedule constraints, moving shots may have to be simplified or bypassed in favor of the static camera positions in the interest of time.

Selection of location sites and the planning and design of stage settings are critical in accommodating camera coverage. It is well to read and analyze the script during the pre-production phase and to lay out prospective camera angles at that time. The size of settings will help determine the type and amount of camera, lighting and grip equipment—and the personnel required to set up, adjust, and operate this equipment.

Summing Up. Selecting, augmenting and executing the many camera angles has the principal purpose of capturing the essence of the action and emotional content of each shot, within each scene, within each sequence, for any type of cinematic production, whether film or video. Understanding the planning process of establishing effective camera angles will help prepare the way to better-looking, more effective and affective productions and, from there, to a smooth transition to an upgrade position.

THE MOVING CAMERA

Every experienced Director stages action with the camera in mind. The camera is then placed in position, sometimes on a mobile platform, with an appropriate lens in place, to capture that action.

Moving Options. Normally, the Director will seldom want the camera both in a fixed position and locked-off, with the possible exception of a glass, matte, process plate, or registration shot or a stop-motion or time-lapse setup. To the Director, the camera represents the intended audience viewpoint and the framing represents an ever-changing proscenium, in effect, transporting the viewer from viewpoint to viewpoint, each shot, in turn, selectively delineating the contained subject matter, as perceived and set by the Director.

The cinema is a dynamic medium. Capturing and conveying physical and dramatic movement, as well as moving people emotionally, is what it is all about. In order to keep the audience in the thick of things, the Director has several options available when it comes to moving the camera during a shot. Principal among the mobile camera platforms are the camera dolly and the studio crane, with its highly mobile boom arm holding the camera platform. These are available in various sizes and configurations, with boom arm extensions and track. Some cranes and jib arms are designed to accommodate a remotely controlled camera. In addition, there are other suitable means and methods of moving the camera, such as: Hand-holding or using camera stabilizing devices like the Steadicam™, Pogocam™, etc; employing wheeled vehicles and airborne or marine craft; utilizing construction cranes, hoists, lifts, swings, cables, conveyer belts, etc.

Modified Camera Movement. With the camera in a fixed (static) position, more often than not the Camera Operator must pan and/or tilt the camera in order to follow and properly frame that action, even though the performer has been adjusting his or her position only slightly. Of course, it is best to select a frame size that will accommodate moderate movement of the actor without having to continually manipulate the camera for framing purposes during a take. The variable focal length capability of a zoom lens is a convenient and quick way to make this minor adjustment, rather than having to reset the camera, change a prime lens, or move the actor. Of course, the trade-off is in settling for the somewhat lower resolution in the zoom lens than in prime lenses. But when the end use of the production is for display on the low-resolution home TV monitor, the resulting image quality produced by a zoom lens is more than adequate.

The Pervasive Zoom Lens. From a fixed camera position, and with a zoom lens in place, the temptation to plan and use only the zoom movement to follow the action, rather than to put the camera on a mobile platform and move in concert with the action, is an all too convenient decision, often made "to save time." And it may accomplish that purpose; but certainly detracts from the aesthetic aspects of the shot. Why? Because the change in perspective which the moving camera gives to the framing is not there in the stand-alone mechanical zoom move. The pure zoom move is like adjusting a cropping template on a still photo. The effect of a zoom-in is more like magnifying or enlarging a portion of the framed material; whereas a zoom-out gives the appearance of a two-dimensional expansion of framed material. The visual effect of zoom movement is one of either pulling the image toward the viewer or pushing the image away; whereas movement of the camera toward subject matter *transports the viewer* toward that subject matter, and movement of the camera away from the subject matter *carries the viewer* to a more distant view of that subject matter.

Making the Zoom Move Work. The zoom move is economical. An extensive zoom move can be made extremely quickly, when necessary, and with little preparation time; whereas, a dolly move has certain built-in constraints, such as, how fast the dolly can be moved, the length of the move, and the time necessary to prepare the track and rehearse the move. Because the perspective is constantly changing when the camera is physically moving, and is unchanging during a statically positioned zoom shot, it is possible to utilize the best qualities of each technique by combining them during the shot whenever possible. Relatively little dolly movement is required to furnish an acceptable change in perspective while the zoom movement is in process. Panning or tilting the camera while making a zoom also takes the curse off pure zoom moves.

Types of Mobile Camera Platforms. The **crab dolly** is the most commonly used carrier. It is relatively compact, sturdy, reliable and versatile. It has multi-directional capability with a three-way steering system which allows rear, crab, and circular steering modes. Its boom arm provides a moderate amount of vertical movement. A jib arm, capable of holding camera and Camera Operator—or just a remotely controlled camera, can be mounted on the riser arm of most studio dollies. Aside from its primary function of simply transporting the camera from one setup to another, the crab dolly requires a smooth surface or dolly track in order to make acceptable on-air moves.

The **studio crane** provides a wide range of movement and angles (viewpoints). Its principal value is in executing moving shots, rising from ground level to full vertical extension or the reverse. The longer the boom arm, the more dramatic the effect of its movement.

The **studio pedestal**, manipulated multi-directionally and vertically by the Camera Operator, is a mobile camera support system used primarily to carry electronic cameras on smooth and level sound stage floors (although it is being used increasingly for film production).

The **helicopter** continues where the crane leaves off. The versatile whirly bird can operate from ground level and then rise to great height, or track vehicles moving at high speed over tortuous terrain, thereby transporting an audience through an emotional (even though vicarious) experience.

Reasons for Camera Moves. The camera is moved during a shot for any one of a number of reasons: To carry complex or extended movement of the subject matter in frame; to follow subject matter that is moving and cannot be covered from a fixed camera position; to emphasize a portion of, or person, in the framed material; to keep audience attention focused on dramatic essentials.

Types and Effect of Camera Movement. Camera moves have direction and velocity, both of which can have a purposeful effect on audience sensibilities. The Director wants to keep the essentials (as he or she perceives them) in frame and framed properly at all times. When the camera trucks ahead of the performers as they walk and talk, or dollies with, or tracks behind, it places the audience in pace with that action. When the camera moves through or past inanimate surroundings, it becomes a very subjective mode for the audience. Moving toward a performer focuses the audience attention on that person. Moving away from a performer orients or reorients the audience concerning the environmental surroundings. Moving across the direction in which the performer is facing or moving—called "chinese-ing"— will change the screen direction of the performer's look or move. Vertical rise movement can also help orient the audience by giving a more complete picture of the environmental layout, or its effect can be to diminish the persona of a character. Vertical fall movement can help bring the audience into the story by going from the general (the surrounding environment) to the specific (the essential action taking place therein), thereby, in effect, grounding the audience.

Summing Up. Of course, the camera can be made to spin, spiral, flip, fall, rise, roll, pitch, yaw, tremble and tumble. It is the Director who sets the requirements for the coverage of each shot and who determines the placement and/or pattern of movement of the camera. It is up to us as Directors of Photography, Camera Operators, Camera Assistants and Dolly/Crane Grips to do our utmost to assist the Director in realizing his or her vision. This is what our jobs are all about. This is what keeps us working.

SETTING UP THE MOVING SHOT

Preparation is certainly the most important part of the process of making a motion picture and also may be the most important aspect in setting up and making consistently well-integrated shots, shots that will cut together seamlessly.

Preparation means: **Planning Ahead.** The shooting script is a good place to start. It should be read and analyzed by all Category Heads and key personnel who should annotate the script carefully with notes pertaining to the respective category elements required in, and visual treatment of, each shot, scene and sequence.

For the **Producer**, preparation is ongoing. The script is the road map, building plan and bible. The script sets the requirements for the settings, locations, cast, crew, logistics, matériel and, most important, the budget and the shooting schedule. Seeing that all required elements are foreseen and provided for is a Producer's principal concern in keeping within budget and comfortably ahead of production schedule requirements.

For the **Director**, preparing/planning the shot is with the actors in mind, concerning the staging areas for stage business and blocking along with guiding their interpretation, character development and emotional level(s).

For the **Director of Photography**, it is planning the lighting level(s) (interior or exterior, day or night) and balance (the desired mood) for the performing area(s) and for the actors appearing in the scene. Selection of the appropriate camera equipment and taking lenses and arranging camera movement to capture the required visuals are additional concerns of the DP.

For the **Camera Operator**, it is the framing (the inclusion of all essential elements, plus the exclusion of extraneous matter, within the camera frame), coordinating camera setting adjustments and camera movement (which is appropriate in range, sweep and velocity) by members of the operative camera crew and seeing that it all comes together seamlessly—and **works!**—In the viewfinder.

For the **First Assistant Camera Operator**, it's a numbers game, measuring the distance to subjects, noting zoom lens sizes and recording the numbers involved. And then artfully integrating the required settings as appropriate during each rehearsal and take.

For the **Second Assistant Camera Operator**, it is being there with a properly prepared and placed slate and then being ready to step in and help during a take by making planned adjustment(s) to one of the camera's variable settings.

For the **Loader**, it is having magazines, loaded with film of the proper emulsion, ready and at hand, to replace expended magazines.

For the **Dolly Grip**, it is having the dolly track level and clear of debris, marked for starts and stops, and having the dolly set in the appropriate movement mode.

Setting Up the Moving Shot. The first step is to carefully observe the movement of the actors during the blocking phase as set by the Director. This will provide a preliminary framework on which to construct the camera movement (panning, tilting, zooming, and/or booming, craning, trucking, tracking or dollying). The Camera Operator should stay very near the Director and DP during pre-setup discussions in order to hear their plans for, or to receive specific instructions regarding, camera positioning and/or movement and the expected framing (or coverage) during the shot. This "eavesdropping" is both expected and necessary in order to save time and energy of the Director by not having to search out and repeat instructions to each one concerned with making the shot.

Laying the Track. Assuming an uneven surface and that a dolly will be used, once the path of the camera movement is determined, the Grips set about laying the dolly track, which can be 3/4″ plyboard, 1″x12″ clear pine, or metal rails. The track must be level and its surface must be even. The dolly should be wheeled onto the dolly track and, with the Camera Operator aboard looking through the eyepiece, moved along the entire length of the track to determine the condition of the surface and solidity of the track.

Rehearsals. The camera dolly is then placed in starting position and the shot rehearsed with camera and actor movement. The starting point and each stop along the way is marked by the Dolly Grip and used as reference for each subsequent rehearsal and take. The First Assistant Camera Operator runs tapes to determine focus distances for stops and camera/actor movement, marking actor floor positions, and also notes zoom size settings, as confirmed by the Operator, during the blocking rehearsal.

Checking. When the lens size(s), camera height(s) and movement configuration(s) have been set with the actor movement, each stopping position and the coverage in between should be carefully checked to be certain that the framing stays within the confines of the setting, whether interior or exterior, and does not shoot off the sides or top of the setting. Other in-frame no-nos to check for are: Set lighting, flares and reflections—of lights, off-the-set equipment and personnel; the microphone and boom or their shadows; technical personnel or equipment; visitors/observers/intruders.

The Camera Operator sees that the dolly movement is fully coordinated with actor movement and that zoom lens sizing, if any, is being finessed so that all camera movement is visually unobtrusive and appropriate.

The Camera Operator should make sure that the adjustable viewfinder and the dolly seat configuration are working to keep him/her properly positioned behind the eyepiece during any sweeping panning or tilting and/or riser arm movement during the move. The proper ratio of gearhead control movement for the shot should be set during rehearsal in order to coordinate with the relative movement of the camera and subject matter. In addition, the camera should be rebalanced on the control head with each new film load and after each take in order to facilitate geared, fluid or friction head operation.

Summing Up. Setting up and executing a moving shot requires the technical expertise of several classifications: A Producer to provide the economic wherewithal—the matériel and personnel; a Director to stage and set the shot; a Director of Photography and Gaffer to light the setup; Grips to shape and control the lighting patterns and to lay the dolly track as determined by the DP; Dolly, Crane or Boom Grip(s) to move the dolly, crane or boom; a Camera Operator, to frame the shot; a First Assistant Camera Operator to follow focus and control zoom lens sizing; a Second Assistant Camera Operator to operate the slate clapper and assist with camera setting adjustments, as needed; and a Loader to assure a supply of camera-ready film magazines.

MAKING THE SHOT

Making each shot an example of perfection is what we strive for, but more often than not, never quite attain. The reason for this is the state of each of the variable elements which combine, on- and off-camera, during the take to make the shot. These elements are: The performers and their positioning and movement; the Director and the blocking; the Director of Photography and the lighting; and the operative camera crew, their preparation for the shot (both the equipment and their state of mind), and their responses to the variable elements in capturing the presented imagery.

During production of a single-camera ninety-minute feature or MOW, we can expect to make several hundred shots from nearly as many setups. For one-hour episodics (42 minutes of program time), up to two hundred shots can be expected (often multiplied several times by intercutting shots during the editing phase). Multiple-camera film or video sitcoms and soaps have three or four cameras participating in each shot, which consists of continuously moving coverage of the action for an entire sequence. In sitcoms, this sequential coverage may consist of takes as long as eight or ten minutes with many camera moves and lens sizing and focus adjustments. In addition, there may be as many as fifteen sequences, all shot in continuity, during presentation to a live audience. In a daily soap opera, using three or four video cameras, there will be even more sequences covered by several hundred on-line cuts of the coverage.

Regardless of the production genre, the process of making a shot is much the same. The first phase is **observation**—watching and understanding the elements of the shot; the second phase is **preparation**—getting ready to make the shot; and the final phase is **operation**—capturing the imagery presented to the camera.

PHASE I—OBSERVATION

Carefully observing, during each shot setup, the process of blocking as the Director and performers work out their movements, stage business, and character interplay and development and then watching the lighting process are important first steps in anticipating the results expected of the operative camera crew—the Camera Operator, the First Assistant Camera Operator and the Dolly Grip or Crane Grip(s).

Blocking the Action. Blocking the movement of the performers by the Director is the first step in the process of setting up a shot for the camera. The extent of movement by the performers will determine the staging area and its background which will require lighting and camera coverage.

Blocking the Camera. It is important to carefully observe and listen in as the Director and Director of Photography work out the movement of the camera in order to cover the essentials of the performed action. The desired camera movement and coverage throughout the shot must be clearly understood by the Camera Operator, the First Assistant Camera Operator and the Dolly Grip or Crane Grips.

Analyzing the Action. There are several elements to look for in the planned action. First, who or what is in motion; a person, animal, object or vehicle? Second, how massive is the movement; how many people, animals or objects are moving in frame. Third, how extensive is the movement; how much latitude, height and depth does it encompass; where does the action begin and end? Fourth, how sudden and fast-moving is the action; is it abrupt, intermittent, or smooth and flowing? Fifth, which direction does the action take; toward or away from the camera, and/or up or down in relation to the camera? Finally, when does the action and/or each aspect of the action occur; when does it begin and end?

Watching the Lighting Process. The process of selecting, placing and connecting lighting units to power is the next phase of preparing the shot for the camera. Each unit will have a specific purpose in covering the background, foreground, midground and/or action portions of the staging area. The Camera Operator should be aware of this coverage in order to call, or confirm, any observed lighting disfunction during a take to the attention of the Director of Photography. Since ours is a check and double-check business in which the details have details, it is well never to assume that any such glitches which can affect the captured imagery have been observed by others.

Placement of the Sound Boom. Noting the placement of the sound boom and its subsequent movement during setup procedures is important in determining where potential mic and boom shadows may occur in frame during the shot. Watch how the Boom Operator moves the boom around to determine where its shadows fall on walls, set dressing and performers.

Understanding the Required Coverage. It is not enough to merely observe the blocking and perform the camera movement. In order to achieve the best results, it is equally important to understand the logic of the coverage desired by the Director. This will help smooth the ebb and flow of properly framing and following the action. The Director will specify what will fill the frame during the shot and the size in frame of that subject matter.

The Director of Photography, having consulted with the Director, and in consideration of the blocking and lighting requirements for the shot, will be concerned about the camera position, its coverage and its movement; will specify the taking lens, its filtration/diffusion, the T-stop, shutter angle and frame rate to be used; and will direct the placement of any dolly track.

After carefully observing the various steps taken in planning and setting up the shot, the process of preparing the camera, mobile camera platform and the operative camera crew in order to make the shot now takes place.

PHASE II—PREPARATION

After having closely observed the blocking of the performers in relation to the blocking of the camera, and with specific input from the Director and Director of Photography, the operative camera crew prepares to ready themselves, the camera and mobile camera platform to make the shot as efficiently and effectively as practicable.

The Operative Camera Crew. Since the responsibility for coordinating the camera moves and settings falls to the Camera Operator, the Operator must make sure that the other members of the operative camera crew understand the elements of the shot desired by the Director and DP: The direction of the move(s); the starting, ending and intermediate positions of the camera in relation to the performers; any variations in the velocity of camera and/or performer movement during the shot; the number and/or specific grouping of the performers in frame; the sizing of the subject matter in frame at given points during the shot; any selective focus, frame rate, T-stop, sliding diffusion or shutter angle variations during the take.

For moving shots, the First Assistant Camera Operator must understand the coverage required, and marks and measures each position of the subjects to be photographed in relation to the camera, noting distance, lens sizing and the selective focus points required by the Director and Cinematographer, and whether it would be better to ride or walk during the shot.

For moving shots, the Mobile Camera Platform Operator, in this case the Dolly

Grip, must understand the dynamics of the shot in order to better move the camera dolly in concert with the action and will mark the start, stop and each intermediate position of the camera dolly and its riser arm during the shot, working under the direction of the Camera Operator.

The Camera. In preparing for the shot, the Camera Operator: Positions the viewfinder to the appropriate level and adjusts its diopters for optimum image clarity; turns on the ground glass illumination for dark settings, as necessary; positions and adjusts the height of the seat; has the Dolly Grip position the dolly chassis in neutral alignment to the action, in order to afford the Operator optimum operating room for broad panning movement, and put the riser arm at the proper starting height; sees that the camera is level and balanced; checks the camera control head, whether friction, geared or remote, for fluidity of movement, adjusting the tension, as necessary; tests each of the gear ratio positions to insure that the geared head is fully and dependably operational; selects the gear ratio setting for the upcoming shot.

The First Assistant Camera Operator makes sure that: The camera is properly set up, tied to power, operative, level, balanced and securely mounted on the operative camera support; for the remotely controlled camera, all electrical connections have been made to the control head; the appropriate taking lens is in place; the proper filters, diffusion and/or diopters are in position; the sizing and focus controls are fully functional; the T-stop, shutter angle and frame rate are set to the specifications desired by the DP; the proper film stock is correctly threaded into the camera; the diopter position for those who look through the viewfinder—the Operator, Director, DP and First Assistant—are clearly marked on the viewfinder diopter adjusting ring and set in place in order to facilitate optimum image quality for whoever is looking through the ocular; essential tools and accessories are near at hand and/or in the Camera Assistant's ditty box; the basic information on the slate is properly and accurately prepared by the Second Assistant Camera Operator.

The Mobile Camera Platform. The Mobile Camera Platform Operator makes sure that the camera dolly, crane or aerial or marine mount is fully operational.

When a camera dolly is used, it is essential that: The wheels are proper for the type of track or surface being used; the directional modes respond properly; the hydraulic system is fully charged, holding the charge, and responsive; the riser arm is functional throughout its range of movement; the camera is securely mounted to the dolly riser arm and level on all planes; accessory seats, sideboards, platforms, risers and support paraphernalia are in place or on hand.

When a crane is used, it is essential that the Crane Grips check that: The tracking surface will support the weight of the crane; the crane boom arm is attended and properly locked off when not in use or when being loaded with counterweights to offset the weight of the camera and camera personnel being carried aloft; the carrying weight of the crane is checked by loading and lifting the arm before personnel get aboard; the crane chassis is properly positioned and aligned for the shot; the boom arm is fully functional throughout its swing, rise and fall movement; the turret can be smoothly panned by use of the turret pan wheel; personnel riding the shot are properly safetied in their bucket seats; no one gets off the boom until the boom arm has been securely locked off.

When an aerial or marine platform is used, with an accompanying state-of-the-art camera mount, it is important that: The respective platform is air- or sea-worthy; the respective camera mount is securely attached to the platform; camera personnel are appropriately attired and properly safetied to the craft.

Ready to Begin. After careful observation of the Director's blocking, and having set up the camera and its mobile support to properly capture the shot which the Director and Cinematographer have laid out, the process of accurately capturing the planned imagery now follows.

Everything that has been done to this point has been to lay a solid foundation for making the shot as effectively and efficiently and as practicable. The blocking, performing and staging parameters have affected the camera, lighting placement and coverage which, in turn, will have a measured effect upon the performance.

PHASE III—OPERATION

The final and decisive phase in making a shot is the operational aspect—the process of image capture. All the previously taken steps during the observation and preparation phases have been prelude to the real thing—presentation of the action to the participating camera(s).

PRE-REHEARSAL

With all lighting and set dressing in place, it is well to make a dry-run with the camera, microphone boom and stand-ins going through the motions at half-speed. This will allow time to check for and correct: Tracking surface irregularities; lighting flare and its reflections in the set dressing; reflections of off-the-set personnel, equipment or activity from set windows and mirrors; camera height (particularly low angles shooting up), to avoid shooting over the set; the mic, its boom and their shadows; and prop and set dressing placement in order not to obscure or distract from the action. If it hasn't already been done, it is well to mark actor stop positions as well as camera dolly or crane chassis as well as crane boom arm alignment, stop and timing positions at this time. This is also the time to check with the Director of Photography to consider having ceiling pieces and set extension flats added to keep from shooting off the set.

THE REHEARSAL

The process of rehearsal is the refining phase, during which it is essential to work out the timing of the movement of cast and camera in order to achieve optimal coordination and composition. It is well to consider each rehearsal as an opportunity to examine, improve and perfect every facet of the part the camera plays in making the shot.

Camera Operator Concerns. During this refining process, the Camera Operator must concentrate on seeing that all aspects of each and every camera adjustment and movement made during the rehearsal combine visually with the movement of the performers in the viewfinder into a smooth and seamless flow of images. If that result is not achieved during the first dry-run, then corrections should be made and another rehearsal requested. It is particularly important in comedy that excessive rehearsals (and retakes) are to be avoided. So it is essential that the operative camera crew consistently collaborate and coordinate effectively and efficiently in order to maintain their welcome.

It is well for the Operator to be constantly aware of the movement of the performers and the moving camera platform in order to compensate for deficiencies in camera platform movement by panning and backpanning as necessary to maintain appropriate framing at all times.

Sizing and focus are important to constantly monitor. If either adjustment appears to be off, the First Assistant should immediately be made aware of the error, when it occurred, and who or what was involved. Equally important when modified during a take, changes in iris (T-stop), shutter angle, frame rate and/or sliding variable filtration or diffusion must be closely observed and assessed in order to assure that these adjustments work together seamlessly and that the desired image quality is consistent throughout the shot.

If the grouping of performers varies at any time from that set by the Director—performers missing their marks, or late getting to their marks, moving off and on their marks, moving from their marks too soon or too late, too spread out, too compressed, or stacked—the Director should immediately be informed so that the problem can be addressed.

Following each rehearsal, the condition of the makeup, hair and costume of each performer should be checked through the lens to be sure it has not been altered during the activity which took place in the scene and if it has, notify the Director of Photography so that the problem can be touched up or corrected by appropriate personnel prior to the next rehearsal or take.

First Assistant Camera Operator Concerns. In preparation for camera participation in dry-runs, the First Assistant Camera Operator, as directed by the Director of Photography, sets the T-stop and places specified filtration or diffusion in the lenticular system. During the dry-runs of pre-rehearsal and rehearsal, the principal responsibility of the First Assistant is to maintain acceptable focus and to manipulate lens sizing controls in order to assure the sizing variations required by the Director.

In addition, when other camera adjustments must be made and attended to during a shot, such as, sliding filtration or diffusion and/or iris, shutter angle and/or frame rate changes, the Second Assistant Camera Operator and other camera personnel may be enlisted to give a hand in riding control on each of the necessary variable settings.

Dolly/Crane Grip Concerns. During the refining process, the Dolly Grip concentrates on synchronizing the moves of the camera dolly—the Crane Grips on crane moves—to the movement of the principal action as enacted by the performers. The Dolly or Crane Grip will check, and adjust as necessary, position marks and/or movement velocity of the dolly/crane chassis and/or crane boom arm as directed by the Director, DP or Camera Operator. The Dolly Grip will maintain operational pressure in the hydraulic system at all times. As a safety measure, a Crane Grip will remain constantly at the crane arm when personnel are aboard, and by the carriage platform when it is near or at ground level in order to monitor transfer of personnel.

Up to this point, this article has been concentrating on single camera coverage. Four-camera film sitcoms are another genre which deserves a comment at this time. Sitcoms achieve comprehensive coverage of the action simultaneously with its presentation. In general, the two centrally positioned cameras cover the action and groupings with wide angle lens settings, while the two wing cameras capture opposing closeups. A Technical Coordinator gives the Dolly Grips audial cues via headset when to move their camera dollies to preset positions. This avoids traffic tie-ups and the danger of playing bumper cars in getting to assigned marks.

Once the final rehearsal has been completed, the performers are groomed for the real thing and the operative camera crew gets into starting position, checks and compares notes, and prepares to make the shot.

TAKING THE SHOT

A shot is the basic building block in the construction of a cinematic product. A shot consists of an unbroken continuity of framed imagery captured frame by frame on a recording medium from the beginning of an action or combination of actions until the conclusion thereof. During the editing process, all or portions of the shot may be selectively used in completing the final version. So it is important that every aspect of the shot work and all its elements blend as seamlessly and effectively as possible.

Master shots require the most extensive coverage and are generally shot with a wide angle lens in order to include all the action and much of the setting foreground and background. Complex action and camera moves are often devised by the Director to adequately cover the overall action to be followed by static camera position selective closeup coverage. It is the complex camera moves which require careful planning, coordination and attention on the part of the Director, Cinematographer, and operative camera crew.

Picture this scenario. All is now ready to shoot. Sound and camera roll. The action begins. Sound and images are captured as the camera and mic boom follow the action. The action concludes. Camera and sound shut down. End of shot; end of take. Was it a print, hold, or no good?

Evaluating the Take. After each take, the Director, Cinematographer and Camera Operator appraise the shot and evaluate the take, often by way of video assist and tape playback. Depending upon their appraisals, the Director may decide that a second take is necessary.

During the take, the Director is concentrating on the performance—actor interactions, character clarity, emotional intensity, and the timing and content of both action and dialogue. The Director of Photography is focused principally on the lighting—that the performers hit their position marks which place them in optimum lighting, that performers do not cast unwanted shadows on each other, that the camera, mic or mic boom do not cast unwanted shadows in the areas being photographed, that lighting units have not moved from their focused positions, and that lamp burnouts are detected.

Camera Operator Concerns. The Camera Operator is concerned with: Appropriately following and framing the action while including essential elements in frame; holding to image sizes set by the Director; monitoring visual focus to assure that essential action and elements are in sharp focus throughout the take; observing when performers vary their positioning in set group shots; noting when and where the microphone, the sound boom and/or their shadows or other extraneous matter intrude, or are inadvertently included, in frame; noting when other on-air camera adjustments—iris, shutter angle and frame rate—lack coordination, thereby varying the density of the images seen in the viewfinder; detecting irregularity in any camera move; and finally, evaluating the take on the basis of how all the elements have come together, as seen through the viewfinder.

First Assistant Camera Operator Concerns. The First Assistant Camera Operator attends to keeping the objective essentials in acceptable focus and within the sizing specified by the Director on the variable focal length lens. After each take the First Assistant should record the amount of footage expended and rebalance the camera, taking note of any changes in coverage, size, focus or timing requested by the Director, DP or Camera Operator. After each print take, the First Assistant should pull and examine the film gate aperture for film chips, emulsion residue, dust, sand granules, or hair particles.

Dolly/Crane Grip Concerns. The Dolly or Crane Grip is principally involved in moving the dolly and its riser, or crane chassis and/or boom arm, along a given path at a velocity which corresponds to the movement of the action being followed and photographed. It is important that the Dolly or Crane Grip ease into and out of movement, to keep dolly and crane movement as steady and consistent with the action as possible, and to avoid abrupt changes in direction or velocity, in order for the Camera Operator to be able to make any necessary corrections by panning or backpanning the action.

Final Appraisal. The moment the take has been made, the Camera Operator should know whether or not the take was technically acceptable, whether or not the operative camera crew coordinated their efforts. This is most important, because the Camera Operator may well be asked by the Director whether or not the take was acceptable (from a photographic standpoint), and if not, at what point the problem occurred. It is important that the Camera Operator give a reasoned but concise response. And whether asked or not, should the Operator feel the take was unacceptable from a technical viewpoint, he or she should ask the Director for another take, making sure the Script Supervisor makes note of the request in the production notes.

Avoid reshooting at all costs. Resetting and reshooting a scene is an expensive alternative to retaking a shot already set up—lit, dressed and prepped. Redoing master shots is the more expensive alternative because most of the setting will be used to cover the action and will require redressing and relighting. Redoing closeups are less labor intensive, but still time consuming. So, by all means, retake rather than reshoot.

If the purpose of the retake is to correct technical coordination problems, it is at this point, before commencing the next take, that the Camera Operator must advise the First Assistant, Dolly or Crane Grip and other camera personnel handling camera setting adjustments during the shot, where the coordination went sour and what might best be done to correct the problem. Input from these participants should be encouraged and considered. The Cinematographer and/or Director may well get involved at this point to resolve matters. Each retake is expected to correct or improve upon certain aspects of the previous take.

Moving On. Once the take has been approved by the Director's order to **"Print it!"** the shot has been successfully made and the process of preparing the next camera angle, or setup, begins. Care, continuity and consistency are the hallmarks of a top-notch operative camera crew and well worth developing by all film and video craftspeople.

SAFETY CONSIDERATIONS

SAFETY is an important consideration when operating a camera under potentially hazardous conditions. Needless to say, if the Camera Operator doesn't concern him or herself about his or her safety, it is not likely others will either. It is wise to take certain steps to insure relative safety during a shot which requires a manned camera position in hazardous proximity to a pass-by, stunt, or special effect.

Pass-bys. Pass-bys or run-bys (those not involving a stunt) can include vehicles, planes, boats, or livestock, passing by, over, or under a camera position. The principal concern is to be positioned a sufficient distance from the planned pass-by path to avoid unnecessarily close proximity to the action. (A longer lens will often give a sufficient feeling of closeness to the action without putting the camera crew in a position of jeopardy.) Any camera position that cannot be placed in relative safety should be unmanned, covered by a fixed, remotely activated camera, or, if the action must be framed and followed, by a remotely activated camera control head setup. These systems either come hard wired or operate from radio frequency.

Stunts. Before operating from a vulnerable camera position during a stunt (or drive-by), in addition to the Stunt Coordinator, it is also advisable to talk to the Stunt Person (whether driver or fall person) who will actually be doing the stunt or drive-by. Why? If that person's head is not on straight (eyes glazed, can't concentrate on your questions, seems to be in another world, etc) then you should not be manning that camera position, unless a remotely controlled camera setup is provided.

Even if you are satisfied that the Stunt Person is clearheaded and competent, you should request the Stunt Coordinator to place a Stunt Assistant on the **action side** of the camera position and have a couple Grips standing by ready to pull your Assistant and yourself out of harm's way, if necessary.

Manned camera positions involving close proximity to fast-moving or stampeding animals usually have sturdy structural protection.

Special effects such as crashes and/or explosions should now be covered by remotely controlled cameras when close proximity to the action is required and when manned cameras with longer lenses are not satisfactory to capture the effect desired.

When in doubt, hazard pay is never worth the gamble of putting your life and limbs in harm's way.

ELEMENTS OF CINEMATIC COMPOSITION

Webster defines **composition** as "The art or practice of so combining the parts of a work of art as to produce a harmonious whole." Assuming that what we do falls into the category of art (even if only occasionally), then the better we understand the process of composing our images, the better able we will be to deliver a quality result.

Cinematic composition varies in several respects from that of still photography and pictorial painting. Whereas pictorial and still photo composition frame a moment in time and space, cinematic composition frames elements *moving* in time and space.

Types of Cinematic Composition. There are two types of cinematic composition—**static composition** and **dynamic composition**. Static composition applies when the elements in frame and/or the camera are not changing position in relation to one another. Dynamic composition occurs when the elements in frame and/or the camera are changing position relative to each other.

Of course, others are involved in this collaborative, compositional process, which follows a cinematic product from concept to final realization. Cinematic composition includes not only the composition of elements occurring within each frame, but also the overall linear arrangement of shots into scenes, of scenes into sequences and of sequences into the major dramatic divisions of "acts" or "movements," comprising the complete and unified whole.

The Compositional Elements. The compositional elements are *everything* which is included in frame from a given camera angle.

Among the compositional elements of most concern **to the Director** are: The setting(s) for the action (whether studio set or location site), set dressing, props, costumes, makeup and hair dressing, and, most importantly, the actors, placed and moving in a way which clearly conveys (through the intermediacy of the camera) the purpose of each shot and scene—the mood, emotional level, character and story development, and continuity clarity; **to the Director of Photography**, it is: Lighting the compositional elements for the camera by applying the appropriate placement, quantity, quality and intensity of light to each setting—its background, midground, foreground and action areas—and planning the placement or movement of the camera, selecting its taking lens, the proper exposure, selective focus, special filtration, shutter angle and frame rate (fps) in order to cover the essential action and to convey the mood and pace desired by the Director; **to the Camera Operator**, it is: All elements which the Director has planned to include in frame for each camera angle and take made therefrom—the setting, set dressing, props, costumes, makeup and hair-dressing, the actors, the action which takes place, the background, foreground or panorama essential to the purpose of each shot or scene and the visual effect each camera angle and camera move may have on these composed elements.

Compositional Balance. Let's clear the air by saying that there are two kinds of camera framing. One kind is **quantitative framing**—simply including the essentials within frame without concern for placement, facing positions or balance. The other is **qualitative framing**—taking the pains to arrange the essentials within frame for a more effective if not pleasing and harmonious result. Arranging the elements (and/or camera angle) for presentation to the camera is critical in optimizing composition.

In cinematic composition, presentation of the elements to the camera is tantamount to presentation to the viewer/target audience. Clarity of purpose is an essential compositional element so that no doubt can be left in the audience's mind as to the purpose of the action occurring within that shot or scene. Proper composition—both static and dynamic— is a means of assuring that result.

Attention may be drawn to the essentials within frame by weighing the effect of, and by manipulating the presentation of, any or all of the following elements: The actors, their positioning and facing; the setting or background; the set dressing; the props; and/or the camera in relation to any or all of these elements. It is evident that certain compositional elements have a greater effect (or "weighting") on compositional framing (and balance) than others.

Placement and Treatment. Placement and treatment of elements in frame may also be used to enhance compositional effectiveness. For example, the eye is drawn to the following: **movement** of elements **toward** rather than away from and **faster** rather than slower; elements positioned **closer** and **higher** in frame rather than farther away and lower; **larger** objects; **frontal** appearances; **faces**, **brighter** objects and areas; elements in **sharp focus** in contrast to those in frame which are in soft focus; elements which are the **focus of attention** of other elements in frame; and a **violent or threatening gesture or action**.

So if one were to maximize the compositional impact of a shot, the following arrangement of those elements to be included in frame might be in order. **Place the subject**: **Facing** the camera, in a relatively **higher** intensity of light and a relatively **higher** and **closer** physical position than surrounding people and elements which are each **focusing their attention** on the subject throughout the shot, while the subject **moves rapidly toward** the camera and the camera **moves toward** the subject, which is in **sharp focus** throughout the shot, until a **full-face closeup** is achieved with the subject **looking directly into camera**, then making a **sudden, rapid and threatening move toward** the camera.

It is not always possible or practical to arrange static composition to ideal artistic standards, but where foreground and background set dressing or prop items can be arranged to maintain a modicum of compositional effectiveness, so much the better.

Dynamic composition frequently begins and ends with a static camera position prior to the start of, and after the completion of, the action. Composing for such a shot is simply a matter of keeping the essential action—moving subjects and objects—in frame with appropriate lead framing in order to accommodate the direction and velocity of that action.

Balancing forms, colors and areas of varying light values are among other compositional considerations. Any cinematic product may be made a more effective communication by close attention from all contributing and controlling parties—especially, the Director, the Production Designer, the Director of Photography and the Camera Operator—to the selection, preparation, placing and framing of the compositional elements.

CINEMATIC STRUCTURE— A VISUAL GRAMMAR

Cinematic structure follows a set of style rules much like those for a verbal or written grammar. These style rules provide a framework for applying non-verbal elements within the parameters of a distinct visual grammar. We should remember that original writing was picture drawing, which evolved into hieroglyphics and then into the symbols we use today.

Understanding cinematic structure is imperative if you wish to make your contribution to the final product as meaningful as possible. Just as it is essential to become entirely familiar with your tools of the trade (the script and storyboard are two essential tools), it is equally vital to know how and where your work will integrate into that final product. The better the understanding by all members of the collaborative team, the better the end result can be.

We will be identifying the elements of visual grammar, syntax and transitions and will indicate their correspondence to written and verbal elements.

The Pictured Elements. Basic to cinematic structure are the **pictured elements** which are selectively arranged to fill the frame with visual and audial information and stimulation. These elements consist of people, animals, things, costumes, settings, set dressing, props, scenery, positioning and movement of these elements and of the camera viewpoint, perspective, image sizing, positioning of focus, lighting, and sound. These basic cinematic elements may be likened to **letters** of the alphabet which are the basic components of words. And, of course, each **pictured element** is made up of myriad **picture elements** called "**pixels.**"

The selection, arranging and rearranging of these visual elements are what bring meaning, added dimension and visual interest to each sequential frame. Closely allied in this process are the Producer, the Writer, the Director, the Production Designer, the actor, the Cinematographer, the Camera Operator and (often, much later) the Editor. If actors, set dressing or props need to be rearranged or replaced, or the camera moved in order to improve compositional framing, now is the time for the Camera Operator to be heard.

The Frame. The **frame** is the basic structure used to present the elements during a captured moment in time and position in space. Each frame, in itself, contains a static representation of the elements, although, since the exposure itself takes a bit of time, movement may be detected by image configuration (as in a pictured runner) and its blurring. The imaged frame may be considered synonymous with the written or spoken **word**. With the exception of the sound element, still photography shares the foregoing structural components with motion pictures. A **frame** may contain **one** (being totally of one color or greyscale value) **or more pictured elements**.

The Camera Operator must be constantly aware of all the **pictured elements** contained in the framed composition. The most important elements—the actor or actors—must be placed and held in important positions in frame. The Camera Operator should add input to enhance the arrangement of these pictured elements so they might add to rather than detract from the overall effect of the production.

The Shot. The **cinematic shot** separates still photography from moving pictures. It adds the dimension of a time continuum by providing a progression of change or movement in a linear series of still photographs. The **shot** is a linear arrangement of consecutively positioned and exposed frames, representing a single camera viewpoint of the subject matter, which makes a statement in time and space. The **shot** is much like a written or verbal **sentence** whose function is to present a complete idea. However, a **gesture** or **movemen--t** within the shot or the **very short** or **intercut shot** may be likened to a **phrase,** which is a fragmented, but integral, expression, comprising a portion of the complete idea or sentence. A **shot** is composed of **one or more frames**.

The **shot** is planned and set up by the Director, who positions the actors and blocks the action and camera movement. Each **shot** has its purpose and must contribute to the progression of the plot line, the action, mood and emotional level of the **shot** and character development. The Camera Operator must understand the script and the Director's intent in these matters and strive to deliver the desired pictorial result on every take. In addition, the Operator is expected to have instant recall as to the content of the frame at any moment in time—actor positions and their direction of looks, costume and/or prop placement and/or condition, and what transpired during the take. Knowing the elemental contents of the **shot** that precedes and the **shot** that follows the **shot** which is being set up can provide the Camera Operator with clues to the most appropriate camera viewpoint as well as the framing and camera movement to help the Editor make a smoother transitional cut from the preceding **shot** as well as to the following **shot**.

The Scene. A **scene** (like an event) is often composed of a series of related shots (of actions and reactions) which occur during a specific time span in one setting and for dramaturgical purposes, having a beginning, middle and end. The **scene**, which is closely related to the **paragraph**, is a distinct subdivision of the visual continuity. A **scene** may be composed of **one or more shots**.

Because of the change of place and time from **scene** to **scene**, visual transitions (which occur at the head or tail end of a **scene**) are an important concern of the Director. Making each transition smooth and seamless is another concern of the Camera Operator. Planning transitions often involves matching action, size, or camera movement.

Review. In likening dynamic visual presentation to written or spoken grammar, **pictured elements** in each frame are like the **letters, vowels** and **consonants** which we use to form written and spoken words and which comprise the basic visual stuff of cinematic presentation.

Each **frame** can then be likened to a **word**.

A **shot** is composed of successive frames of the same subject matter from a given camera viewpoint, occurring at a certain time and place. A very few frames (presenting a reaction or gesture) might make a **phrase**, while a substantial number of such frames covering that action would present a complete thought or **sentence**.

A **scene** presents a complete series of actions and reactions which take place in real time and in a contiguous setting; it can be composed of **one or more shots** and serves grammatical purpose similar to that of a **paragraph**.

The Sequence. A **sequence** (like an episode) is usually composed of a series of scenes and conveys a complete statement or action with a beginning, middle and end. **Sequence** is directly related to the term **chapter**, which is a principal subdivision of a larger written work. A **sequence** may be composed of **one or more scenes**.

The Act. The **act**, like an **act** in a play (or a main **movement** in a symphony) represents a completed action, series of actions (or theme) with a beginning, middle and end. An **act** may be composed of **one or more sequences**.

It is the Writer who puts the scenario into a **one- or multi-act** format. In a **three-act** movement, the **first act** is the beginning, the **second act** the middle and the **third act** the ending segment of the total work.

The Motion Picture. The **motion picture**, of whatever genre and length, is the final product in the process of recording and assembling the parts and segments to make the completed whole. The **motion picture** (also called a: movie, film, flick, picture, video, production, program, show) is a term synonymous with the terms **play** or **book**. A **motion picture** may be composed of **one or more acts**.

The Editor is the person who finally arranges the recorded **shots** into **scenes** and the **scenes** into **sequences** and the **sequences** into acts and the **acts** into the completed **motion picture**.

The Camera Operator should be aware that every **shot, scene, sequence, act** and the **motion picture** itself has a beginning, middle and end, along with a certain appropriately varying emotional level. This knowledge can help in determining optimum camera placement, height, movement and composition.

VISUAL SYNTAX

Syntax is a grammatical term applied to sentence structure, and is, as *Webster's New Universal Unabridged Dictionary* so succinctly puts it, "the arrangement of words as elements in a sentence to show their relationship." Visual syntax then is the arrangement of the **pictured elements** in a **shot** to show their relationship. That relationship is the result of planned **action and camera blocking, stage business, production design, lighting** and **composition**.

The relative positioning and length of each shot also relates to a syntactic structuring of visual elements comprising the scene, sequence, act and total picture.

VISUAL TRANSITIONS

The **cut** is an abrupt transitional device between two **shots** (two ideas) and is the visual equivalent of a **period**.

The **dissolve**, depending upon its length, is a more deliberate transitional device, indicating a change in time and/or place, equivalent in meaning to "in the meantime." This effect gradually takes out the **preceding, or outgoing, scene** while merging it with the gradually apparent **following, or incoming, scene** and is the visual equivalent of **a paragraph break**.

The **wipe**, a variation on the dissolve, is a visual device used to show a change in time and/or place, by wiping out the preceding scene while wiping in the following scene. The wipe can take on several configurations and movement from a straight-across movement left to right, right to left, down, up, diagonally, circularly, spirally, saw-bladed, checkerboarded, etc.

The **superimposure** is a visual device used to combine images from a variety of different shots to add layers of meaning to the recomposed shot. This technique is somewhat similar to a stream-of-consciousness narrative.

The **split or multi-framed shot** is similar to the superimposure in that this technique can show several distinctly framed actions and how they relate, simultaneously. Multi-level staging in theatre presents a similar effect.

The **fade** is a distinctly deliberate transitional device which indicates the beginning of a **motion picture**, an **act** or a **sequence** (the **fade in**) or the conclusion of an **act**, **sequence** or **motion picture** (the **fade out**). The length of the **fade** gives symbolic indication of the duration of the passage of time it represents. It is the visual equivalent of the separation of **chapters** in a book.

The **iris in** and **iris out** are dated equivalents of the **fade in** and **fade out**.

Summing Up. The elements of cinematic structure will work for those filmmakers who understand the grammar and syntax of the structural application of these elements, and who then use their own creative talent to apply that knowledge and manipulate those elements in order to make each cinematic moment the most affective possible.

PACE, TIMING & RHYTHM

Each production and script has a distinctive continuity—a pace, timing and rhythm—of its own. The Director operates at a certain pace consistent with his or her experience and understanding of the script along with the ability to block and motivate the performers. The script carries a certain sustaining mood and requires appropriate pace, timing and rhythm during each scene from the performers and from the camera. At the close of production, with the shooting script, exposed footage and recorded sound in the hands of the Editor, the production begins to take on its distinctive internal pace, timing and rhythm as it is shaped, shot by shot and scene by scene, sequence by sequence, into its final form.

Pace, as applied here, has to do with the rapidity of movement and/or development in either the production or performance process. **Timing** has to do with regulating the pace of the production or performance process. **Rhythm** has to do with manipulating the pace in order to establish, by recurrent accents and pauses, an ebb and flow in the overall pace of the production and performance processes.

Production Mood by Type. It is important that the crew be tuned into the mood, pace and expectations of the Director, for it is the Director who establishes the ambient mood of the set and the pace with which the production progresses. Generally, the established on-set mood correlates with the nature of the subject matter— light, loose and jovial for comedy; quiet, intense and serious for drama. The actual pace of the production processes depends upon the production genre—slow-paced and highly detailed for big-budget features and commercials; fast-paced and compromised for tight-budget episodics and other TV programming. It is then the First Assistant Director's job to see that the mood and pace are adhered to. It is up to the production crew to fit in and deliver.

Performance Pace. The performance, as orchestrated by the Director, will carry the mood and the action to be photographed. The performers understand and have internalized the persona of the characters they are portraying. Therefore, they will move with the pace and characteristics of their respective character. The Director will block their movement, help plan their stage business, arrange their groupings and orchestrate their performances with both the story and camera (and shooting schedule) in mind.

As Camera Operators, we are expected to observe, frame and follow the action whether slow, fast or intermittent while maintaining optimal composition. Each character role has its intrinsic rhythm and pace which the performer personifies by performing the movement and gestures of the assigned character. In order to adequately anticipate and go with the flow, the Camera Operator should take every opportunity to study the type, repetition and intensity of movements and gestures of each performer during rehearsals and dry-runs. This "homework" will pay off in anticipating and following otherwise unexpected moves of the performers.

Each department head must be thoroughly familiar with the script and be prepared to deliver the required results in a seamless collaboration with other crafts. Personnel and matériel must be ready to function and fully operative.

Generic Pace. In comedy, timing is everything. Its scenic pace is relatively rapid. Since first takes in comedy are generally the best from a performance standpoint, it pays to be prepared to deliver a perfectly acceptable shot the first time around. This requires a thorough understanding of the scene (and of Directorial instructions) by members of the operative camera crew.

In drama, patience prevails. Its scenic pace is relatively deliberate, except during climactic/action scenes during which pace becomes progressively more rapid and coverage more extensive. Depending upon the amount of pre-production rehearsal time, scenes may require several takes to achieve the results desired by the Director. Nevertheless, an operative camera crew that delivers the goods with each take—in focus, in frame and thoroughly coordinated with the action—never missing a take, will prove an asset to the production.

Production Pace by Type. With features, the production pace is quite deliberate. Budgetary allowances are relatively liberal. There is time to rehearse and shoot takes until a state of perfection is reached before moving to the next setup. The average production pace of high-budget features amounts to one-and-one-half to three pages or so of shooting script a day; of lower-budget features, up to six pages per day.

With television programming—episodics, movies-of-the-week and sitcoms— the production pace is rather rapid because there is not the budget for extended shooting schedules. The average production pace for television programming—episodics, MOWs and epic series—is 8-12 pages per day (ppd); for sitcoms, 40-50 ppd; for soap operas, 75 ppd.

Summing Up. It is well to be aware of how the factors of pace, timing and rhythm can affect our work, and how the quality of our work can affect the pace, timing and rhythm of a production as well as that of the production process. It pays to stay in sync with the ongoing pace of the production. It also pays to understand the importance and function of pace, timing and rhythm in the performance process and to blend in and support those dramatic elements with the best work we can apply to the production.

MANIPULATING THE IMAGE

The old saying, "There can be many a slip between the cup and the lip," could just as well apply to the work we do. Just as the cup can be jostled or dropped by those handling it, resulting in spilled contents, the visual image can be accidentally or purposefully blemished, altered, distorted, manipulated and/or modified in the process of capture. And, of course, after capture, the size, position, form, color, hue and brightness of the image can be further manipulated and modified by optical or electronic means in the frame it occupies.

The Blemished Image. Capturing an image which is out-of-focus is one of the most obvious forms of accidental blemishing, one which cannot be corrected in post. Framing into the head area of the subject when not in extreme closeup mode is another non-correctable capture. Being off in exposure three to four stops or more can result in irreparable loss of image quality. Faulty internal film movement while the camera is running and/or positioning and holding the film in the film gate, will result in a weaving or bobbing frame. A faulty shutter can cause blanking, image smear and/or exposure deviation. Any of these can result in unfixable footage. Variation in frame rate during a take due to irregular drive motor speed also results in unusable shots. In addition, extreme diffusion of the captured image by filter, fog or smoke can render a take useless. These are some of the more obvious causes of creating unusable, uncorrectable, worthless footage.

Manipulating the image. On the other hand, purposeful blemishing and/or modification or manipulation might include: Controlled use of diffusion filters to soften facial features and/or use of smoke to create atmospheric ambience; application of under- or over-exposure to create an atmospheric effect; use of split diopters and/or swing-focus lenses to selectively manipulate depth of field; employing a fish-eye lens to purposely distort the image field; use of graduated filters to selectively manipulate exposure balance of areas in frame and/or their color quality; use of graduated diffusion to selectively alter the sharpness of portions of the frame; use of a star filter to add sparkle during image capture; varying the frame rate during, or for, various shots, resulting in purposeful variation in the projected speed of subject movement; varying the shutter angle to provide more image smear (wide angle) or more image crispness (narrow angle); and varying the lens iris setting during a take to accommodate desired exposure while moving to capture contiguous subject matter or an adjoining area which is receiving significantly more or less light.

A blemish, accidental or intentional, modifies the captured image. If the modifications fall within the parameters of acceptability, there will be no problem. However, if the modifications are unacceptable and uncorrectable, the consequences may be severe.

KEY ELEMENTS

Consider the elements comprising the process of image capture and how variations in their application can affect the result:

Exposure. Exposure is the product of the intensity and duration of light striking the film and the sensitivity of the emulsion to that light. The exposure setting places the brightness tones of principal persons, objects and/or areas at an optimum level for appropriate reproduction of the overall image on the recording medium. Overexposure tends to burn out details in the highlight areas. Underexposure tends to lose detail in the shadow areas.

Exposure is determined by the Director of Photography; the lens aperture (T-stop) setting is then made by the First Assistant Camera Operator.

Shutter Angle. The normal fixed shutter angle on most professional cameras is set at 170° to 180°. Those professional cameras with variable shutters provide the capability of setting the shutter angle from 0° up to 230°. A narrower than normal shutter angle combined with a longer taking lens while rapidly panning the camera can result in an objectionable strobing effect of the projected image.

The shutter angle is determined by the Director of Photography and set by the First Assistant Camera Operator.

Frame Rate. Any frame rate other than the (US) standard of 24 fps will affect the reproduction of image movement at the (US) standard 24 fps during projection. A slower taking frame rate will result in apparent greater velocity of movement during projection at the standard rate; a faster taking frame rate will slow any movement during projection.

The Director and/or Director of Photography make the decision as to any variance from the standard film taking rate; the First Assistant Camera Operator then adjusts the camera taking rate to conform to the desired frame rate.

Focus. Overall focus can vary from sharp to soft. Soft focus can occur during image capture; during the contact printing process, if the emulsion side of both the camera negative and print negative are not in direct contact; or, during optical transfer, if the focus is deliberately altered. The focus of an object in frame can be manipulated, depending upon its relative position of depth in the field of view and/or its relative compositional importance from time to time. Sharp focus can be transferred from one object or person located at a distance to another much closer in frame, or vice versa, during a take by a manipulation termed "**rack focusing.**" **Split focus** is attained with two objects not in the same focal plane when there is sufficient light to place both within an adequate depth of field, thereby keeping both in acceptable focus.

Production focus is the responsibility of the First Assistant Camera Operator.

Sizing. Sizing applies to adjusting the amount of frame space occupied by a person or object. When using a prime lens, and the subject size in frame needs adjusting, several options are available: Changing to a lens of appropriate focal length; or positioning the subject nearer the camera lens; moving the camera closer to the subject, or using a variable focal length (zoom) line. Maintaining a given object size, even though the subject is approaching the camera, requires either a compensating camera move and/or use of a zoom lens. Matching size and perspective in opposing closeups is important in order to maintain visual balance. Sizing is most efficiently accomplished with the use of a zoom lens. **Resizing** can be carried out as well during optical or telecine transfer.

Again, production sizing, sizing during each take, is the responsibility of the First Assistant Camera Operator, under the direction of the Director and/or Director of Photography.

Framing. While blocking is the process of arranging elements to be photographed, framing is the process of composing those elements within the appropriate aspect ratio, whether static (still) or dynamic (moving), during each take. **Reframing**, repositioning/resizing of subject matter in frame, can be done during optical or telecine transfer. The image can be enlarged or reduced in size and/or repositioned in frame. Further, digital manipulation can exclude selected elements which were captured in frame during the production process, or include elements not photographed.

Production framing during takes is the sole responsibility of the Camera Operator, under the direction of the Director and Director of Photography.

Coordinating Camera Essentials. It is the direct responsibility of the Camera Operator to coordinate dolly or crane and camera and sizing moves with that of the action taking place before the camera lens. It is the Camera Operator who sees it all coming together in the reflex viewfinder during a take. It is he or she who must advise the Camera Assistant and Mobile Camera Platform Operator when corrections or adjustments are required in order to assure that camera movement is seamlessly coordinated with the action.

Summing Up. Manipulating the image, advertently or inadvertently, during or following principal photography, has an effect on the final product. Mistakes which destroy image integrity are to be avoided, and must, at the very least, be immediately recognized and reshot. Modifications which contribute to image integrity and to the intent of the storytelling are to be welcomed and utilized either during production shooting or in the post production phase.

MANIPULATING THE EMOTIONS

Carefully planned and empathetically well-executed camera moves can aid greatly in evoking desired emotional responses from the viewer.

THE MANIPULATORS

Although it is true that motion pictures is a Director's medium, and it is **the Director** who plans and blocks the action, orchestrates the performances and determines the scene-by-scene emotional level and overall rhythm and pace of the production, it is the cast which characterizes and conveys the action and emotions, and it is the camera, in static and moving configurations, which captures and records that imagery for posterity.

It is the **Writer's job** to use the written word to affect the interest and emotions of the reader. This is best done through interesting and carefully constructed, developed and orchestrated characters, interacting in arresting settings and situations, with an ever-progressing logical plot and story line construction.

It is the **Production Designer's job** to provide settings conducive to and appropriate for eliciting the best performances from the players; settings within which the Director can logically and conveniently block the action and within which the Director of Photography can effectively light the action.

It is the **Director of Photography's job** to light the settings, action and actors and to plan camera movement with the Director in a style consistent with the story content—its period, action and character development.

It is the **Camera Operator's job** to frame and, along with the Dolly and/or Crane Grips, to follow the action in a manner consistent with the movement of the subject matter relative to the position and/or movement of the camera platform.

It is the **First Assistant Camera Operator's job** to maintain focus and manipulate the zoom lens in order to hold the various framing positions during each take, coordinating and synchronizing those adjustments with the movement of the subject matter being photographed as well as the movement of the camera relative to the subject matter.

It is the **Editor's job** to create rhythm and pacing from the shots that have been made of the action, using only those takes and portions thereof which convey the action and intended mood, excising all footage which does not constructively contribute to the final version.

Camera movement should be motivated by the action and should not call attention to itself. Camera movement which is motivated by, perfectly coordinated with, and follows the action is seldom obvious to the viewer. On the other hand, camera movement which is out of synchronization with the action or uneven and/or uncoordinated in following the action will distract and upset the viewer.

This non-obtrusiveness of the camera is particularly important in dramatic films. People come to see movies to be entertained, that is, to exercise and enjoy the stimulation of their emotions—and the more the better. They enter a movie theater, willing to suspend disbelief and to be emotionally manipulated for a period of time while expecting to be rewarded with a worthwhile and entertaining experience.

If, during a dramatic moment, unsteady camera movement or inappropriate framing should occur, the spell would be broken, even if momentarily, and the viewer would return to reality with his or her concentration on the production distracted or destroyed.

Consequently, it is of vital importance that all parties to the creation of the production experience do their utmost to avoid inconsistencies in the planning, preparation, staging and execution of cinematic productions.

THE EFFECT OF CAMERA

Aside from cast performance and set design and dressing and, of course, the sound effects and music scoring, the greatest emotional impact from a technical standpoint probably comes both from lighting and from camera placement and movement. Let's consider the camera.

Camera Placement. Placement of the camera is a commentary by the Director/Director of Photography as to how the audience is to view and, therefore, to feel about a particular shot. An eye-level camera position is normal and therefore neutral in its emotional effect. A low-angle camera position (angled upward) may emphasize height of the subject or visually imply its dominance of some order. A high camera angle (angled downward) may diminish the height of the subject or visually imply subjugation or a demeaning of some degree. The more extreme the angled position of the camera lens, the greater the potential emotional impact and effect on the viewer.

Selection of the taking lens can have an effect on the emotional manipulation of the viewer. A lens having an angle of acceptance approximating that of the human eye is considered a normal lens and would have little effect on the emotions of a viewer. A wide angle lens, having an angle of acceptance greater than that of the human eye, generally fills the frame with more clearly discernible visual information than lenses of narrower angles of acceptance and would keep the viewer's interest up and the eyes busy absorbing the displayed imagery. Narrow angle lenses tend to compress the planes in which the subject imagery resides, concentrating focus, and therefore viewer attention, within a narrow depth of field on one relatively shallow plane while imagery on other planes, in the near foreground and more distant background, become progressively fuzzy and visually less important. Use of telephoto lenses concentrates viewer attention on limited imagery.

Subject Movement. The motion of subject matter relative to the lens position can have an emotional impact on the viewer. Static positioning of subject matter has a neutral effect on the viewer's emotions. Movement arouses interest and attention and, depending upon the direction, mass and apparent velocity of that movement, can stir the emotions of the viewer. A lateral movement of a subject is reasonably neutral in its emotional effect. However, subject movement toward the lens position may well evoke an apprehensive or fearful viewer reaction. On the other hand, movement away from the lens position is non-threatening and may release emotional tension.

The apparent velocity of subject movement is affected by the angle of acceptance of the taking lens and the direction of movement relative to that lens. For example, a so-called normal lens would not have an effect on approaching or departing movement. A telephoto lens would compress the movement as though it were moving in place. But a wide angle lens would appear to increase the velocity and mass of the movement toward or away from the taking lens. The velocity of lateral movement would not be affected by any of the lenses. Viewer emotions would most likely be most affected by rapid subject movement toward and "into" a wide angle taking lens.

Camera Movement. If the camera is mounted on a mobile platform, such as a dolly or crane, the camera may be moved up, down, in, out, around and/or sideways during a shot. Each direction of movement will tend to evoke an emotional viewer response. The intensity of that response will depend upon the angle of the camera to the subject matter, the direction of the move, the velocity of the move, the duration of the move, and, of course, the subject matter and the direction, velocity, intensity and duration of any move made by the subject matter. Maximum effect on viewer emotions might be expected to result from rapidly accelerating subject movement directly toward and "into" a reciprocally rapidly accelerating moving camera shooting with a wide angle lens from a low angle viewpoint, shooting upward toward the, by now, frame-filling subject matter.

For maximum emotional effect on the viewer, all camera moves should be well-framed, in focus, and unwaveringly on target throughout the shot. In effect, the Camera Operator can make the camera an emotion-conveying entity—a member of the creative cast of performers, if you will.

Summary. Viewer emotions may be manipulated by carefully planned and executed camera moves. Selection and positioning of the taking lens can also have a pronounced effect on viewer emotions as can the direction, configuration, velocity and duration of camera and subject movement. Creatively used, the camera can provide substantial support for the emotional continuity of a cinematic story.

EDITING CONSIDERATIONS

The key to contributing most effectively to the cinematic process is a thorough understanding of the process of editing. The editing process is what makes the cinematic process work.

The editing process begins with the development of the concept; then to posing and juxtaposing structural story elements during the script writing stage; continues throughout the production process with the selection and preparation of shot setups, the blocking of actors and camera, the decisions to print or retake shot by shot; then on and into the final stage of the physical cutting, arranging and rearranging of the printed takes shot by shot, scene by scene, sequence by sequence until the cinematic entity has achieved a pace and rhythm, a form and identity, intended by the Writer and realized by the Director, with the aid and abettance of his or her production collaborators—the staff, cast and crew.

Everything we put on film or tape eventually finds its way to the film or video Picture Editor. As Camera Operators, how do we contribute to this editing process? In several essential ways. We see the immediate result of the interplay among the actors, the directed action, the makeup and wardrobe, the setting, set dressing and props, the special effects, and the lighting and any special filtration or diffusion used to modify the images we are framing. We can contribute to this process by spotting any inconsistencies we may observe in these production elements and apprising the Director and/or Director of Photography thereof (for this is indeed a check-and- double-check business we are involved in). Film Camera Operators do *"see it first"* (unless a video assist tap is used, and then that first view is shared with others at the floor monitors, sometimes referred to as "TV village"). By concerning ourselves with consistent framing and composition, carefully executed camera moves, smooth zooms and proper image sizing, and by giving careful attention to lens perspectives and camera positioning in relation to the **action line**, camera operation can make a major contribution to the image-making process from an editing standpoint.

Consistent, meaningful framing gives any picture a balanced look insofar as the composed images are concerned. Inconsistent, haphazard framing makes a hodgepodge of the visuals—an Editor's nightmare. Expensive and time-consuming optical or electronic repositioning and/or resizing can sometimes be used to correct this at the cost of some image denigration.

In order to maintain consistent image sizing, it is best, when doing opposing closeups, to use the same lens (or the same focal length on a zoom lens) for both setups, and at the same distance and T-stop.

Composing foreground objects in shots intended to be intercut can be an editing problem. For example, a prominent foreground object that is camera left in one angle can be on camera right in the reverse angle, thereby distractingly jumping left to right and back again when intercut. It is better to reposition the camera or object in order to exclude that foreground object in both such angles.

Keeping the frame on the set, while excluding from that frame all extraneous matter, such as, production equipment, the microphone, its boom and their shadows, is important from an Editor's standpoint. Off-the-set shots, or shots with extraneous material therein, can result in optical or electronic resizing or repositioning (with resulting loss of image quality) or expensive reshooting.

Maintaining proper image sharpness is another editing essential. Soft images, whether out-of-focus or too heavily diffused, cannot be significantly sharpened in post and will probably have to be reshot. (The captured imagery can be more safely diffused, as desired, in the post-production process.) Proper placement of focus (when depth of field won't carry), whether at foreground, midground or background, is also an important consideration. Staying with (focusing on) the essential action is a good rule of thumb.

Smooth and flowing camera movement—dollying, arming the crane, panning, tilting, or zooming—closely coordinated with actor movement, cuts very well into a static shot of the actor(s) at rest at the point that the camera/actor movement stops. Without camera movement at the cutting point, a smooth-looking cut can be made. In juxtaposing shots with camera movement, the result is optimal if the camera movement at the cutting point is in the same frame direction and at or near the same velocity in each shot. (On the other hand, in order to obscure the cuts, Editors frequently cut on actor movement or other matching action.)

Allowing actors to make clean entrances and exits, both through portals and into and out of frame, gives the Editor additional editorial options.

Guarding the **action line** (that imaginary line bisecting two individuals during an action or dialogue face-off) is essential in order to insure that it is not violated (crossed over by a static camera position—most often placed there for an opposing angle) thereby incorrectly placing the direction of each actor's look in the same screen direction—an editing headache, often requiring a reshoot in lieu of a seldom-possible optical flip.

So by being aware of the consistency required of the numerous elements appearing within frame—subjects, objects and movement—or affecting the frame— panning, tilting, dutching, rolling or moving the camera platform—the Camera Operator can be an important guarantor that the quality and consistency of these production values is being maintained and that they are being composed in an optimal manner, fulfilling the vision and intent of the Director. By so doing, the Camera Operator has contributed significantly to the production and to the process of editing—finalizing— that production.

WORKING WITH OTHER CAMERA OPERATORS

The only opportunity Camera Operators have of working together is when two or more cameras are to be utilized simultaneously on a film or video production. This might involve an extra camera on a feature or episodic, or extra cameras on stunts, chases and special effects, or the multi-camera audience participation, specials, sports and news events, or the three- and four-camera audience situation comedies, or the three- to five-camera soap operas.

When this happens, a certain protocol applies in order to keep the production process flowing as smoothly as possible.

Features and Episodic Production. On feature and episodic productions, the "A" camera is the principal camera, which usually frames the wider, more inclusive master angle, while the "B" camera is assigned the tighter, closer-view angles.

It is important for the B-camera Operator to be aware that the B-camera is a "guest" on the production and will only be used to the extent that the Director requires the additional coverage. This mandates that the extra Operator remain more or less in the background, all the while being alert to what is going on, until called upon to make a shot.

The B-camera, the #2 camera on the production, can be expected to be positioned after the A-camera has established a position or positions (if a moving shot) required by the Director to cover the blocked action. The Director will then place the B-camera to capture a closer view of selected portions of that action. In serving this function, the B-camera must never intrude on the operational area required by the A-camera. It is the B-camera Operator's responsibility to see that this does not happen.

Multi-Camera Chases, Stunts and Special Effects. On multi-camera chases, stunts and special effects shooting, several Camera Operators and Assistants are utilized. Whether working on an insert car, or positioned for a run-by, or deployed to cover a stunt or a special effects extravaganza, each Camera Operator must take care that his or her operative camera crew is positioned in a safe location, properly placed to make the required shot, and at the same time ascertain that no other camera crew or extraneous equipment, personnel or scenery is in frame, or likely to be so, during each planned shot.

Multi-Camera Audience Participation, Specials, Sporting Events and News Coverage. Multi-camera audience participation shows, specials, sporting events and news coverage provide another opportunity for Camera Operators to work together and to get to know each other and their work. Usually these particular types of productions are video events, staffed by video Camera Operators. During specials and sporting events, each Camera Operator is usually being given specific instructions by the Director (and/or Associate Director) regarding the coverage and positioning desired, although much of the positioning aspect is left up to the Camera Operator. Care should be taken to keep out of another camera's angle of view during taping or live broadcast..

Multi-Camera Sitcoms. On multi-camera sitcoms, whether film or video, three to four Camera Operators have the opportunity to work together, show after show, for an extended period of time. Because the cameras are moving much of the time during filming or taping, the Camera Operators must take care during the blocking phase to position their cameras in such a way as to avoid interfering with another camera's view/coverage of the action.

Nearly without exception the master camera (the camera with the 5- or 6-to-one zoom lens—20mm-to-100mm or -120mm) holding the wide, more inclusive master angle) gets the first opportunity to position for the coverage of the action. The camera holding the cross master then gets positioned for its coverage. The two wing cameras, which generally hold the closer view angles with their ten-to-one—25mm-to-250mm—zoom lenses, then are positioned well out of the angle of view of the master camera(s). It should be noted here that some DPs use a 5- or 6-to-one zoom on each of their four cameras, while other DPs use four 10-to-ones. This decision is usually based on the size of the standing sets, the size of the cast, the configuration of the operating apron and the visual quality desired.

Multi-camera sitcom Operators cooperate fully with each other to facilitate the shot-making process. To be sure, a lot of give-and-take goes on, for it is understood that the better each shot angle can be, the better the production can be.

Multi-Camera Soap Operas. Soap operas are multi-video camera events which produce a half-hour episode on television five days a week. As on any multi-camera show, but particularly because of time constraints, soaps require that each

Camera Operator be alert, flexible, and ready to make instant adjustments in position or coverage in order to help insure a desirable result.

Summing Up. Multiple camera shoots afford Camera Operators the opportunity to work with each other. There is always the principal or master camera which must be accommodated first, followed by the positioning of the additional camera(s). On episodics, features and other single camera productions, extra Camera Operators are guests on the production and should conduct themselves accordingly. Camera Operators on multi-camera sitcoms must demonstrate a high degree of flexibility and cooperation in order to help each other get the shot angles needed.

WORKING WITH DOLLY/CRANE/BOOM GRIPS

Dolly, Crane and Boom Grips are important functional members of the operative camera crew. Working closely with the Camera Operator, the work they do is essential to the proper execution of mobile camera moves, whether the camera is mounted on a dolly or a crane boom. The Dolly/Crane/Boom Grips move, drive and/or guide the direction of these mobile platforms from which the camera is operated.

Dolly/Crane/Boom Grip Responsibilities. The Dolly/Crane/Boom Grip is directly responsible to the Key Grip for setting up and maintaining mobile camera mounts and dolly track, and to the Camera Operator while setting and executing moving camera shots during rehearsals and takes, operating the mobile camera platform smoothly and accurately hitting position marks, in order to help make each take as technically perfect as possible.

Dolly/Crane/Boom Grip Duties. The Dolly/Crane/Boom Grip is responsible for setting up and checking all mobile camera platforms for proper and safe operation, maintaining proper pressure in the mobile camera platform hydraulic system and tires, and operating and/or moving the camera dolly, crane or boom during moving shots.

The Dolly Grip attends to and operates the camera dolly. The Crane Grip attends to and drives the camera crane, while the Boom Grip moves the camera crane boom arm in elevation (rise and fall) and azimuth (swing) movement.

Extreme care must be exercised in laying, leveling and cleaning dolly track, or in preparing the crane tracking bed, all done under supervision of the Key Grip. Accurate marking of the start, intermediate stop(s) and final stop position for mobile camera platform moves (by the Dolly and Crane Grips) and marking elevation and swing positions of the boom arm (by the Boom Grip) or marking elevation for the dolly arm (by the Dolly Grip) is essential to the effective result of a moving shot.

Safety of personnel is a primary concern of the Dolly/Crane/Boom Grip who: Weight-checks the lift capability of cherry-pickers, forklifts, hoists, construction cranes and similar lift mechanisms prior to allowing human loads aboard; determines the position placement of the boom arm post; maintains proper counterbalance weight load on the crane boom arm; locks the dolly riser arm or crane boom arm when not in use, when making a static shot, or when changing the personnel or equipment load, and until proper counterbalancing weight can be applied to the crane boom arm; and stands by the boom arm at all times when personnel are aboard.

Interpersonal Relations. When a dolly or crane is utilized as a mobile camera platform, one or more Dolly, Crane or Boom Grips, as appropriate, is/are used to operate such equipment and become part of the operative camera crew, working closely with the Camera Operator (and the First Assistant) in order to coordinate the movement of the mobile camera mount with the movement of the action. The Camera Operator, who is framing and riding the shot, is the final word on how each moving take looks and feels; hence, the Dolly/Crane/Boom Grips must pay close attention to the instructions from the Camera Operator regarding modifications to be made in dolly, crane and/or boom moves.

Feature, Episodic, Special Event and Commercial Production. Camera dolly and crane work on feature, episodic, TV specials and commercial production is pretty much the same. The requirements, parameters and procedures for moving camera shot execution are similar: Lay, set or prepare the track or tracking surface; operate the dolly/crane/boom arm; mark position start, stop(s) and direction change(s), dolly riser arm or crane boom arm elevation and crane boom arm swing positions for each moving shot.

Multi-Camera Film Sitcoms. The three- or four-camera film sitcom may have 6 to 14 or more sequences, any one of which may be up to ten minutes in length—in effect, a ten minute take, involving three or four 35mm or 16mm studio cameras, each mounted on a dolly, each making as many as 8 to 20 moves or more. So the Dolly Grips are busy moving a McAlister, Fisher or Chapman dolly with a Mitchell BNC or Panavision PSR or Panaflex on a geared head, a Camera Operator and Camera Assistant aboard and, on some shows, a hundred pounds or so of batteries for an on-board OB light.

The Dolly Grip needs to know and keep track of eight things during a rehearsal or take: **1)** That, at the start of each sequence, the dolly chassis is properly aligned relative to the set, **2)** the riser arm is at the proper starting height, **3)** exactly which mark the dolly is on at any given time, **4)** where (in what direction) the next mark is, **5)** how far away, when the move (and/or riser arm rise and/or fall) is to be made, **6)** how much time is needed to get there, **7)** whether the move is to be made straight, banana and/or variable speed, and **8)** whether or not the move is "on-air" (expected to be used in the final cut).

That is why each dolly position is carefully floor-marked by each Dolly Grip with a strip of 2″ masking or heavy white tape on which the Grip prints the sequence letter (A, B, C, etc), followed by the number of each sequential stop position, an arrow indicating the direction in which the next position mark is located and a subscript number, indicating the distance that move will be. Fast (color coded) or specially configured moves (a curved arrow shaft) are also noted. Each camera is assigned a color for floor-marking purposes by the Key Grip (red, blue, black or green), because by the time camera blocking is completed, the working floor area will be virtually covered by myriad tape markers.

Video Productions. When a dolly or crane is used on video productions, the

Dolly/Crane/Boom Grips usually have a video monitor which is mounted on the dolly, crane and/or boom arm for convenient visual access, in order to enable each Dolly, Crane or Boom Grip to follow the framing and movement being composed by the Camera Operator. (Film productions are increasingly using video assist to plan, verify and help expedite moving camera shots.)

Camera Operator Expectations. It is the Camera Operator who sees and feels the effect of each dolly, crane or boom move, so it is encumbent on the Dolly/Crane/Boom Grip to heed suggestions and instructions given by the Operator and to modify any move accordingly. The Camera Operator expects all dolly and crane moves to coordinate closely with the action. This translates into smooth and accurate starts and stops, which are delicately feathered in and out, and a duplication of the pace of the action which is being tracked.

Summing Up. In understanding the responsibilities and duties of the Dolly/Crane/Boom Grip, the Camera Operator can better coordinate the efforts of the Camera Assistant and the Dolly/Crane/Boom Grip(s) in following the planned action.

USE OF
RADIO COMMUNICATION

Ever been up on the business end of a crane and, because of a tight schedule, without adequate time to fully prepare the shot(s)?

At that time you would have given your left knuckle for a convenient, quiet and efficient way to communicate with the Crane Driver and/or Boom Grip during rehearsal and during the shot.

The solution is at hand, provided the production and sound departments are given adequate notice of your needs. Ask for four hands-free, two-way RF (radio frequency) radios (MAXON, or similar make)—one for you the Camera Operator, one for the Director, one for the Crane Driver and one for the Boom Grip. These units have a clip-on transmitter/receiver and a single earphone headpiece with a flexible boom mic attached.

Set your audio PWR (Power) on VOX (voice activated), the incoming VOL (volume) on M (medium) and MIC output on HI. Have the two Grips and the Director set their radio PWR on PTT (press-to-talk), their VOL on HI and their MIC on M. It is essential that both Grips can hear the Camera Operator at all times during the shot.

Once hooked up, the Camera Operator can talk or whisper the Crane Grips through the shot during rehearsals and takes without removing the hands from the control wheels. Any slight modifications needed in crane or boom movement can be immediately implemented by the Grips with a word from the Camera Operator or Director. Use of radio communication means that the boom arm need not be lowered in order for the Camera Operator to communicate with the Director or Grips after each dry-run or take.

These small and effective radio communicators are great time-savers and a lot less expensive than video-assist monitors for the Crane and Boom Grips. The use of RF communication for electrical and grip rigging and production procedures could also prove an efficient energy and time saver as well as promoting a less noisy working environment.

WORKING WITH CAMERA ASSISTANTS

Most film Camera Operators have at one time or another been Camera Assistants, starting as a film Loader, then going to Second Assistant Camera Operator and on to First Assistant Camera Operator before becoming a Camera Operator. When first becoming a Camera Operator and dealing with the new and increased responsibilities and pressures of the upgrade classification, it is easy to come down hard on the Assistant for a minor mistake. It is easy to forget, but well to remember, the pressures that the Assistant is under before lowering the boom too severely. And remember also that no one is perfect all the time; everyone is going to goof now and then—even the Camera Operator. The important thing is to catch the error promptly, know **why** it happened, and make the necessary correction and/or retake on the spot so it won't happen again.

First Assistant Camera Operator Responsibilities. The First Assistant Camera Operator is directly responsible to the Camera Operator, assists the Operator in various aspects of camera operation, operating the ancillary adjustments—focus, zoom sizing, variations in T-stop, frame rate and/or shutter angle and sliding graduated diffusion or density filters—during the shot, and is responsible for setting up and preparing the camera equipment for operation.

First Assistant Camera Operator Duties. It is well to remember that the First Assistant Camera Operator has a host of duties to perform which constantly keep him or her occupied. In fact, throughout the shooting day, the First Assistant is probably the busiest person on the set or location site—checking, setting up and moving the camera equipment, taping distances, changing and cleaning lenses and filters, changing film mags, threading film in the camera, using the inching knob to carefully engage the registration pin(s) and the pulldown claw cleanly into the film perforations, adjusting pitch control, keeping camera reports and much more. So far as the First Assistant's relationship to the camera and its optical elements is concerned, cleanliness is next to godliness, for if a speck of dirt, a film chip, a grease smudge or finger print is allowed to remain on a lens element or in the film gate aperture, the captured image could be flawed.

The First Assistant assists the Camera Operator during a take by following focus, sizing the image on the zoom lens, riding the shutter angle control, adjusting the T-stop, varying the frame rate (fps) on a variable-speed (wild) motor, and/or sliding the graduated filter or diffusion. Assuming all of these adjustments are working at the same time (and it can happen), the First Assistant can handle two and the Second Assistant can manage two; if other Camera Assistants are not available, the Director of Photography has been known to lend a helping hand for the remaining settings.

The Second Assistant Camera Operator. The Second Assistant Camera Operator is directly responsible to the First Assistant Camera Operator and assists the First Assistant in certain duties, namely, unpacking, setting up and wrapping the camera equipment, fetching camera gear requested by the First Assistant and returning that gear to its proper place, loading and unloading film magazines (when a Loader is not used), preparing the camera slate and slating scenes for the camera(s), and keeping Camera Reports for the First Assistant. The Second Assistant should have the slate properly filled out and ready for each take, and place the slate so that the Camera Operator does not have to search for it, then voice identify the take clearly and completely and hit the sticks distinctly, but (ever aware of the microphone placement) with less intensity for closeups than for long shots.

Check-and-Double-Check. Making motion pictures (an activity wherein the details have details) is and always has been a check-and-double-check process, which means: **CVR**—**C**heck to **V**erify and, if not right, **R**ectify. It is always better (and a lot less traumatic for all concerned) to catch a glitch while shooting the scene than it is to discover the problem during dailies the next day. Returning to a set or location to redo a setup is much more time-consuming and expensive (and unforgiving) than remaking a take at the time.

In other words, it is a good idea to check thoroughly and regularly after each printed take that the film gate (and chamber) is free of emulsion build-up, hair, dirt or film chips, that the film is properly threaded and has not lost a loop, that the footage counter is properly zeroed with each fresh film magazine and correctly read following each take, and that the camera is rebalanced (if the magazines are bi-axial and/or displacement type) when approximately half the film load has been run through the camera. (A camera running a 2,000´ film magazine should be re-balanced following each take.) The camera and its settings should be thoroughly checked following a meal break or at any other time when it has been standing unattended.

Operator Expectations. The Camera Operator expects the First Assistant to know the responsibilities and duties of that classification and to do that job competently and expeditiously at all times. On the other hand, the Camera Operator should expect no more of the Assistant than the example set by the Operator's own work ethic.

Operator Responsibilities. It is the responsibility of the Camera Operator to see that the camera is ready for each take, which means that the First Assistant has finished threading film in the camera and/or checking the film gate, has the proper lens up, has measured and noted all camera-to-actor distances, has noted and marked all zoom lens sizings, has set the T-stop to the Director of Photography's specifications, has placed any specified filtration and/or diffusion in the lenticular system and has taken a position by the camera, ready to make the moves; that the Second Assistant is out front with the slate all properly and completely filled in and placed; and that the

Operator has hands on the control wheels, ready to switch on and roll film. It is the expectation of the Assistant Director that the camera is ready to roll when the lighting is set and the Director is ready. When the Camera Operator tells the AD that the camera is ready, **it had better be ready.**

Keeping Sharp. The Camera Operator must see that the operative camera crew—Operator, First Assistant and Dolly/Crane Grip(s)—is on its collective toes during dry-runs, rehearsals and takes. Each of the crew members should pay close attention to the blocking of both actors and camera in order to maximize job performance. (Synonymous with optimal job performance is **job security**.) A well-executed dolly or crane move during a complex shot is a thing of beauty to behold—on the set or on the screen—the result of concerted and harmonious coordinated effort of all concerned.

Safety. In order to avoid collision and resulting injury to either the person or eye of the Camera Operator (which is pressed to the camera ocular), the First Assistant (when riding the dolly) should keep tucked in to the dolly during moving takes past set pieces, furniture, obstacles and set props. For rapid dolly moves, the First Assistant should be encouraged to walk the shot in order to decrease the inertial weight load which the Dolly Grip must start and stop, and also to reduce dolly yaw and wheel squeal during fast starts and turns caused by the unbalanced weight distribution on the dolly.

Catching Errors—Avoiding Problems. We all have days when we're not as sharp as we would like to be. The First Assistant may miss some focus or zoom positions, or the Dolly Grip may be late in moving the dolly or may miss a dolly stop position during a rehearsal. *Then* is the time for the Camera Operator to let the offender know that an error has been detected. If the same error occurs during a subsequent rehearsal, a more pointed comment is in order, along with some assistance in helping to analyze why the problem is recurring and what might be done to eliminate it. The Camera Operator sees the combined effect of a shot through the viewfinder and is the only one who can judge the technical and aesthetic aspects of what is being framed in the viewfinder (unless, of course, a video assist tap in the camera ocular system is being used).

Make it a practice to let the First Assistant know when focus buzzes (softens) or sizing needs adjusting during rehearsals and takes so that he or she is aware exactly when and where the problems occur and can make appropriate correction before or during the upcoming rehearsal or take.

The very nature of filmmaking requires a close collaboration and coordination between the Camera Operator and the rest of the operative camera crew—in particular the Operator and the First Assistant. An attitude of mutual respect and cordiality helps make the process work even better.

CAMERA ASSISTANT BASICS

In the very early days of motion picture making, the Cameraman did it all. He was a true and complete Cinematographer, a motion picture taker and maker. He planned the shoot, placed and propped it, directed and shot it, souped, duped and printed it, edited it, and screened it.

Help was not far away. To lighten the load, Assistants were hired to carry, move, set up, clean and wrap the camera and its related equipment. In return, if they were observant, they became privy to the "secrets" of the master Cameraman unfolding before them during each set up and take.

As equipment and production techniques developed and became more complex and as the production process became more time/money-driven, a second camera was put to use for the foreign version. The First Cameraman, who always operated the principal camera, determined the camera positions and then lit the setup. A Second Cameraman was brought aboard to operate the second camera. A Camera Assistant (Third Cameraman) was often used to carry and set up the camera, pull focus and/or manipulate any special effects settings on the camera in addition to loading mags and changing lenses, filters and f-stops at the First Cameraman's direction.

Gradually, under the pressure of budget and schedule, specialization became the norm and from this working relationship evolved the job titles in use today: Director of Photography, Camera Operator, First Assistant Camera Operator, Second Assistant Camera Operator and Loader.

Today, the First Assistant directly assists the Camera Operator in the functions related to the camera and its operation—setting it up, checking out its lenses and operation for facility and function, and riding certain of the camera adjustment controls—usually focus and image sizing—during rehearsals and takes.

The usual job progression is from Loader to Second Assistant to First Assistant to Operator to DP. Each level is built upon a solid foundation of myriad learned and applied detail—of consistently doing the assigned job efficiently, consistently, and well. At each step of the learning process, watching, listening and doing goes on. To the degree that sufficient knowledge and understanding of the responsibilities and duties of related job functions takes place, the progress continues apace and the goals are reached.

Making a certain setting or adjustment and, at the same time, understanding the reasons for doing it are not always part of the equation. But for those experienced and motivated Camera Assistants it nearly always is. Doing an adjustment by rote may get the job done, but knowing why it is being done and the visual effect it will have, and then artfully finessing that adjustment during a take, can help make the visual result a memorable event and the doer a person in demand.

For the Camera Assistant just starting, or on his or her way up the experience/ job ladder, a working knowledge of the responsibilities, duties and functions of the job classification held, as well as the job being worked toward, is essential. Of basic importance is a thorough knowledge of: Camera components and their function, film emulsions and their capability, cinematic theory and definitions, optics, camera accessories and their function, production procedures—the testing and proving ground for that practical knowledge—and last but not least, *safety*.

RESPONSIBILITIES & DUTIES

The five classifications in the camera category involved in principal film production are the Director of Photography (Category Head), the Camera Operator, the First Assistant Camera Operator, the Second Assistant Camera Operator, and the Loader. Each classification has its specific responsibilities and duties. Each classification relies upon the others to function in completely responsible fashion in order to keep the level of efficiency high and consistent.

Knowing what to do, when to do it, and how to do it—safely—is important for each craftperson to understand when making his or her contribution to the production. A clear understanding of the levels of authority and lines of communication is also necessary for the collaborative cinematic production process to function efficiently and well.

Although all production personnel in the Camera crew are under the direction of the Director of Photography, each classification, because of the working relationship among the camera crafts, is directly responsible to the craftsperson being directly assisted, as follows: The Loader is directly responsible to the Second Assistant, who is directly responsible to the First Assistant, who is directly responsible to the Camera Operator, who, in turn, is directly responsible to the Director of Photography.

It is the responsibility of the **Loader** to care and account for all film charged to his or her care and to load, download, can and properly identify all exposed film and unexposed short ends.

In addition to helping the First Assistant set up and wrap camera equipment, the **Second Assistant** has the responsibility of preparing the slate, slating each take and keeping an accurate record in the Camera Report for each film roll of footage exposed during each take for each scene.

The **First Assistant** is responsible for seeing that all ordered equipment, accessories and expendables are present and accounted for, for setting up and checking out the integration and operation of each item of equipment, and, among other duties, mounting the taking lens and filters on the camera, and, finally, making those adjustments (T-stop, frame rate, shutter angle, variable filtration, focus and zoom control) necessary during each rehearsal and take.

Framing the action as well as checking and coordinating the focus and sizing by the First Assistant and the camera movement provided by the Dolly or Crane Grips are the principal responsibilities of the **Camera Operator**.

The **Director of Photography** works closely with the Director and has responsibility for the overall look of the production—the lighting, exposure, equipment and lens selection, and camera movement—and for efficiently utilizing technical (principally camera, electrical and grip) personnel under his or her direction.

Traits. Perhaps the three most important traits a Loader or Camera Assistant should develop are **cleanliness** (of the workplace and equipment), **attention to details** (seeing, checking and double-checking that all necessary steps during set up and production are taken) and **accuracy** (doing it right the first time—and every time thereafter).

Tools of the Trade. Every beginning Camera Assistant seriously interested in moving up/up grading starts accumulating items essential to help in doing the job better. Among those ditty-bag items are: A 50´ cloth measuring tape, small flashlight, Swiss army knife, tweezers, scissors, chalk, powder puff, pens, pencils, grease pencils, marking pens, air blower (syringe or can), sable-hair brush, lens cleaner, lens tissues, black and white camera tape, electrical tape, orange stick, Q-tips, magnifying glass, current ASC Manual, Philips and standard screwdrivers, jewelers screwdrivers, assorted Allen wrenches, needle-nose and standard pliers, wire stripper, spirit level, camera oil and grease, electrical adapters, camera reports, spirit gum, spring-loaded clamps, clothes pins, Velcro strapping, changing bag, extra black film roll bags, cores and cans, plus personally preferred items.

As equipment and techniques have become more complex, and as shooting schedules and logistics have become more demanding, the work of the Assistant Camera Operator also has become more complex and demanding, requiring up-to-the-minute knowledge of how to assemble and service newly introduced equipment while working at top accuracy and efficiency.

CAMERA COMPONENTS & FUNCTIONS

Camera Components. It is well to know and understand the function of each of the major components of a motion picture film camera. The camera consists of a **light-tight dark chamber** (including the external **film mag**, if any) through which the film is moved from a **feed axis** over **guide rollers** by a **motor**-driven constant-speed **sprocketed drive wheel** with **drive clamps** to keep the film in secure contact with the drive, briefly converting the film flow to intermittent movement as it is pulled into and then over a **recessed metal path** with **side rails** through the **film gate** at the camera **aperture** by the **pull-down claw** and, while held in place by the **pressure plate** in the gate and **registration pin(s)**, exposed to light passing through the **lens** and its light-controlling **diaphragm**, past a rotating **shutter** and through the camera **aperture**, after which the exposed film is advanced, past a **film buckle-protector** to the film **take up axis** in the camera or external film magazine. An **on/off switch**, **inching knob**, **pitch control knob**, **buckle protector/indicator**, **footage counter** (mechanical or electronic) and a **viewfinding system** complete the major components.

Component Functions. The purpose of the **side rails** bordering the recessed pathway in the film gate, under the pressure plate, is to keep the film laterally aligned while it is stationary in the film gate.

The purpose of the **pressure plate**, in applying force across the base side of the film, is to keep the entire emulsion surface of the film stock perfectly flat and in the focal plane during the exposure interval.

The purpose and function of **pin registration** is to consistently immobilize, hold and vertically align each frame relative to the film perforations (sprocket holes) during the exposure interval.

The purpose of the **taking lens** is to collect light reflected from the framed subject matter thereby forming a properly exposed, undistorted and focused image on the film emulsion at the focal plane of the camera.

The **lens diaphragm** controls the amount of light passing through the lens and camera aperture and striking the film while it is being held steady and motionless in the gate during the exposure interval.

The **shutter** functions as a light control mechanism, stopping all light from reaching the camera aperture while the film is being transported through the film gate. A standard **fixed angle shutter** is normally set and rated between an angle of 165° and 180°. A **variable angle shutter** can be adjusted to control the amount of time that light has to strike the film during the brief period it is immobilized in the gate (thereby controlling the amount of light affecting the film). By varying the shutter angle, the action of the image can be blurred or sharpened, strobing can be minimized and the entire image can be made to fade in or fade out.

The purpose of **intermittent film movement** is to allow the film to be momentarily held at rest while being exposed to light passing through the lenticular system in order to keep the recorded image stable and the exposure consistent. (**Frame rate** has a direct effect on image quality at a given shutter angle setting—the slower the frame rate the more moving image blur will occur and the more rapid the projected action will appear.)

Proper sizing of the **film loops** (and accurate setting of the pull-down claw pitch control) is important in order to avoid excessive film movement noise, tearing and scratching the film and/or hindering free film movement (and claw engagement), thereby resulting in poor imaging and possible mechanical damage to the camera. (**Frame rate** has a direct effect on noise creation/emanation—the higher the frame rate, the more noise produced.)

Film Mag Types. There are four general types of professional film magazines: **Double-chamber bi-axial** (Mitchell, Panavision, Auricon, MovieCam, UltraCam), **double-chamber co-axial** (ARRI 35BL, Eclair NPR and ARRI 16 with 1200´ mag), **single-chamber bi-axial** (B&H Eyemo, Auricon, Ciné Special, ARRI 16S), and **single-chamber bi-axial displacement** (all ARRIs [except BLs], Eclair CM3 and Camerette, Panavision, Moviecam, Ultracam, Aaton).

There are five types of **lens mounts**: The bayonette, "C," "S," "T," and rotary.

Readouts. There are several external readouts on the modern ciné camera. These are the **on/running light**, the **footage counter** and the **frame rate.**

CAMERA CONTROLS

There are a number of camera controls which adjust the operating function of various of the camera components.

External Controls. The principal external controls of ongoing concern to the First Assistant Camera Operator are **T-stop**, **focus**, **sizing**, **frame rate**, **shutter angle**. Of secondary concern are the **sliding graduated diffusion/density**, **polarizer rotation**, **footage counter reset**, **ground glass illuminator**, **inching knob**, **off/on switch**, **viewfinder magnifier** and **viewfinder cut-off**.

Internal Controls. The principal internal controls of concern to the First Assistant are the **film buckle protector** and the **pitch control**. The buckle protector must be reset following each film buckling episode and with each fresh load of film. The pitch control, which adjusts the pull-down cycle of the pull-down claw, must be reset with each fresh load of film in order to minimize the noise of engagement of claw with film stock.

CAMERA ACCESSORIES

Camera Assistants must be thoroughly conversant with the care and use of support elements which contribute to camera operation. Camera accessories include lenses, film magazines, batteries, matte boxes, optical filters, auxiliary lens attachments, control heads and camera supports.

Lenses include primes and zooms. Prime lenses are of a specific focal length and include super wide angle fisheye lenses to extremely narrow view telephoto lenses, whereas zoom lenses are variable focal length lenses.

Film magazines come in various load capacities: 200′, 400′, 1,000′ and 2,000′ sizes for 35mm and 65mm; and 200′, 400′; and 1,200′ for 16mm.

Batteries must be kept charged and ready, and replaced at the first signs of losing power.

In addition to protecting the lens from direct sunlight and artificial illumination, the **matte box** holds the Director of Photography's filter pack, with **filters** and **diffusion** (optical glass, gels and gauzes) arranged in specific designated order.

Auxiliary lens attachments such as extension tubes, diopters or trick lens attachments add to the DP's bag of visual options.

Included in the general types of **camera control heads** are the friction head, the ball-and-socket, the spring-loaded, the counterbalanced, the fluid, geared, gimbal and gyro heads and combinations thereof.

Camera supports are of two types—static and mobile. **Static supports** include the tripod, unipod, chain or rope pod, hi-hat, pancake and stand. **Mobile supports** include the body-mounted pod and shoulder pod as well as camera stabilizing devices such as the Steadicam™ and Pogocam™. Among the free mobile supports are the Tyler mount, aircraft, boats, insert cars, wheeled pedestals, crab dollies and cranes.

STANDARDS TO CONSIDER

Standards represent international agreements reached by technical standards organizations and adhered to by manufacturers, producers, technicians and exhibitors. These standards guarantee that equipment, accessories and film (and certain production procedures) which are provided can be utilized with confidence that uniformity is guaranteed and that consistency can be maintained. Some standards to consider are standard sound speed, motion picture camera and film dimensions and perforations, and light transmission measurement in calibrating lens stop settings.

Frame Rate. Frame rate refers to the speed with which the film runs past the camera (or projector) aperture as measured in frames-per-second (fps).

Frame rate has a direct effect on the rate of recorded (and projected) movement and on exposure. For example, double the fps taking rate (requiring one stop more exposure) and the projected action slows down fifty per cent at the standard projection rate; halve the fps (requiring one stop less exposure) and the projected action doubles in rapidity.

Standard sound speed is 24 fps and standard projection speed is also 24 fps (25 fps is the standard used in Europe), resulting in one-to-one representation of the recorded sound and movement.

At standard sound speed, **16mm film** runs through the camera at 36 feet per minute, **35mm** goes through at 90 fpm and **65mm** at 112.5 fpm. (Exceptions to this are 3-perf 35mm Moviecam pull-down which runs at 67.5 fpm, 2-perf pull-down 35mm Techniscope at 45 fpm, 35mm VistaVision which moves film 8 perfs horizontally at 180 fpm, and 65mm Showscan which devours film at the rate of 60 fps and 225 fpm. And then there is the IMAX system which drives 65mm film horizontally at 15 perfs per frame and 337.5 fpm.)

Standard motion picture film width dimensions are 8mm, 16mm, 35mm, and 65mm (70mm is for print only), but only 16mm, 35mm and 65mm films are considered for most professional purposes.

16mm has 40 frames per foot and 1 perforation (sprocket hole) at the horizontal frame line on each side per frame. 35mm has 16 frames per foot and 4 perforations on each side of each frame. (Exceptions to this are the two-perf pull-down of Techniscope and 8-perfs on each side of the frame for the horizontal pull-across film movement of VistaVision.) 65mm has 12.8 frames per foot and 8 perfs on each side of the frame.

Each full **T-stop setting**, from the largest to smallest diaphragm opening on any given lens, is calibrated to admit (to reduce or stop) all but half the amount of light compared to its adjacent next smaller full T-stop scribed setting. Each full T-stop opening in size admits twice the light to the film plane.

Assistant camera personnel would do well to constantly strive for a more complete understanding of production processes and the reasons therefor. Camera Assistants are there not only to manage the equipment but also the various camera settings and adjustments—some given to them by the Director of Photography, others required by actor and/or camera movement. Camera Assistants should be aware of why they are making certain settings and adjustments and of the visual result which can be expected.

THEORY & DEFINITIONS

Although practical application of craft work is the bottom line in film and video production, a basic knowledge of theory—of what makes the process work—is important for those who wish to move ahead and do the best work possible. Having a practical working knowledge and basic understanding of terms used in, and the effect on, production work processes is also extremely helpful in getting along and doing the job better.

The psycho-physiological phenomenon which makes the motion picture experience possible is called the "**persistence of vision**." When the retina receives a series of intermittent visual images, each image remains on the retina for a fraction of a second, said to be about 1/25th of a second. This is the reason frame rates of 24 fps (1/50th sec) or more make the visual display appear to be a continuous, unbroken image flow. That's also why the early films shot and projected at 12 or 16 fps appeared jerky and were often called the "flickers," because each frame held on the screen for too lengthy an interval then went to a brief black interval before the next frame would be presented. The taking/projection rate of 12 to 16 fps was simply too slow. (The development of the double-bladed projection shutter along with the present 24 fps standard has definitely enhanced the visual display of cinematic product.)

Stops. **F-stops** are determined mathematically as the ratio of the lens internal diameter, within its mounting and diaphragm setting, to the focal length of the lens. **T-stops** are determined by measuring the amount of light that actually passes through the lens at respective diaphragm settings. Of the two, T-stops are the more reliable and accurate settings.

T-Stop Determinants. Several factors can affect the determination of a T-stop setting: **Amount** of light illuminating the subject matter; the **quality** and **direction** of that light; the **greyscale position** and/or **reflectivity** of the subject; the desired **visual relationship** of subject to the background and/or foreground; the desired **mood**; the type of **lens**; **lenticular additions** (optical filters, diopters, diffusion and extension tubes); the **emulsion qualities** and **sensitivity** (ASA, ISO, or EI) rating of the film being used and its **reciprocity factor**; the **frame rate**; and **shutter angle** selected.

Depth of field is that area in front of the taking lens within which all subject matter is within the range of acceptable sharpness, before and behind the point of principal focus. At a given T-stop, wide angle lenses have greater depth of field than longer lenses. The depth of field of any lens will increase as the lens is stopped down. The result can be determined by subjectively judging the overall sharpness of the projected film.

Depth of Focus is that area behind the lens, bracketing the film plane, wherein the image is in acceptable focus. At a given T-stop, long lenses have a greater depth of focus than wide angle lenses. This means that it is very critical that a wide angle lens be properly seated in the camera lens mount or it will not focus an image properly on the film plane. Dirty, dented, distorted or marred seating surfaces can put a wide angle lens out of focus. The depth of focus of any lens will increase as the lens is stopped down.

Hyperfocal Distance is the nearest distance from the film plane at which a subject will be in acceptable focus with the lens focused at infinity.

Focus is most critical when shooting a scene with a long focal length lens which is set wide open while focusing on a nearby subject which is approaching the camera. **Acceptable focus** is a function of the diameter of the circles of confusion which represent points or picture elements, and which make up the image at the film plane. The smaller each circle of confusion, the sharper the image will appear to be. Acceptable focus is subjectively determined in screening and is dependent upon the focal length of the projection lens, the scale of enlargement, screen brightness, and the viewing distance from the screen.

Aspect ratio refers to the dimensions of the framed or projected image. Aspect ratio is determined by dividing the horizontal dimension by the vertical dimension. Academy and TV aspect ratios are each 1.33. Theatrical is currently 1.66 to 1.85. Anamorphic is 2.35 to 2.55. Proposed framing for hi-definition television programming is 1.78.

Pitch is that distance measured from the leading edge of one perforation to the leading edge of the immediately following perf. Standard camera negative has a short pitch as compared to special-order long pitch negative or to standard positive film.

Exposure Equivalents. There are several variables which can be set to allow either more or less light to strike the film as it is held motionless in the film gate during the exposure interval. Doubling the frame rate, or decreasing the shutter angle by half, or decreasing the subject illumination by half, or placing a filter with a factor of 2 in the lenticular system: Any of these adjustments (with a constant light level) require opening the lens diaphragm by one T-stop in order to maintain proper and/or consistent exposure.

Two adjustments can be made to artificially increase the sensitivity of a film emulsion (but at some cost in quality). By doubling the manufacturer's ASA (EI or ISO) rating of the film emulsion being used or by push-developing the exposed film one stop, the light sensitivity of that emulsion has been effectively doubled (increased one T-stop).

OPTICS

Optics deals with the behavior of light—physically, physiologically and geometrically—that is, with the composition and character of light, light as related to human vision, and the pattern of the paths traced by light rays under specific conditions, respectively. Here we will deal only with optical capability and effect of certain of the lenticular elements used in cinematic production techniques—lenses and filters.

The optics being employed determine the quality and perspective of the image being recorded on film, assuming, of course, that the subject matter has been properly lighted and exposed and that the film stock being used is appropriate and not faulty.

Because of the optics involved, the image being recorded on film is upside down and reversed from that of the subject matter which is being presented to the camera. The reflex viewing system, of course, corrects this anomaly and provides the Camera Operator with a correctly oriented image of the framing.

Light reaching the lens may be either relatively specular (sharply defined, having nearly parallel rays, such as direct sunlight) or diffused (having scattered rays, such as daylight on a cloudy or overcast day). The former is termed "hard" light and the latter "soft" light. Each light source, natural or artificial, will tend to produce either a hard or soft image on the film. The light may be modified at any point, either by filtering at the source, by striking and being reflected from objects or material with surfaces of varying color and/or texture, or by filtering the light rays before they reach the film plane. Filtering can also take place during optical reproduction, or in the film lab during the printing process.

All lenses are light valves, accepting and passing a given amount of light through varied optical elements and an internal volume-controlling diaphragm, then on to the film plane. To function properly, the surface of front and rear external elements of the lens must be clean and the movement of the diaphragm and focus (and zoom) mechanisms on the lens must move freely and accurately and the lens barrel must be light-tight.

Three classes of lenses are used in straight cinematography: The **wide angles** (including super-wide fish-eyes), the so-called **standard, normal,** or **midrange** lenses, and the **telephotos**, the narrower angle-of-view lenses.

Perspective is related to physical distancing between viewpoint and object. It has to do with the relative size of near and distant objects from a given viewpoint. In general, from a visual perspective of static objects in frame, the wider the angle lens used and/or the closer to the subject matter the viewpoint is placed, the greater the chances of size and form distortion, especially of obliquely presented close foreground subjects and of tall, vertical structures and objects, particularly from low-angled viewpoints. On the other hand, the longer the lens used, and/or the farther away from the subject matter the viewpoint is placed, the greater the apparent compression of objects in frame. In both cases, the visual effect has to do with the physical distance of the camera viewpoint from the subject matter and not to any particular characteristic of the lens used. From a given viewpoint/distance, a wide angle lens includes more information in frame because its viewing field is broad; however, the viewing perspective, with subject(s) at a given distance, is no different than that of a narrow angle lens with its relatively limited field of view.

The so-called **foreshortening** effect—a forced technique whereby the size of near and obliquely positioned portions of a subject are presented to appear disproportionate and exaggerated in order to give the visual illusion of proper perspective—is the result of placing the camera viewpoint in close proximity to the subject matter and is not due to the characteristics of the taking lens itself. This technique has been used to create humorous or horrifying imagery by placing the subject extremely close to the taking lens which, in effect, visually enlarges and distorts the nose and mouth in relation to other facial features.

Considering **movement perspective** within the frame, any object movement crossing the lens field of view on a plane parallel to the film plane will appear to be moving with the same velocity whether using wide angle, normal or telephoto lenses. At a given distance and with object movement relatively toward or away from the camera, wide angle lenses, because of their relative forced perspective effect compared with lenses of narrower view, will provide a relatively higher apparent velocity of linear subject movement than normal lenses, and telephoto lenses will provide visually substantially less apparent advancing or retreating movement of subject matter than normal or wide angle lenses. Again, this relative movement velocity is a function of the camera viewpoint (distance from the subject matter) and not of the lens itself.

A **zoom lens** is a variable focal length lens which has the capability of being set at any of the focal lengths within its range, or of being moved through any part of its range, during a take.

A **doubler** is a supplemental lens attachment which is placed behind the lens in order to extend the effective focal length of the lens. For example, a 20mm-100mm zoom lens could be doubled to 40mm-200mm range. Doublers require additional exposure compensation.

An **extension tube** is a lens extender which is used behind a standard taking lens in order to focus on very close objects. Its use serves to contract depth of field and requires additional exposure, depending upon the length of the tubular extension.

A **macro lens** is a lens whose elements can be moved an extended distance away from the film plane thereby making it possible to focus on extremely close objects. Its use serves to enlarge the recorded image size and to contract depth of field, and requires additional exposure, depending upon the amount of lens extension used.

A **diopter** is a weak supplementary lens which is used in front of a standard taking lens in order to focus on very close objects. Its use in effect shortens the focal length of the prime lens, serves to contract depth of field and requires no exposure compensation. A **split diopter** is used to selectively enhance the focus on close foreground objects while maintaining focus on objects in the background which are not covered by the diopter. The split diopter must be carefully placed, with due consideration for objects in the foreground, midground and background. For example, objects in the foreground (covered by the split) and background (covered by the prime lens) may be in sharp focus while objects in the midground will be out of focus. And so, some set redressing or object/actor repositioning may be in order.

Ciné cameras are reflexed either by a **front surface mirrored spinning shutter** or by a **pellicle**, positioned in the lenticular alignment. The pellicle is an extremely thin, specially coated, flat glass element which passes two-thirds of the light striking it on to the film plane, while reflecting one-third on to the viewfinding ocular. A pellicle requires an additional exposure of 1/3 stop. Cleaning of the surfaces of the pellicle must be done with great care.

The **viewfinder ocular** is the eyepiece through which the Camera Operator sees, judges focus, frames (excluding extraneous elements) and follows the action. That inner and outer elements of this system are kept clean helps make the Operator's job go smoother.

The **ground glass** is particularly important for the Camera Operator. Its proper positioning in the ocular (ground surface facing forward, toward the lens) is critical to determining eye focus for objects in frame. Also important is that the ground glass to be used is accurately inscribed with the proper aspect ratio to be used to frame takes for a given production. That it be kept clean and free of fingerprints and dust particles goes without saying.

Optical filters come in optical glass or gel, can be used in front of or with gels behind the taking lens, and may be classified in five general categories by the effect they have on the film image. These functional categories are: **Color compensators**, **color temperature balancers**, **color tonal modifiers**, **light suppressors** and **special effects**.

The three basic **color compensating** filters, used to correct emulsion bias, are **cyan**, **yellow**, and **magenta**. **Color temperature balancing** filters are used to correct the color temperature of the light source before it reaches the film. The principal physical characteristic of filters which are used to **modify tone** is color and these filters are used to give the frame an overall color modification, or in the case of black and white emulsions, to emphasize or de-emphasize certain colors by shifting their greyscale position. Filters which suppress light but do not affect color rendition are termed **neutral density**. The five types of filters used for a **special visual effect** are: **Diffusion**, **fog**, **star**, **polascreen**, and **prepared surface** (oil/grease/paint/other material applied to an optical flat).

Since colored and light suppressing filters stop a certain amount of light from reaching the film plane, a certain factor relating to that light-stopping quality is assigned each of these filters. For example, a **filter factor** of 2 is equivalent to 1 lens stop, 4 equals 2 stops, 8 is 3 stops, etc.

The four basic types of **diffusion** are: **Optical glass**, **gel**, **gauze/netting**, and **lubricants** applied to an optical flat. Diffusion scatters light rays thereby softening the recorded sharpness of an image.

PRODUCTION PROCEDURES

Performing production procedures in an efficient and effective manner is the key to successful camera assisting. The name of the game is attention to details, details, and more details.

The principal steps leading up to actual production use of rental camera equipment are: **1)** Prepare a list of all camera equipment and accessories needed for the production schedule; **2)** list all equipment by category, beginning with the specified camera; **3)** place the order for the camera equipment and accessories; **4)** after completing the placing of the itemized order, have the order-taker read back the order as you check off each item; **5)** upon picking up or receiving the order (preferably at the rental facility), check in all equipment ordered on the production order list against the contract fulfillment order of the supplier; **6)** set up the camera to be sure all elements are present, fit properly and are functioning; **7)** only then accept the order and remove the rented equipment from the rental facility.

The principal material causing camera malfunction and/or image pollution is the **film chip**, generally found either in the film chamber, in the gate, in the claw cam and/or in the drive gear.

Legibility, accuracy and **inclusion of all essential information** must be of prime concern when filling out the Camera Report or preparing the Slate.

Appearing on both will be: The Production Company; the Production Title and/or Number; Date; the Director; the Cameraman; whether Exterior or Interior; Day or Night; sound or MOS (mit out sound); "**U.P.**" (under protest); the scene and take numbers; special frame rate, shutter angle, or effect.

Appearing only on the Camera Report will be such information as film type and emulsion number, order number, magazine number, roll number, scene and take number, footage for each take, printed (circled) takes, processing and printing instructions, special technique notation (process, registration, split screen, filtration, wire gags, explosives).

The film laboratory receives the original (first sheet) of the Camera Report; the Production Company gets the second sheet; the third sheet goes to the Editor; a fourth sheet, if any, would go to the Camera Department for its record.

When **setting up** a camera on a tripod, be sure that the tripod legs are firmly seated and locked off, then be sure that the control head is securely attached to the tripod and that the pan and tilt movement are locked off; finally, make certain that the camera is firmly secured to the head and is sitting level.

Marking actor static positions with "T"s (exteriors, and on loose or granulated surfaces, such as dirt, sand, or grass), or chalk or tape (interiors, and on loose surfaces) helps assure proper positioning of cast members in order to accommodate the planned-for coverage and composition during a take.

In **slating** synchronous sound takes, first, check to be certain that all pertinent info is accurately entered and legible on the slate, then, place the slate in the camera framing area (avoid causing the Operator to search for the slate) with sufficient light on its face (or backlight, if translucent) to properly expose the slate information. When the camera has attained speed, and after announcing the scene and take number, the clapper arm should be brought down only hard enough to be picked up by sound, especially when slating for tight head closeups.

The **pitch control** should be adjusted with each fresh load of film with the camera running until the engaging noise of the pull-down claw(s) is minimized. There are six settings or adjustments on the ciné camera which the First Assistant may be called upon to make or monitor during a take: **Focus, zoom sizing, diaphragm opening, shutter angle, frame rate, sliding diffusion** and **sliding graduated filtration**. Of these variables, only diaphragm, shutter angle, frame rate and sliding graduated filtration settings affect exposure.

The **film gate** should be removed and examined after each print take. There are at least six undesirable conditions you look for when you examine the film gate and film chamber. These include: **film chips, dust/dirt/sand/hair, emulsion build-up in gate, scratches on gate/plate/film,** and **excessive oil/grease.**

In **cleaning** an optical surface, first, use a blower syringe to remove dust particles; second, apply lens cleaner in order to dissolve grease; then use lens tissue to dry the surface.

In checking a lens for proper focus, **1)** be certain the lens is properly interfaced and seated in a debris-free camera lens mount, **2)** open the diaphragm all the way, **3)** set the lens at the desired distance, **4)** have the Second Assistant attach a tape measure at the film plane and move to the desired distance, holding the tape with the desired footage number showing to the lens, **5)** adjust the ocular diopter to your eye, **6)** focus the lens on the tape number, using the magnifier, and **7)** check the resulting footage at the witness mark on the lens barrel to confirm that it conforms precisely to the taped distance.

If this does not check out exactly, either the lens is not properly seated, or the ground glass is reversed, or the lens footage marks are incorrectly calibrated, or the lens is damaged with its elements, focusing ring or both out of adjustment, or the tape measure itself is faulty.

To avoid getting fogged or light-struck film, the camera, its film magazine and optical elements should be protected from direct light and reflections striking front and rear optical surfaces, open filter slots, an open reflex viewfinder and/or untaped film magazine covers.

The principal atmospheric condition causing emulsion deterioration is **heat**, closely followed by **humidity/moisture**.

Desiccants are drying agents used to remove (absorb) moisture. **Condensation** (moisture formed on the surfaces of lenses and metals) is caused by a sudden variation in temperature (cold to hot). To avoid production delays due to condensation, the camera equipment and film should be placed, for a reasonable time before shooting, in the temperature/humidity environment in which they will be used.

Nose grease is a convenient agent to apply to the film path track in the film gate and aperture plate to minimize emulsion build-up and/or static electricity (during periods of very low humidity).

When shooting in **extreme hot or cold** locations, special lubrication must be used on all moving parts. In **extreme cold** all lubrication may have to be removed from all moving parts. One should avoid touching metal with the bare hands (or skin) and film must be loaded and threaded carefully because it becomes very brittle and breaks easily.

In **high-speed cinematography**, it is important to take up all slack in both feed and takeup rolls before each take, then to check lubrication, film loop size, and for film chips in the film chamber and gate after each take. In extreme high-speed photography, the film should be brought up to speed with a variac in order to minimize stress on the film and possible breakage.

The purpose of **registration shooting** is to perfectly align a subject in two sequential shots. This technique requires extreme care in making measurements, alignment and perspective. The reference film frame must be placed in the registration punch heads down and emulsion down before cutting. Then the excised reference frame is placed against and in front of the ground glass heads down and emulsion toward the taking lens. The camera is then positioned and lined up so the subject matter to be photographed coincides with the image in the inserted registration frame. Procedure to follow includes: Placing the camera lens at the same height as the originally photographed subject, the same distance from the subject, with the same lens, at the same exposure and T-stop, with the same lighting balance and quality as in the original setup.

In setting up a camera for **single frame time-lapse exposures**, the camera must be securely immobilized and the shutter must be in closed position over the film aperture between exposures.

A First Assistant receives the T-stop setting from the Director of Photography, and the scene/take number from the Script Supervisor. The Director determines which takes to print. During sound takes, the Camera and Sound Reports must conform as to scene and take numbers and printed takes.

The following information should be placed/taped on each can of **exposed film**: Production Company; production title & number; film stock type; roll number; amount of exposed footage; clearly marked "EXPOSED" and "PUSH (or) PULL X-AMOUNT STOPS" (if applicable); and the Camera Report for that particular roll of exposed film.

The following information should be placed on each can of **short ends**: Production Company; type of film; clearly marked "UNEXPOSED"; roll footage; date canned; and name of the canner.

The production process is where all the training and preparation pay off. It is the true test of dedication and ability. It is, in fact, the testing ground and R & D laboratory for working with and manipulating the production elements in the on-going practice of our filmmaking crafts.

ACTION AND THE
PARALLAX VIEWFINDER

The development and implementation of the reflex camera in professional motion picture production was a large step forward in honing the efficiency of the image capture process.

It also resulted in putting a good share of the responsibility for focus on the Camera Operator who, after all, was looking through the lens and could *see* that the First Assistant Camera Operator was keeping the out-front essentials in acceptable focus. It was as though the Camera Operator didn't have enough to do already—such as properly composing and following the action, seeing that the composition remains "on the set" and does not include mics, boom shadows or extraneous equipment or personnel. *And*, if the Director should ask, whether the looks, gestures or positions of the actor(s) were "correct/appropriate/passable" (choose one), the Camera Operator is expected to respond with an opinion.

Well, the parallax viewfinder may be ready for a comeback of sorts. With all the chases and run-bys being filmed today, which often require fast and/or sweeping pan/tilt moves, the reflex viewfinder, which requires keeping the eye centered in the eyepiece, is not the most convenient mechanism to follow such action. Instead, for such shots, use a camera which will accept a Mitchell-type parallax viewfinder (cams and all). By using this type finder, following close and fast-moving action will be much more convenient for the Camera Operator, provided that prime lenses are used. (The parallax viewfinder will not function properly with a zoom lens unless it is placed in a fixed focal length position.)

The First Assistant, of course, must maintain focus on the moving subject at all times in order to keep the parallax viewfinder properly aligned with the taking lens so that the composition, as seen through the finder, is what is being captured on film. There is no immediate double-check on the focus. The proof will be in the dailies— another day—and the First Assistant will have one more thing to worry about.

WORKING WITH DIRECTORS OF PHOTOGRAPHY

Probably most Camera Operators have, at one time or another, thought about being or aspired to be a Director of Photography. Having worked with many DPs over a number of years, having observed the lighting procedures, crew management and collaborative techniques which they have employed, and having shot inserts at the DP's behest, the Camera Operator may or may not feel, and **be**, ready to function as a Director of Photography, under the full pressures of production.

But while this process is happening, it might be a good idea to consider the responsibilities and duties of the Director of Photography.

DP Responsibilities. The Director of Photography is directly responsible to the Director (and ultimately to the Producer) for the efficient functioning of those categories and classifications under his or her technical direction, and for assisting the Director in translating the screenplay into appropriate visual imagery, within the creative and budgetary latitude afforded, for optimal aesthetic visual effect.

DP Duties. If you have been paying attention, you know that the Director of Photography, as leader of the technical production crew, sets the pace of lighting and camera-ready procedures. To accomplish this, the DP selects his or her "production family"—the camera crew, the Gaffer, the Key Grip and Dolly Grip—as well as the camera equipment, accessories, lenses, filtration and film stock(s) to be used. The DP either selects or approves the type and amount of lighting and grip equipment, checks and/or film-tests (and may be called upon to approve or pass judgment on) scenic art, settings, set dressing, props, special effects, costumes, makeup and hairstyling.

The Director of Photography works closely with the Director in the general lining up and matching of both action and screen direction for each setup, and collaborates with the Director in setting the camera positions, angles and moves.

The Director of Photography originates (in consultation with the Director, Production Designer and/or Producer) the lighting plan and supervises all production lighting procedures; selects the film stock(s), camera(s), lens(es), filtration and diffusion to be used for each take; determines all exposure settings; and may check composition with the Camera Operator during the setup process.

Because the Director of Photography is responsible for an effective and consistent visual look of the production, mood (lighting quality, direction and ratios appropriate to the dramatic content and action) and consistency (balanced continuity lighting and color/density timing) are essential elements. So viewing all dailies and supervising the timing of the work and answer prints (during the film process) or the colorization process during transfer from negative to 1″ tape (during the film-to-video telecine process), is of great importance in order to maintain quality control and a reputation for quality work.

Interpersonal Relations. The PR and political aspects of what is expected of a Director of Photography should not be overlooked or their importance underestimated. The movie-making business is a community of people with strong convictions, imposing personalities and enormous egos. Working with such individuals can be a challenge to anyone. The Director of Photography, besides having a well-grounded knowledge of the technical and artistic aspects of the cinematographic craft, must bring to the fore what may be the most important talent—that of dealing with powerful and often volatile individuals, namely, the Producer, the Director and the starring actor(s). How well he or she interrelates with this triumvirate pretty well determines how well and/or how long he or she functions on a given production.

Of course, there are many Producers, Directors and stars who are neither temperamental nor inconsiderate and, so long as the production is on schedule and within budget allowances, *and* the stars look good in dailies, the Director of Photography is not likely to have troublesome encounters. It is when a production is on a tight schedule, perhaps even running a bit behind schedule, that the powers-that-be start pressing—**hard**. It is then particularly important to observe how the DP handles the situation. There is no school for this type of on-the-job training.

Observe and Learn. As a Camera Operator, you have the opportunity to observe how the various Directors of Photography you work with go about lighting sets, people and things; how they interrelate with people—their crew subordinates, the cast and management; how and why they react as they do under pressure situations, and the result of those reactions. Observe and deposit it all in your memory bank to draw compound interest. It's all an important part of professional practice. That's why there is no substitute for experience. You can't buy it, but you can certainly absorb and bank on it.

DP Expectations. On features and episodics, because the Director of Photography is usually very involved in closely collaborating with the Director and with supervising lighting procedures, it is encumbent upon the camera crew to have the camera set up and ready for the take. The DP expects the First Assistant Camera Operator to have the camera assembled on the appropriate mount, with the specified lens, filter(s), diffusion, shutter angle, frame rate, and film stock in place; expects the Camera Operator to listen in while the Director explains the shot and to be at the controls and ready to operate the camera for rehearsals and takes; expects the Dolly Grip to have checked out the dolly track for a smooth and level ride and to have marked the limits and each stop position of a complex dolly move.

On multi-camera film sitcoms, the Director of Photography also expects the cameras to be set up promptly and completely and the operative camera crew— Camera Operators, Assistants and Dolly Grips—to be prepared to perform their respective functions efficiently and well.

In addition, most Directors of Photography appreciate the fact that there are at least three pairs of experienced eyes examining the set and its action area—those of the DP, the Gaffer and the Camera Operator(s). Should a light burn out during a take, should an actor step out of the key light area or improperly shadow another actor, should a light flare or bright reflection appear in frame, the Director of Photography wants to be apprised immediately (and discreetly) so that evaluation and appropriate adjustments can be made and another take arranged, if necessary.

QUESTIONS TO ASK YOURSELF

Some of the questions to ask yourself as you observe the Director of Photography at work might include the following:

• **Film Stock**. Why does the Director of Photography favor: One brand of film over another? One emulsion over another for interiors, for exteriors, for night shooting, and for special effects? Varying the manufacturer's recommended exposure index (EI) and under what conditions? A certain film gauge for one job and a different gauge for another project? One aspect ratio rather than another for a given production?

• **Camera Equipment**. Why and under what set of circumstances does the DP use a particular camera or camera system?

• **Lenses**. Why and under what conditions does the DP favor: A particular brand of lenses? A specific range of focal lengths? Prime or zoom lenses and under what circumstances? A specific lens in a specific situation? The use of diopters?

• **Lenticular Filters and Diffusion**. Why does the DP prefer a particular brand of lenticular filters and diffusion? Why and under what circumstances does the DP employ a given degree of lenticular filtration and/or diffusion? Is it placed in front of or behind the lens? Why?

• **Camera Settings**. When and under what circumstances does the DP employ variations in: The frame rate (fps)? The shutter angle? The T-stop (iris) setting? Variable, sliding filtration or diffusion?

• **Exposure**. What are the criteria the DP uses when determining exposure for a given scene? (Then go to dailies and see the result while the setup is still clearly in mind.)

• **Lighting**. What type and quantity of lighting equipment, gels and diffusion are favored by the DP: For studio interiors? Studio exteriors? For location interiors? Location exteriors? For night exteriors? How does the DP maintain consistency in continuity lighting in view of the out-of-sequence shooting on an episodic or feature? How, in what order and to what comparative ratio does the DP light the background, midground and foreground areas in relation to each other and to the principal action area(s)? How is each lighting unit used—its type, output and placement? How and why are certain luminaires trimmed?

•**Grip**. What type and quantity of grip and light control matériel and mobile camera mounts are favored by the DP: For studio interiors? Studio exteriors? For location interiors? Location exteriors? Exterior night shooting? How is the equipment applied to each setup?

• **Film Tests**. Under what circumstances does the DP make film tests? What are the parameters set by that DP for each specific test?

• **Interpersonal Relationships**. How does the Director of Photography interrelate with crew subordinates? With the Director? With production management? With the cast? What performance level does the DP expect of camera crew personnel? Does he or she set the example? What criteria has the DP used in selecting the particular individuals in his or her production crew family? Does the Cinematographer fully support camera personnel in the relationship with production management? Does the DP insist that "safe" set practices be maintained during working procedures?

Summing Up. Each Director of Photography may handle his or her responsibilities and duties differently, but no less responsibly and effectively, than another experienced DP.

Be mindful that the more complete the understanding which the Camera Operator has of the responsibilities and duties of the Director of Photography, the more valuable that Operator becomes to each successive production and DP, and the more successful that Camera Operator is likely to be when moving up to Director of Photography.

THE FUTURE OF CAMERA OPERATING

Operating cinematography is a skill unto itself, just as are lighting cinematography and the many support functions of camera assisting. Preparation, dedication and skill are the prerequisites for performing and excelling at any of these essential production team roles. Maintaining these skills at a dependably high level tends to make the powers-that-be aware of the essential importance of each member of the camera crew.

Indeed, as long as cameras are used to capture images, there will be a need for camera personnel. But what will be the potential demand down the road compared to the present state of activity? Should one strive to become a Camera Operator? If already a Camera Operator, should one develop the skills of a Director of Photography, or remain in the business as an Operator? And if so, what are likely to be the work opportunities and the manipulative control mechanisms one will work with? Lastly, and most importantly, what effect will the consumer marketplace have on the work we do?

Where We've Been. Time was, during the beginnings of motion picture time, when the Cameraman did it all. He was the only member of the camera crew. He *was* the camera crew. He was film Loader, Focus Puller, Camera Operator and, later, Lighting Technician. He positioned his camera; changed the lenses; loaded, downloaded and changed film magazines; marked side lines in accordance with the coverage angle of the lens; cranked the camera while the actors performed; then processed the exposed film.

As the equipment and productions became more complex, sophisticated and demanding, as crews and budgets became larger and shooting schedules tighter, the need for specialization and collaboration became necessary in order to save time, money and energy.

As a result, camera crews were formed and augmented to fit the need: First Cameraman, Second Cameraman, Focus Puller, Slate Boy, and Film Loader became, respectively, Director of Photography, Camera Operator, First Assistant Camera Operator, Second Assistant Camera Operator, and Loader.

The Director of Photography was responsible for the lighting and for supervising the technical crew; the Camera Operator was responsible for framing and following the action; the First Assistant Camera Operator was responsible for setting up the camera, putting the accessories in place, following focus and operating the zoom sizing control; the Second Assistant Camera Operator for slating the scenes; and the Loader for loading and down-loading film magazines. And so, the tasks of cinematography were separated and given individual responsibility, thereby making the filming process a more efficient, effective and collaborative operation.

As motion pictures captured the interest of audiences, consumer demand continued to grow, more pictures were made, more equipment was developed and manufactured, and more crew people were trained and put to work.

Where We Are. Yes, once upon a time, there was a beginning to our craft techniques. As the dynamics and popularity of the silver screen grew apace with the sophistication of movie audiences, ever more sophisticated production tools were developed until today we are the beneficiaries of the innovations and developments in equipment, materials, services, distribution, exhibition, and production techniques.

In addition, television came to be and brought us into the electronic age with the convenience of watching visual entertainment while in the comfort and convenience of our homes. Programming and audiences have proliferated, resulting in more equipment being developed and manufactured and more people being trained and put to work than ever before.

We regularly work with the latest in cameras—both film and video—descendents of earlier product, designed to make the jobs of the Camera Operator and, for film, the First Assistant Camera Operator more efficient and effective. Improved high resolution lenses, film and video stocks and high fidelity electronic components and controls have helped enhance the process and assure an optimal result of image capture.

Camera supports, both fixed and mobile, with tripods, pedestals, dollies, cranes and remotely controlled cameras mounted on these camera supports have been developed and refined to afford ever greater reliability and flexibility in capturing the imagery in all types of shot setups.

The remotely controlled camera set up, in addition to being able to place the crane- or jib-mounted camera in otherwise inaccessible positions in various moving configurations to best get a shot, has also proven to be a boon to the safety of the camera crew. The camera can now be placed and effectively operated in the path of, or in proximity to, hazard without endangering the camera crew. On the other hand, robotic cameras, which require reduced staffing to operate, are already in use at several television stations.

Throughout the world, there has never been more cinematic material being shot on film or video tape than there is today. The production pace is continuous and unrelenting, primarily to feed the hungry maws of broadcast and cable television programming and commercials, the video cassette market, and to a somewhat lesser degree, the theatrical and industrial markets.

Where We're Headed. If the distant and recent past are any guides to what we can expect in the future, we will see a continuing movement toward electronic components in, and controls of, camera heads and cameras.

Again, the greatest demand for cinematic product will continue to be from television display facilities. This will include the proposed 500-channel interactive networks with their multiple specialized sub-channels for shopping, information and entertainment and the continual updating of programming and/or display visuals which will be required. This will place even more demand on production facilities and afford opportunity to those prepared to provide cinematic material for display on the many available channels. In other words, the future seems assured for those who are trained in the capture and refinement of the moving image. After all, someone has to operate the image capture machines, and it might as well be those prepared.

Will We Have Arrived When We Get There? Much of this potential demand is in the process of happening. And when it is all finally in place and the programming requirements are clear, we may think we have arrived; but wait. Be assured that status quo is an illusion. Expect other innovative concepts to be brought to light which, to varying degree, will capture the imagination, unleashing a flurry of creative energy and product, resulting in further refinement and accommodation and a trip to the next plateau, where the process will repeat itself. In these circumstances, "arrival" is a relative term, representing an ongoing process of doing, discovering and adapting to innovative techniques and procedures.

During this age of information and communication, of two things we can be reasonably confident, and that is that there will always be a need—indeed, an ever-growing need—for visual communication and display, and that the product appearing on the various cinematic display media will have to be framed and followed while it is being captured on camera. And that requires a Camera Operator. So the future of camera operating seems assured.

OTHER COLLABORATING CRAFTS

There are more than one hundred fifty film and video crafts which can be used in a cinematic production. Each active craft is important to the production during either the pre-production, production and/or post-production phases. Each is a contributor to the final result in the collaborative image-making and capturing process.

As a film or video craftsperson, it is well to have a good understanding of the responsibilities and duties of colleagues in some of the other collaborative crafts who contribute to the cinematic process. A number of these essential crafts are included in this section with sub-sections focusing on the categories of directorial, producing and production management, art, and several of the key crafts in other craft categories.

The principal emphasis in this section is from the perspective of those working in the camera category.

APPRECIATING OTHER CRAFTS

Because we are so thoroughly involved in what we are doing during production, we often tend to feel that our contribution to the production is the most important and that efforts of other crafts are somewhat less significant. Indeed, that may be so at any given point in time, but certainly not when everything is taken into consideration within the context of the overall production. Each craft contribution, whether we are aware of it or not, is important to some degree, if not essential, to the end result.

Film and video production (like life and living) are collaborative processes, requiring the skills of dedicated craftspeople and artists in many specialties. At any given time, from the conceptual through marketing phases, each involved craft is doing its bit, at its own pace, to contribute significantly to the production. During pre-production very few outside the crafts directly involved are seeing things happen. Even during production, while other crafts may be marking time, each craft takes its turn out front, on stage, doing its thing: Either preparing a setup, doing a take, or moving the company to a new location site. Post-production finds the rather compact editorial staff in its privatized grotto assembling the footage into meaningful form.

Each department or category of work has its on-going off-stage preparation time in order to pick up, prepare or return matériel with which its craftspeople work. While many of these activities may be happening out of our sight, it does not mean that other crafts are dogging it or goofing off or not contributing. Quite the contrary. This off-stage preparatory attention to detail is essential to the effectiveness of the image-making process.

By and large, we know what the personnel in our category of work are responsible for and we know what to expect from each of them and when they have delivered. After all, most of us who moved up through the ranks from Loader to 2nd Assistant Camera Operator to 1st Assistant Camera Operator and, whether now a Camera Operator or Director of Photography, have an understanding of and appreciation for the work of the Camera Assistants (having been there before).

But such is not the case as it relates to the other collaborative crafts. To be sure, we understand many, if not most, of the responsibilities and duties of the Dolly/Crane/Boom Grips because we work closely with them on a daily basis; perhaps, to a degree, even of the work of the production Electricians and Grips as well. However, the same cannot be said of most of the other crafts. We simply are not that close to or tuned in to their efforts, most of which happen either off-stage, or on-stage while we are involved in dealing with our own duties and responsibilities. So we generalize their functions in our mind by classifying them neatly by job title; the specifics of their work often conveniently, if understandably, elude us in the focused pursuit of our own endeavors.

The question, then, is how much should be known about the responsibilities and duties of crafts both inside and outside our own craft category? And why?

The answer to the second part depends upon where you are in your own craft at a particular point in time and on where you want to be in both the near and distant future.

In the near view, Loaders want to be, and move to become, 2nd Assistants, 2nd Assistants to become 1st Assistants, 1st Assistants to become Camera Operators, Operators to become Directors of Photography. DPs may opt to go ex-category and become Directors. And many from other crafts want to get into the camera category in any classification in order to work their way up the craft ladder. So it behooves each aspirant to learn as much about the responsibilities and duties of the craft aspired to as possible while doing a creditable job in the current working classification.

In the long view, a Loader may have in mind eventually becoming a Director of Photography and realistically regards the intermediate steps as simply means to a desired end. Others are perfectly satisfied and fulfilled functioning with a high degree of assurance and expertise in an Assistant capacity with no need to seek further responsibilities and duties in a more elevated position. The higher the position, the more important and time-consuming the politics—the attention to interpersonal relationships with superiors, peers and subordinates—become. Many craftspeople opt not to get involved at this level, preferring instead to devote their energies to the techniques of their craft. How far to move along, if at all, is a very personal decision.

Assuming that the desire and decision is to advance in the craft however far, it then becomes imperative to learn as much as possible about the responsibilities and duties of the next higher classification while performing one's own craft with dedication and perfection.

Since we are involved in a highly collaborative art, the more we know about, and the better we understand, the contributions of our colleagues in other craft categories the more satisfying our feelings can be about our own contributions to the production. Knowing and understanding the contributions of others in the image-making process can give us a better appreciation of the kinds of varied and valued expertise that goes into a production and a fresh perspective on how our own craft impacts on the work of others where it all comes together—**in front of the camera**.

A prime purpose of this book is to focus reader attention on that perspective— to help make the total contributory, collaborative procedure a more understandable and satisfying shared experience for all who are involved in the production process.

ART CATEGORY

The prime responsibility of the Art Category is to provide adequate, appropriate and thoroughly prepared settings in which the action/performance will take place for presentation to the camera.

The contributions made to the production by the Art Category personnel are extremely important to the success of the final product. Without specially designed settings, set dressing, props and special effects, a picture may have lost the production values so important to audience sensibilities.

Properly designed and dressed settings can add immeasurably to the visual effect on the audience while helping the lighting and camera phases happen more efficiently.

ART DIRECTION

Art direction is a key element in establishing the mode and mood of the settings—whether for a real life or an impressionistic effect—thereby significantly contributing to the final pictorial result. The art of creating a cinematic experience for an audience is the art of designing, planning, managing and executing myriad integrated details which are prepared for presentation to the camera in a carefully and consistently orchestrated way.

The Art Director is an integral element in the process of mounting a production—of conceiving and designing settings, set dressing, props and costumes, thereby preparing a production for the camera(s).

The Art Category consists of an Art Director (who may also be Production Designer) as Category Head, a Set Designer and Assistants, a Set Decorator with supporting Lead and Swing Persons, a Scenic Artist, and Artists who sketch and craft color renderings of settings and/or storyboard details.

Art Director Responsibilities. The Art Director is directly responsible to the Producer, works in close cooperation with the Director, and is responsible for maintaining consistency and accuracy in the renderings of the art elements and execution thereof in order to insure the optimum aesthetic and photographic effect of those elements in the production.

Art Director Duties. The Art Director does the following: Reads and analyzes the script in order to determine and note portions requiring special attention and/or treatment insofar as the design and specifications of the settings, dressings, props and costumes are concerned, in order to insure the optimum aesthetic and photographic effect of these elements; consults with the Producer and/or Director (and the Director of Photography, if available) regarding the settings, dressings, props and costumes to be designed and executed for the production; plans, oversees and coordinates the execution of the **complete** production design of the production if called upon to do so, receiving credit as Production Designer; prepares a schedule breakdown from the script pertaining to set design and construction requirements—the building and finishing materials, furniture, floor covering, properties, drapes, fixtures and other set dressing—in consultation with the Set Designer, Key Set Builder, Set Decorator and Property Master; specifies and/or selects and/or designs furniture, properties, backdrops, scenic cycloramas, greens and other set dressing; provides color sketches and renderings, construction specifications and/or diagrams, floor plans and elevation drafts and/or detail drawings for the Key Set Builder and set construction personnel; sees that the sets are accurately installed on the studio floor and that each element—walls, corners, ceiling pieces and floor coverings—is aligned and properly positioned with regard to the overhead electrical rigging; may be called upon to supervise the storyboarding of given sequences of the production; otherwise carrying out the duties normally required of this classification.

The Art Director/Production Designer specifies and supervises all set, furniture, model and prop design and construction, scenic artwork and set dressing, and coordinates costume, makeup and hair styling associated with the production.

Way the Process Works. The way the art direction process works is generally as follows: The Producer hires an Art Director to oversee the design and realization of the settings for a cinematic project that is set to go. If a big budget feature, the Art Director presses for credit (and compensation) as Production Designer. Once resolved, the Art Director/Production Designer reads and analyzes the script, making notes regarding the practical and aesthetic requirements bearing on both overall production design and/or set design and construction, scenic design, set dressing, set props, costume design and the design for makeup and hair styling.

The next step for the Art Director is to provide a Set Designer with sketches and renderings (with the help of Artists) and specifications of the sets. The Set Designer then reduces this input to plan and elevation drawings (with the help of Draftspersons). Upon approval by the Art Director, the p/e (plan and elevation) drawings go to the Key Set Builder for construction, which is detailed and finished by Carpenters, Construction Specialists, Specialized Craft Artisans and Painters. At the same time, the Art Director consults with the Scenic Artist regarding requirements for specially executed backings, matte paintings and glass-shot art. And this work commences.

Next, the Art Director discusses the parameters for wardrobe with the Costume Designer, who then sets about the designing process. Upon approval by the Art

Director of the design sketches and renderings, the Costume Designer oversees the execution of wardrobe items.

Models, working props and special decorations are specified, designed and executed by Model Makers, Prop Makers and Specialized Artisans, respectively.

The Art Director as Production Designer may sketch out the entire production or critical and complex action or stunt or special effects sequences by storyboard (assisted by Artists), indicating camera and actor positions in relation to the settings and effects, for optimal photographic realization of all production elements on all sets, settings and location sites.

The Art Director supervises and approves each step of the production art fabrication processes underway—preliminary to final sketches and drawings, choices of set decor and the material, color and patterns of wardrobe. Film tests may be made to determine the fidelity of photographic reproduction of set and costume items, and to redesign and/or alter form, colors or patterns as necessary.

The Art Director, in turn, keeps the Producer and/or Production Manager posted on the progress of all work being carried out under art direction.

As the sets, special furnishings, props, and costumes approach completion, the Set Decorator is brought in to make a list of all set dressing, and the position of placement of each item on the set, required to fully express the period and character of each set as conceived by the Art Director. Upon approval by the Art Director, the Set Decorator then brings in a Lead Person to go about shopping for and selecting the items from prop shops, thrift and antique stores, office and furniture suppliers and personal collections, among many other sources. The Lead Person brings the items back to the studio set (or location site) and, after all items are inventoried and listed (as to condition and placement in, on and about the settings), the Set Decorator and Swing Persons place the items in their appointed place in, on and about the setting(s). With the approval of the Art Director, the setting is ready for final lighting, the actors, and the camera(s).

Special thanks to Jim Claytor (Art Director) for his constructive input.

WORKING WITH
THE SET DECORATOR'S CREW

An apparent set decoration item needs to be moved. But is it really a set dressing, or is it (has it become) a prop? And who do you call on to move it?

Since Camera Operators are often required to request the repositioning of props and set dressing, it is important to know whether to call on Assistant Props or the Set Decorator's Swing Set Dresser to move, remove or replace the offending piece.

Before dealing with that question, it is a good idea to consider what set decoration entails.

Set decoration involves the art and technique of determining and selecting appropriate items and materials with which to dress the setting—whether a studio set or location site—within parameters established by the Art Director/Production Designer. Set dressing addresses the placement of set decoration items, as specified by the Set Decorator.

Set decoration items are selected for each setting by period, style, size, shape, and color, in order to help establish and convey the mode and implied mood of the setting, as specified by the Art Director.

The Set Decorator's crew consists of a Lead Set Dresser (Lead Person), who shops, helps select, and brings the set decoration items to the set or shooting site, and the Swing Set Dresser (Swing Person), who, with the help of additional Swing personnel, places each item on or about the setting, as specified by the Set Decorator.

Set Decorator Responsibilities. The Set Decorator is directly responsible to the Art Director for the visualization, selection and placement of set decoration items in a manner best suited to provide optimum aesthetic and photographic realization of the settings.

Set Decorator Duties. The Set Decorator does the following: Reads and analyzes the script and/or storyboard; makes a scene-by-scene breakdown of set decoration items; examines and analyzes the Art Director's set decoration list, sketches, renderings and blue prints of the settings (or photos and dimensions of the location sites); researches the period for appropriate items to acquire (or have fabricated); prepares a list of set decoration items which conform to the period, style, size, shape and color required by the setting, each scene of the setting, and for the overall production; checks with the various supply sources for availability of the required set decoration items; supervises the Lead Set Dresser in the selection, ordering, placement and inventorying of all items of set decoration; consults with the Art Director regarding changes, revisions and/or modifications of set decoration; carries out any other duties normally required of this craft.

Lead Set Dresser Responsibilities. The Lead Set Dresser is directly responsible to and works closely with the Set Decorator in shopping, selecting and arranging the pick up and delivery of set decoration items to the set or production site, and then caring for, inventorying and returning same to their proper suppliers.

Lead Set Dresser Duties. The Lead Set Dresser does the following: Reads the script and/or storyboard; examines the list of set decoration items prepared by the Set Decorator; helps determine where each item can be obtained; calls to determine availability and cost of each item; accompanies the Set Decorator in shopping, selecting and ordering set decoration items; personally picks up, or causes to be picked up, all set decoration items from the various supply sources; sees that all set decoration items are brought to the set or location site; inventories and/or photographs each item for condition; lists, numbers and colorcode tags each item as to its precise placement on the set for each scene and sequence in which it belongs; places corresponding numbered and colorcoded tapes on the set to indicate each item and its precise placement; gives a copy of the set decoration list to the Swing Set Dresser for the physical placement of set decoration items; picks up and delivers replacement and/or additional items as required; inventories and checks each item for condition before returning such items to the originating supply source; carries out any other duties normally required of this craft.

Swing Set Dresser Responsibilities. The Swing Set Dresser is directly responsible to the Set Decorator and works in close cooperation with the Lead Set Dresser in listing, tagging, and finally placing each item in its assigned place on or about the setting(s).

Swing Set Dresser Duties. The Swing Set Dresser does the following: Reads the script and/or storyboard; examines the list of numbered/colorcoded set decoration items, noting the setting and scenes in which each item appears, and the position where each is placed; physically places each item in its specified position; moves and re-marks set decoration items, as necessary, in order to accommodate actor, camera or special effect positioning, or to help achieve better lighting or composition, or to facilitate moving camera shots; makes note of each change in position of any set decoration item, whether made at the request of the Director, an actor, the Director of Photography, a Camera Operator, or the Key Special Effects Technician; physically removes each set decoration item and returns it to the care of the Lead Set Dresser; carries out any other duties normally required of this craft.

How the Process Works. The process of decorating/dressing the set is generally as follows: After the Art Director has consulted with and given (copies of) the sketches, renderings, models and blue prints of the settings (with placement of key furnishings indicated thereon) to the Set Decorator along with any list of specifically essential and special preferred items of set decoration, the Set Decorator then prepares his or her own list of set decoration items, and the specified placement thereof, based on a scene-by-scene breakdown of the script, and on careful study of the Art Director's concept for the mode and mood of the various settings.

The next phase in the process is for the Set Decorator to turn the list over to the Lead Set Dresser, who then, with the Set Decorator, determines where to get each item on the list of set dressings.

The Production Manager has already given a go-ahead on the amount of expenditure for set decorations based on the Art Director's cost estimate and on the duration of shooting time expected for each setting.

The Set Decorator and Lead Set Dresser then contact the supply sources in order to determine the availability of each item of set decoration required. Then the Set Decorator, accompanied by the Lead Set Dresser, personally selects each item and negotiates the rental/lease rate for the length of time each item will be required for the production (which is usually **until returned**, because it is important to keep such items available for photography, including reshooting, until the picture is finalized).

The Lead Set Dresser now acquires, inventories, lists and colorcode tags all the items of set decoration and, with the Swing Set Dresser and, under the supervision of the Set Decorator, marks the position for each item on and about the setting where the Set Decorator has designated that a set decoration piece is to be placed. Each position is marked and numbered to correspond with the number and/or color-coding of **that particular piece** for **that particular scene**.

The Swing Set Dressers physically place each set decoration item and take over during the actual placement of set dressing which takes place when the set has been completed (and the paint is dry). The Swing Set Dresser is particularly evident during blocking and shooting, when the need to move, remove, replace or adjust the position of set dressing is greatest. Set dressing items may be moved or replaced at the request of the Director (at any time), by an actor (for blocking convenience), by the Director of Photography (for lighting purposes), by the Camera Operator (for purposes of composition) and by the Special Effects Technician (for reasons of safety and damage prevention). When modifications occur, the Swing Set Dresser makes note of the changes, moving or removing position marks, as appropriate.

So, when the need arises to have a carpet, sofa, chair, table, floor or desk lamp, wall hanging, cabinet, desk top or greens item moved, and you call for "**Set Dresser!**" a Swing Set Dresser will materialize and do the deed.

When A Set Decoration Item Becomes A Prop. Remember, once an item of set decoration has been handled or used by an actor, that item becomes a working prop and falls under the aegis of the Property Category during the production process.

Special thanks to Andy Klaiman (Swing Set Dresser) for his constructive input.

WORKING WITH PROPERTY PERSONNEL

According to Webster's New Universal Unabridged Dictionary, **property**, insofar as the theater and motion pictures are concerned, is defined as "any of the **movable** articles used as part of the setting or in a piece of stage business, except costumes, backdrops, etc." So, under the proper circumstances, almost anything can qualify as a prop.

Since every production using actors also uses props for the actors to manipulate and/or interact with, props are essential items in helping create the desired reality of a setting and of the performed scene which takes place therein.

By present industry practice, once an item of set decoration or a special effect device has been handled, moved or used by an actor in a bit of staged business, that item is considered a prop and is placed, moved and stored by Property personnel during the production process. Because of this overlapping of jurisdictions, there is considerable give-and-take among Property, Set dressing and Special Effects personnel.

There are usually large numbers of set decoration items mixed in with numerous property items on a given setting or production site, so it pays to pay attention to what are set dressings and what are props in the event one or the other needs moving for compositional purposes.

An item of wardrobe, such as an accessory, jewelry, a hat, a glove, a shoe, can also become a prop when it is used, or has to be specially rigged or prepared, for a piece of acting business.

The Property Master is the person in charge of all props used or to be used at the production site and is supported by Property Assistants and, when needed, a Food Stylist for on-camera edibles.

Property Master Responsibilities. The Property Master is directly responsible to the Producer and is responsive to the Director and actors for the utility of provided props and to the Art Director for the appropriate style of props, and is responsible for acquiring and maintaining the count and condition of all items of property entrusted to his or her care in order to help optimize stage business and its presentation to the camera(s).

Property Master Duties. The Property Master does the following: Reads and analyzes the script and/or storyboard for the type and number of property items required; prepares a scene-by-scene breakdown of all hand props (by character name) and set props by scene numbers; examines and analyzes the Art Director's prop list, sketches, renderings and/or storyboards; researches the period for appropriate items to acquire (or have fabricated); prepares a list of props which conform to the use to which each will be put as well as the period, style, size, shape, texture and color required by the setting and the action which takes place therein; checks with the various supply sources for availability of the required props; prepares a budget for property items and presents it to production management for approval; orders fabrication of specially designed and rigged working props; selects and secures necessary hand and set props (straight, special, breakaway, and weaponry); supervises Assistant Property personnel in the pickup, placement, removal, inventorying, storage and return of all props; maintains all props and related items in good condition while retained or in use by the production; consults with the Art Director and/or Director regarding changes, revisions and/or modifications of property items; purchases and prepares all food and liquid props to be used on-camera and places these items for performance and photographic purposes; for TV commercials: is custodian of and physically handles all product items to be used and/or photographed, pouring beer and other liquids, as necessary; receives advance monies from the Production Manager for procuring needed property items prior to and during production, and is accountable therefor; acts as custodian of, and assumes responsibility for personal jewelry and accessories, money, and other valuables receipted to his or her care by cast members while in costume and/or performing; carries out any other duties normally required of this craft.

Property Assistant Responsibilities. Also called Assistant Props, the Property Assistant is directly responsible to the Property Master for helping facilitate the work of the Property Category.

Property Assistant Duties. The Property Assistant does the following: Reads the script and/or storyboard; examines the Prop Master's prop list; color codes and/or numbers and polaroids each prop item to note condition in receipt thereof; lists each prop item, and each scene in which the prop works, and the character who uses that prop; secures from the Property Master all property items needed for the day's shooting; helps dress the set with prop items, placing and positioning same; lists and marks the position of each set prop by number, colorcode and polaroid of its position in the setting; gives hand props to each actor using same in a scene and collects these props after such use in that scene; marks the floor, wall, ceiling and/or ground position of each set prop in order to facilitate resetting of such items, as required; moves and repositions all prop items, as necessary; dusts, cleans and polishes props, as necessary, prior to the take in which such items are employed; strikes all prop items from the set after their use and returns these prop items to the care of the Property Master; assists the Property Master in the performance of category duties.

The Food Stylist is an occasional addition to the Property Master's staff, and is used when significant amounts of specially prepared foodstuffs are required for photographic display or for consumption by cast and/or atmosphere people while performing on-camera.

Food Stylist Responsibilities. The Food Stylist is directly responsible to the Property Master for having all required food items ordered, prepared and arranged, sufficiently in advance of photography, in the manner desired by the Director, so that production time is not wasted and the desired photographic result can be obtained.

Food Stylist Duties. The Food Stylist does the following: Reads the script and/or storyboard noting scenes involving food items; prepares a proposed menu of food items (appropriate to the period, time-of-day and setting) to be prepared for on-camera consumption by cast and/or atmosphere personnel; prepares a preliminary budget for food items and presents it to the Property Master and/or Production Manager for approval; selects, orders, prepares, places and arranges food items to be consumed, displayed and/or otherwise utilized for photographic purposes; maintains proper sanitary conditions during the preparation and handling of any and all food items to be consumed, whether the food is prepared on the set, at the production site, or elsewhere; cleans the utensils and food preparation area before and after use thereof, dispensing of leftovers.

How the Process Works. The process of properly propping a production is generally as follows: After the Property Master has become familiarized with the script and storyboard and has consulted with the Producer, Director, Art Director and key actors regarding special prop needs, he or she prepares a list of all hand, set, rigged and breakaway props by making a scene-by-scene breakdown of all required prop items. The Prop Master researches the period to determine the appropriate design and style of the props to be used, then begins shopping.

The Property Master personally contacts the various sources for the props needed for the production. Once the availability of the required props and the rental/lease/purchase price for each item has been determined, a detailed prop budget is prepared and presented to the Production Manager for approval. Upon approval, the Prop Master personally selects, reserves, and may pick up the props and bring them to the shooting site for preparation and storage. The props are each tagged and identified by scene number and by the character using it.

The Property Assistants then place each prop in its designated position on the set, or on or with the actor who uses that prop. Should it be necessary to move any prop for purposes of lighting, framing composition, or blocking modifications, Assistant props will be called upon to do the deed.

An item of set decoration, costume or special effects may also become designated a prop should that set dressing, costume or special effects item be manipulated by an actor on-camera. It is then transferred from the responsibility of Set Decoration, Wardrobe or Special Effects, respectively, to that of Property, until shooting is completed and release is given by the Production Manager.

During production shooting, the Property Assistant is present on the set or shooting site at all times in order to place, replace, move or remove property items as expeditiously as possible at the behest of the Director, an actor, the Art Director, the Director of Photography, a Camera Operator, or the Special Effects Technician.

If a dressed set (includes set decoration, prop items and special effects) must be returned to for additional photography, the set is cordoned off and plainly marked "**HOT SET!**" in order to keep unauthorized persons off that set and avoid the possibility of altering the set, its dressings, props or special effects rigging in any respect.

When shooting has been completed on a set, all property items are removed by Property personnel and returned to the care of the Property Master for inventorying, storage (until release is given by production management), and returned to the sources from which these items were acquired.

Variations. There are a few notable differences in managing props on the various types of productions. For example, on TV series and commercials production, the Prop Master may go for all prop items (excluding product items for TV commercials); whereas on feature or TV programming production, one of the Property Assistants may be assigned that task.

Because there is usually much more prep time for features than for other types of production, the Property Master will work more closely with the Production Designer in the selection of prop items than with an Art Director on other types of production. The abbreviated prep time for television programming production generally does not allow for much of this detailing interchange.

In TV commercials, the Property Master usually works very closely with the ad agency Art Director because of the importance of positive product identification in all respects.

Summing Up. Since each motion picture, whether film or video, is an accumulation of contributions by each working category and classification of myriad interrelated detail, set decoration and property contribute importantly to that mosaic of detail which builds the planned-for and desired audience response.

Special thanks to Pat Moudakis (Property Master) for his constructive input.

COSTUMING AND WARDROBE

The design, execution and application of costume for the performers is an essential process in the production of a cinematic story product. Whether drama or comedy, each item of costume must conform to the period, the geographic location, the climate, the weather, the time of day, to the particulars of each character and to the specific action which will take place. Appropriate costuming ranks in importance with that of set dressing. Each process contributes fundamentally to the perceived reality of the action and the story elements and helps enhance the performance and characterizations of the actors.

Pre-Production. The process of costuming begins with the script and/or storyboard. From the character descriptions, action and inferences drawn therefrom by the Costume Designer from a reading of the script, design ideas emerge and are elaborated upon. A script breakdown of costume requirements by character and scene is done to determine the style, quality and quantity of costume items which need to be designed, purchased and/or rented. If the production is a period piece, research is done in order to assure historical accuracy. Input from the Production Designer/Art Director, the Director and/or the Producer will help set parameters for the design and execution and/or selection/acquisition of the costumes and accessories.

Provided that costumes are available from costume shops, or are currently in fashion and can be supplied by the performers from their personal wardrobe, the **Costume Supervisor** authorizes and coordinates the selection and acquisition by the Key Costumers of wardrobe for all those actors and atmosphere people required by the production.

The actual selection, procurement, arranging, cataloging, handling, fitting and altering of costumes are done by the **Key Costumers**—Key Men's Costumer for male wardrobe and Key Women's Costumer for female wardrobe—and their Assistants, coordinated by and under the supervision of the Costume Supervisor.

The Key Costumers, having acquired the physical measurements of the actors and their clothes, shoes, glove and hat sizes, proceed to call each actor in for a fitting. As a result, costumes are marked, pinned and altered by **Cutter/Fitters** and **Seamstresses** in order to properly fit and dress the actor in each respectively required costume.

After the first fitting and alterations, each actor is called in for a final fitting. If no other alterations are required, each costume is duly catalogued by actor and scene along with the accessories selected to go with it.

Production. During production, each actor is assisted in getting into costume by a Dresser. The **Dresser** makes sure that all required items of costume are in place on the person of the actor for the scene to be shot.

The **Set Wardrobe** person, on the set at all times during shooting, sees that the costume is kept clean (or maintained in an appropriate condition of wear or disrepair, as necessary) and that each item of wardrobe is appropriately adjusted and positioned from take to take. Equally important is that Set Wardrobe make certain that all listed costume items are on the person of the actor (and that personal or inappropriate items are not) and are positioned and adjusted in order to present an accurate and consistent appearance from take to take and scene to scene.

The **Assistant Costumer** assists the Key Costumers in the procurement, handling, maintenance and return of costume items and serves as a liaison between the Key Costume and the Set Wardrobe person in order to bring costume items to the set or from the set to the Key Costumers for repair, conditioning (aging, dusting, soiling, tearing, etc), adjustment, exchange or cleaning.

If it should appear that considerable personnel attention is directed toward the appearance of wardrobe, it most certainly is. Inadvertent omission of a scheduled costume item or inclusion of an unscheduled item as well as letting an inconsistency in costume/accessories arrangement slip by unnoticed during production can result in an expensive reshoot (and often has).

Post Production. After the production has wrapped and all additional shooting has been completed, the **Key Costumers** collect the costumes and the accessories, have them cleaned and repaired, and prepare them for return to their actor-owners, vendors or studio inventory, as appropriate. Petty cash is reconciled with receipted cash pay-outs and turned in to the Production Manager by the Costume Supervisor.

Summing Up. The care and attention devoted to costuming and wardrobe serve to emphasize the point that each category operation in the image-making process is an accumulation of details woven into the fabric of the total picture.

The cinematic process is, and always has been, a check-and-double-check operation in order to assure integral accuracy and consistency within the visual product. To assure a high degree of accuracy and consistency, constant vigilance and attention to detail is essential to help facilitate the visual integrity of a production. That is the hallmark of cinematic craftsmanship.

Special thanks to Shannon Litten (Costume Supervisor) and Tom Baxter (Key Men's Costumer) for their constructive input.

DIRECTORIAL CATEGORY

The cinematic media are the Director's media. This means that the film or video Director has virtually total control of the use of production elements—performers, sets, locations, set and site dressing, camera placement and movement, and the editing of the captured imagery.

Since it all comes together at the camera, it is important that all those in the camera contingent be aware of the responsibilities borne by this group of people.

The Directorial Category is composed of personnel who direct the performance of actors, set the operational parameters for the production, and establish and maintain the mood and pace of the operation.

As the title implies, the Directorial Category gives direction to the production. In addition, the Director gives purpose to the project by sharing his or her vision of the final product with the performers, Production Designer, Cinematographer and Editor.

The several Assistant Directors with whom the Director works are there to help maintain scheduling by seeing that all the elements are at hand or in place, ready for the Director's attention in developing the picture, shot-by-shot, scene-by-scene and sequence-by-sequence.

WORKING WITH DIRECTORS

The cinematic media (film and video) are Directors' media. The Director sets the shot and blocks the action, and the actors play it for the Director, an audience of one. The Director either prints (film) or accepts (video) the take or orders additional takes until satisfied with the results—the totality of the shot.

The Director sets the mood and pace of the production. The mood sets the ambience on the set. It can be a quiet set, a noisy set, a fun, no-nonsense or even grim set, depending on the Director. It is well to heed the signals given by the Director (and the Director's alter ego, the First Assistant Director) and to follow their lead.

The production pace is also a directorial function, aided and abetted by the

Assistant Directors and the Director of Photography. The production process can be organized or disorganized. It therefore behooves all crew members to get in sync with, and help maintain, that pace. To the degree that crew personnel understand and perform their own responsibilities and duties efficiently, as well as being sufficiently aware of the Director's responsibilities and duties, that desired pace can be maintained.

Director's Responsibilities. The Director is directly responsible to the Producer for directing the production activities of the cast and crew as creatively and efficiently as possible in order to obtain optimal (dramatic) interpretation of the script (or screenplay) within the constraints of time and budget, while obtaining optimum photographic coverage thereof, so that each shot, scene and sequence will cut together, flow and give life to the finally realized production.

Director's Duties. Much of the Director's work is done during pre-production, before principal photography begins. During the time that is budgeted, the Director studies the script and may work with the Writer(s), and Producer in suggesting sections to be rewritten.

Once the script has been finalized, the Director's attention focuses on breaking down the script into individual shots, comprising scenes and sequences, and then plotting camera angles and movement and actor blocking for each shot as well as notating the desired mood, time of day, season, etc, in addition to the energy and emotional levels expected of the actors throughout each shot, scene and sequence.

During the pre-production period, the Director has the opportunity to confer with the Producer, Writer(s), Production Designer, Art Director, Costume Designer, Production Manager, First Assistant Director, Director of Photography and Music Composer to assure that the creative concept is clearly communicated and understood and will be consistently carried out by each of these principals and their respective departments.

Casting is another area in which the Director may get involved, as well as location scouting. Selection of locations is given as much care and attention as is the choosing of performers. Attention to set construction and set dressing and/or dressing the location site(s) is essential so that the desired "look" is apparent and that actor and camera blocking can be accommodated. Design and/or execution of costumes, makeup, hairstyling and props must also be carefully considered and locked in at this early stage.

The Director then confers with the Director of Photography in order to establish and convey a sense of the pictorial mood—the look—which the Director desires. The DP may shoot film tests to provide points of reference and to help set the aesthetic parameters for principal photography.

On the set, the Director personally sets the camera position(s) and blocks the action of the actors as well as camera moves, working closely with the Director of Photography to achieve the desired coverage and look. At dailies, the footage is mutually evaluated by the Director and DP (and Producer) and modifications planned and thereafter shot or reshot, as necessary.

During the production phase, the First Assistant Director (the Director's chief assistant, the on-the-set expediter and time manager) generally monitors the various production procedures and sees that the shooting schedule is met and the production pace maintained.

Some Directors, in some single-camera productions and in nearly all multi-camera sitcoms, with the full accord of the Director of Photography, like to work routinely and closely with the Camera Operator(s) in plotting camera movement and setting composition, while the DP concentrates on lighting and mood (as in the British system of Lighting Cameraman and Operative Cameraman).

The Director is particularly mindful of getting the coverage needed to provide sufficient editing options for the Editor during the post-production phase in developing the pace and rhythm of the finalized production and must also keep track of elements in matching action, such as: The energy level(s) of the actor(s); direction and velocity of movement of actors, vehicles and camera; the facing direction of looks; the physical position and condition of the actors, their makeup, hair and wardrobe; the props and set dressing. With this myriad important detail to keep track of, the Director relies on the Script Supervisor to maintain a complete, current and accurate record (shooting script) of each take made, the timing of each take, each take printed, and all deficiencies and/or changes noted in no-print and print takes. During post-production, the Director and Editor rely on the shooting script, which is like an architectural blueprint, in putting the pieces of the cinematic mosaic in place.

Interpersonal Relations. The Director is the production leader, and everything possible is done or delivered which the Director needs or requests in order to get the production fully realized. The Director sets the tone and ambience on the set by his or her own attitude, often influenced by the type and level of emotional presence in the scene being shot at any given time. Because the Director's principal concern is for the actors, it behooves each crew member to do nothing which conflicts with that desired ambience. After all, it is the Director's set when working with the actors.

Director's Expectations. The Director expects each crew member to deliver consistently professional work and to be non-disruptive of the production process. Most Directors are mindful that making a motion picture is a collaborative process and are open to discreetly made suggestions in order to give a full sense of participation to production personnel. Never forget that everyone is there (including you) to collaborate with, and help, the Director get his or her visualization on the screen or tube as efficiently and painlessly as possible. So give each Director your best. And remember, Directors often form a "production family" of skilled, cooperative and congenial craftspeople of their own to work with.

Feature Production. In feature production, the Director has more time to refine the scenes and, at a pace of a page-and-a-half to 3 pages a day, is more patient with the technical procedures and allows ample time for the Director of Photography to refine the lighting and for the operative camera crew to refine camera moves. The Director is therefore more accessible and open to crew input.

Episodic Production. In episodic production, at a pace of eight to twelve pages per day, the Director (or the DP or operative camera crew) has little time to refine scenes and is under constant pressure to get the show in the can, so is much less accessible or open to crew input.

TV Commercial Production. In most commercial production, the crew is relatively small, and the pace is quite slow and deliberate. The Director and Director of Photography/Camera Operator work very closely together at the camera in developing the shots. In general, the TV commercial Director is quite open to pertinent crew input.

Film Sitcoms. In multi-camera film sitcoms, the Director works from the shooting floor, blocking the movements of the actors and cameras and setting camera coverage and/or composition and observing rehearsals and takes, during which collaborative input from the Camera Operators is an acceptable part of the process.

Video Sitcoms. In multi-camera video sitcoms (or in nearly any scripted video production for that matter), after preparing the shot coverage desired from each camera for each scene, the Director then blocks the actors from the floor. Thereafter, the Director marks in the shooting script the desired camera coverage by sequential shot numbers associated with specific cut points (before the camera blocking and taping days). The Director spends approximately eighty per cent of production time in the control booth, so most communication—audial and visual—with the Director is via the headset and control booth monitors. The Camera Operators are closely in touch with the Associate Director who gives them the shots (as specified by the Director's notations on the shooting script) during FAX and once again on the floor with the Camera Operators during the first walk-though by talent; and then calls the shots over headset intercom during rehearsals and tapings. The video Director does appreciate suggestions (and "selling" shot ideas via the monitor) and often makes modification in the coverage from the booth.

Summing Up. Directing has many facets, among them being a thorough understanding of: Cinematic and dramaturgical principles, the capabilities of the camera and its optics, the strengths and frailties of creative and technical people, and working with the ever-present time and budget constraints. To deal with this, the Director must often wear many hats, often simultaneously—that of psychologist, negotiator, tyrant, judge, jury, politician, advocate, adversary, comrade, warden, critic, artiste, traffic cop, therapist, and so many more—as each occasion demands. For a person wanting to be tested to the limits, directing is one sure way to that goal.

WORKING WITH THE TECHNICAL COORDINATOR

A Technical Coordinator (also called Camera Coordinator) is used on a multi-camera film sitcom during camera blocking and rehearsals (or during the block-and-shoot process) and on through show time with the audience, in order to help coordinate camera movement and thereby facilitate getting the show on film as effectively and efficiently as possible.

Technical Coordinator Responsibilities. The Technical Coordinator (TC) is directly responsible to the Director, sometimes assisting the Director in plotting the movement (and coverage) of the cameras for each sequence, and is responsible for coordinating all camera dolly movement during rehearsals and showtime filming.

Technical Coordinator Duties. The Technical Coordinator may or may not be called upon by the Director to assist in setting camera positions. In any event, the Coordinator makes careful and complete notation in his or her shooting script exactly when each camera dolly moves, the number of each move, the direction in which each move is to be made, what or who each camera is framing, and whenever a camera is "**on-the-air**" (its footage to be used in the final cut) during the move. (It should be noted that both the Camera Operator and the Dolly Grip for each camera are on RF headset intercom with the Tech Coordinator at all time during run-throughs, dress rehearsal and showtime.) Either a line cue or an action cue is given verbally via the headset intercom to each Dolly Grip by the Coordinator prior to each move so that each dolly move will be made in a planned, timely and safe fashion.

Working from the floor and using a quad-split monitor, the Technical Coordinator is constantly aware of the positioning of each camera as well as the facility with which each on-air move is made and, if a certain move is causing problems, suggests modification of that move to the director. In general, on-air moves should flow smoothly and be closely coordinated with the pace of the action.

The Technical Coordinator should exhibit a high degree of attention to detail, concentration and patience along with a working knowledge of camera coverage as it applies to editing considerations. Having the ability to make accurate assessment of the capabilities of each member of each operative camera crew—Camera Operator, First Assistant, and Dolly Grip—is a skill which can greatly facilitate the production process. In a sense, the Technical Coordinator seems something like an air traffic controller. When all the cameras are moving, at times frantically about the set like a squadron of airplanes coming in for a landing, he or she must be calm and decisive in delivering cues, instructions and reminders.

Camera Blocking. The Technical Coordinator works closely with the Director during the slow-paced camera blocking process in order to help assure optimal coverage of the action. The Coordinator makes notation in an updated script of each dolly move for each of the three or four cameras used on the sitcom, and when that move is to be made. From these notes, the Coordinator will alert each Dolly Grip (via headset intercom) prior to each move so that each move will occur in a timely and coordinated manner during rehearsals and filming.

The Technical Coordinator must be promptly apprised of any modification made in a dolly move by the Director or Camera Operator, and this responsibility falls to the Dolly Grip for that camera. In addition, the Dolly Grip may ask the Coordinator for special helpful verbal cues or reminders during complex moves; the Camera Operator may also utilize the Technical Coordinator to issue helpful verbal cues regarding complex coverage situations such as dumping off framing one actor onto a passing actor, swish panning to a different composition, rack focusing in frame from an element in one focal plane to an element in another focal plane, etc.

Camera Rehearsals. Once the camera blocking is completed, the scene or sequence is run in real time to see whether any problems arise as to actor and/or dolly movement or positioning and/or camera framing; dolly and/or actor marks are changed, if necessary, in order to accommodate the problem. During these run-throughs, including the dress rehearsal, modifications can be and are made. The Technical Coordinator is principally concerned with getting timely, planned moves from the Dolly Grips and avoiding "bumper cars" syndrome at all costs. A Dolly Grip who does not pay attention and consistently misdelivers the planned and expected dolly moves cannot expect to last long on a film sitcom.

During run-throughs and rehearsals, the Technical Coordinator addresses each camera by its designation (from left to right, facing the set) Camera A, Camera B, Camera C and Camera X (which can be on either end). Moves are referred to in numerical order from 1, 2, 3, 4, etc. When modification in an originally blocked move is made—say, an additional stop occurring between floor positions 2 and 3—a stop position at 2-1/2 will be designated by the Technical Coordinator, floor-taped by the Dolly Grip, and so indicated in the Coordinator's script.

Dress Rehearsal. By dress rehearsal time, all modifications in action blocking and dolly movement have been made and set. Some sitcoms run film during the dress rehearsal and may even have an audience in attendance for reaction purposes.

Show Time. The audience assembles. The actors are made up and costumed. The cameras, now loaded with film, roll with the Director's call for "ACTION!" The Technical Coordinator, now in a soundproof isolation booth, keeps the RF intercom channel filled with cues and comments to the Dolly Grips and Camera Operators as he or she follows, by means of a quad split monitor in the booth as well as a clear view of the stage floor, both the action and the dialogue of the actors as well as the movement and positioning of the camera dollies, comparing all this with the cue notations in the Coordinator's shooting script.

It is interesting to note that audiences have commented on the flowing grace of the camera dolly choreography on film sitcoms. This is a special tribute to the Director, the Technical Coordinator and the operative camera crews.

WORKING WITH
ASSISTANT DIRECTORS

During pre-production planning and especially production, nearly everything that is done revolves around decisions made by the Director in response to the never ending attention to myriad details which comprise the cinematic process. In fact, cinematic details have details *ad infinitum*.

In order to conserve the Director's energy and allow his or her full attention to focus on the most important aspects—working with the actors to perfect their performances and with the Director of Photography to get adequate camera coverage and to maintain the desired and planned-for "look"—much of the Director's time management, detail and paperwork is handled by the First Assistant Director who is in turn assisted by Second Assistant Directors.

First Assistant Director Responsibilities. The First Assistant Director (1st AD) is directly responsible to the Director, assisting in the performance of directorial duties—administrative and technical—during the pre-production and production phases, and works in close cooperation with the Unit Production Manager (UPM). The First AD is the **on-the-set expediter** and is responsible to the Producer for maintaining optimum coordination among crew categories and actors in order to maintain the production pace required by the shooting schedule (and budget).

First Assistant Director Duties. Beginning with **pre-production,** the First Assistant Director does the following: Reads the script; times out the shooting script scene-by-scene and estimates the final running time and footage; prepares a script breakdown, listing the probable requirements for bit actors and extras in each scene; analyzes the script breakdown tear-sheets for items required by each department; works out a more refined budget with the Production Manager; and develops a probable shooting schedule with the Director and UPM.

During the **production** phase, the First AD does the following: Demonstrates a comprehensive understanding of Union and Guild working rules and of the responsibilities and duties for the technical craft categories and classifications; handles organizational matters and time management procedures; expedites setup and shooting for the Director; conforms to the day-to-day shooting schedule as closely as weather, logistics, setup time and cast availability permit; informs the unit Production Manager each day of the shooting schedule for the following day; arranges background and atmospheric action; assists the Director in the blocking and direction of groups of extras, mob scenes and stampedes; coordinates the activities of Second Assistant Directors; directs second units and/or inserts shooting which may involve stand-ins, doubles, special effects, working props, rolling and/or live stock, and/or special rigging; cues cast and crew either manually or electronically; obtains photographic releases—personal and property—during production; signs employees' (cast and crew) start slips, time records, pay vouchers, deal memos and reimbursement (mileage, per diem and cash pay-outs) authorizations; authorizes overtime and hazard pay for cast and crew; makes sure that everything and everybody needed during the production will be on hand in the right place, at the right time and in the proper condition to perform their designated function; sees that only authorized people are on the stage or in and around the shooting area; insures that doors, vents, fans and/or air conditioning are secured prior to each sound take; requests a warning bell and quiet on the set or shooting site prior to giving the order to roll sound tape; maintains an orderly and efficient operation during production.

During **post-production,** the First AD sees that all records are complete and properly routed or filed, that all bills are paid and that cash accounts balance, that all rental items have been returned, and that all additional shooting—pick-ups, inserts, process plates, wild takes, second unit—is completed.

Second Assistant Director Responsibilities and Duties. The Second Assistant Director (2nd AD) is responsible to, and is there to assist, the First Assistant Director in the performance of First AD duties. Large crowd or battle scenes may require several

Second ADs in order to properly plan, stage and coordinate the atmospheric action.

Features and Miniseries. In feature and miniseries production, the First Assistant Director is a close collaborator with the Director and an advocate for the Director's needs and concerns, and he/she remains so for the duration of production.

Episodics and Sitcoms. In episodic and sitcom production, although the First AD is mindful of the requests and needs of the Director, the 1st AD acts more like an Assistant Production Manager in order to keep costs in tight control and the production on schedule. This is principally because there is usually a different Director for each episode or show and much has been determined—the budget, the script, shooting schedule, the regular cast, guest and supporting players and bits, and the sets, set dressing and props—before the Director arrives to do the show. This is particularly true of sitcoms where a regular returning cast, two or three standing sets and only one or two swing sets are standard parameters.

Interpersonal Relations. The First Assistant Director must, at all times, see that a professional and proficient decorum is maintained on the set or shooting site. As the Director's alter ego, the First AD sees that the tone and ambience desired by the Director is not exceeded by those working in or about the shooting area. To achieve this compliance, the First AD must be firm and fair—but a loud and penetrating voice does help get everyone's attention.

First AD Expectations. The First Assistant Director expects each crew member to report to work on time, to be at his or her post ready to spring into action, and to do so in an efficient and non-obtrusive manner. When the First AD asks the Camera Operator if he or she is ready, and the answer is affirmative, then the operative camera crew had better be ready to roll. During the production phase, time is of the essence and, since time is money, the First AD is ever concerned with making the most efficient use of the time at hand.

Summing Up. Because nearly all production decisions revolve around the Director, the First Assistant Director is there to oversee myriad details which are affected by every decision the Director makes. The First AD (assisted by the Second ADs) attends to much of the detail and paperwork necessary to keep the production moving ahead on track, on schedule and on budget. An understanding of the responsibilities and duties of the Assistant Directors by the operative camera crew can help facilitate the production process to the benefit of all.

Special thanks to Rusty Meek (UPM) and Rick Allen (1AD) for their constructive input.

OTHER CRAFTS

It is sound practice to become more aware of the contributions made by the other crafts in the motion picture making process. Quite often this craft work is done before principal photography begins, and it is usually done offstage and brought to the photographic arena and set up prior to actual shooting.

The degree to which these crafts recognize and understand the requirements of the film or video camera will have a direct effect on the efficiency and effectiveness with which the camera can capture the required imagery.

The responsibilities and duties of several of the key collaborating crafts are presented in this subsection.

WORKING WITH ACTORS

Whether you operate a film or video camera, you've no doubt encountered actors who almost never: Hit their marks, or make a move, cross or gesture in the same way for each take (at the same place or point in time, at the same velocity, at the same magnitude).

These same actors are likely to cover each other from camera view, throw key light shadows on each other, bounce into and out of chairs (and other derriere receptacles), hide their upstage eye from the camera, "banana" into and out of group shots, bounce up and down or sway side to side (particularly when in a tight closeup), or, when on either end of a group, lean or move away from the others in the line up, in addition to executing any other anomaly either likely or even remotely possible, all the while (in multi-camera sitcoms) the Technical Coordinator (film) or Associate Director (video) is pleading with you through the headset to get clean singles, to keep the head shot or group in frame, and so forth.

Some actors are not even aware which is their close-up camera; however, mercifully for all concerned, after a few shows they soon get this straight.

Assuming that the offending actor is interested in maintaining and growing in craft competence, it is not as difficult to get that actor's attention and cooperation as one might imagine. Once an actor is assured that s/he will look much better on camera if s/he conforms to certain parameters of movement and positioning, you've immediately got that actor's attention.

An effective way to impress an offending actor with the error of his or her ways is to invite that actor to switch places with you and to operate the camera, looking through the lens and following the action, while you proceed to demonstrate the specific shortcomings (as your Camera Assistant follows focus and sizes the image for the guest). Assure the actor that this is in no way a put-down, but to help him or her look better on film/tape—which, of course, is the very purpose of the exercise.

WORKING WITH
THE BOOM OPERATOR

Ever since the advent of motion picture synchronized sound which ushered in the "talkies" in 1926, sound pick-up by microphone has caused modification in the way in which film (and subsequently video) is lighted and framed, resulting, not infrequently, in conflict between camera and sound personnel.

The principal concern of production sound—particularly the Production Mixer and Boom Operator—is to capture absolutely optimal sound at all times, which generally translates to: get the mic as close to the principals as possible. The principal concern of the production camera personnel—particularly the Director of Photography and Camera Operator—is to light and frame the actors and action in the most optimally appropriate way consistent with the style and mood of the production.

As you have no doubt experienced, these "sacred" missions have at times run at cross purposes, and sharp conflicts have occurred between camera and sound, particularly when the sound boom on its perambulator is put in place before the Director of Photography is ready for it or has picked a spot for it (and the camera) around which to light the set-up. Another problem area is when the Boom Operator moves the mic closer to the actor(s) than the limit allows and the mic gets into the composition framed by the Camera Operator.

If a compromise cannot be worked out, such as having the actor(s) speak up, changing to a more sensitive, directional or RF mic, or tightening the actor's positioning and/or framing thereof so that the mic can be brought closer to the actor, then the production sound may have to be voice dubbed/looped later by ADR or other technique. During post-production, several foreign countries voice dub all their pictures, seldom using production sound techniques, thereby not having to light and frame around a sound boom.

One thing is certain: Motion pictures, whether film or video, is a visual medium first and foremost, and sound, as important as it is to the final result, is adjunct to it. Beautiful sound with a mic and/or its shadow in frame destroys the illusion entirely. And so if flack is to fly, it is the ever-present Boom Operator who takes the brunt of the abuse even though he or she may have been told by the Production Mixer to get the mic in closer to the actor(s).

Boom Operator Responsibilities. The Boom Operator is directly responsible to the Production Mixer and is responsible for operating the microphone boom or fishpole, or the shotgun or parabolic microphone, in order to pick up the desired voice(s), sound(s), sound effect(s) and/or music at the perspective desired by the Mixer, giving special attention to the frame line limits given by the Camera Operator, thereby causing no microphone or boom equipment or shadows therefrom, to appear within the camera frame.

Boom Operator Duties. The Boom Operator does the following: Sets up, mounts, adjusts and breaks down the microphones, microphone boom, fishpole, stands, cable and associated equipment; assists the Production Mixer in attaching the proper microphone to the mic boom, fishpole, stand, or to the person of actors, or hiding the placed mic behind set dressing; assists the Mixer in setting up, testing and adjusting RF transmitting equipment; **for video production**, positions the boom perambulator behind, and clear of, the working area for the camera pedestals and/or camera boom; **for film and video**: adjusts the boom monitor contrast, brightness and peak picture for optimum image results; checks all operating functions and limits of the boom—tilt and swing, extension and retraction, left and right facing limits of the mic in its harness, and makes adjustments as necessary; when set lighting is completed and prior to the take, moves the mic boom around the action area of the set for each set up to determine where mic and boom shadows will be falling at all times, noting which lights to avoid with the boom during the take; works closely with the camera, electrical and grip crews to assure that the microphone, boom, or their shadows will not appear in the composed frame; while operating the boom or fishpole, keeps the microphone placed and faced in the proper position at all times in order to achieve the acoustic results required for each sound take and wears earphones to facilitate this; voice slates wild sound takes; otherwise assists the Production Mixer in the performance of production sound duties.

The Boom Operator wears a headset through which (in addition to two-way communication with the Mixer) production sound is fed by the Production Mixer which enables the Boom Operator to monitor the quality and perspective of production sound as it is being delivered and recorded. This is helpful in determining and maintaining proper positioning and facing of the microphone during a sound take.

Checking Procedure for Boom Mic Positioning. A good Boom Operator always checks his or her lower mic boom limits with the Camera Operator for the widest shot (often the master shot) and then visually lines those heights up with background reference points in order to keep the microphone and its boom (or fishpole) out of camera frame at all times during rehearsals and shooting.

In single camera production, this should be checked at the head end of every setup.

In multiple-camera **film** sitcoms, the Boom Operators work above from the front parallel of each set, holding master or wide angles of the action during the run-through phase for each scene and sequence.

In multiple-camera **video** sitcoms, each Boom Operator operates from a boom perambulator on the stage floor with a picture monitor mounted thereon. By referring to the monitor, he or she can easily determine during run-through whether the boom is in or out of frame and set safe limits well ahead of taping.

Summing Up. Even with the checking procedures, the Camera Operator must be ever alert for the "monkey" appearing unexpectedly in frame, or its shadow flitting furtively across an actor's person or across a wall or furnishing or set dressing in the foreground, midground or background.

Camera and sound should always work closely together in order to deliver the very best visual and audial result practicable. Often this can be achieved without undue compromise, providing egos don't get in the way. After all, we're all professionals striving at all times for the best result possible. But never forget, it's the picture that sound is serving, Each frame of the picture must be pristine in appearance to have maximum effect on the viewer.

WORKING WITH
SPECIAL EFFECTS

Most of the injuries and fatalities experienced in our industry seem to occur during special effects and stunt sequences. We, as the **operative camera crew**—Camera Operator, First Assistant Camera Operator and Dolly Grip—are on the front line, vulnerable to any miscalculation or outright foul-up in stunt or special effects execution.

In the cinematic media, there is an abiding and overall respect for the expertise of our supervising colleagues in their abilities and concern for the safety and welfare of their staff, cast and crew. At times, this respect is neither warranted nor deserved, as events have proved. Cutting corners to save time or money has resulted in mishaps. Working long hours with short turn-arounds for rest has taken its toll. Inexperience and ego have often been to blame. Drug abuse, too, has occasionally been faulted. Fortunately, most of the time our supervising colleagues are safety-conscious and watch carefully over our safety in conceiving, planning and executing potentially dangerous special effects and/or stunt setups. We must do the same.

Working with special effects (as with stunts) is a matter of taking due precautions for both personal and operating camera crew safety. It is safer to assume that whatever can go wrong may go wrong, than that the entire special effects and/or stunt sequence is only an illusion, not happening in real time and space. Distancing the operative camera crew farther from the special effects and/or stunt by use of remotely controlled, wired or radio activated camera control head setups is always a viable option.

Understanding the Key Special Effects Technician's job may help to objectively evaluate the potential hazard associated with any camera setup involving special effects.

Key Special Effects Technician Responsibilities. The Key Special Effects Technician is directly responsible to the Director for planning and executing the special effects display and, when operating on a set or production site during production shooting, may function within the Property Category and is responsible for safely, efficiently and effectively planning and rigging all special effects—explosives/incendiaries/mechanical/miscellaneous—in a manner designed to help achieve optimum photographic, and safe, realization thereof.

Key Special Effects Technician Duties. The Key Special Effects Technician does the following: Reads the script, concentrating on scenes and sequences involving special effects; confers with the Director and Production Designer to determine the type, volume, quality, placement and action of explosives, incendiaries, mechanical, or other type of special effect; consults the storyboard of each action sequence which involves special effects; with the Director, walks the action area in which special effects are to be placed and activated, plotting and marking the position of each special effect; orders, cares for, manages and inventories all special effects matériel; supervises Assistant Special Effects Technicians in the handling, rigging and use of firearms, explosives, incendiaries, mechanical and wire gags, man-made rain, floods, wind, dust, snowfall, etc; takes adequate precautions to insure the safety of all personnel and livestock coming in close proximity to potentially hazardous setups, clearly specifying safe positions and pathways; clearly identifying all hazardous areas and installations for the protection of production personnel—cast, crew, staff—and visitors; once special effects have been placed, marks and points out to the Director and Assistant Director(s) safe paths for actors and/or livestock to traverse, and also establishes with the Director and AD(s) a non-ambiguous system of signals and commands for coordinating the special effects with the action; running tests on rigged installations to check (and/or demonstrate for the Director and Director of Photography) the volume, shape and color of explosive charges and incendiaries and to check on the effectiveness of rigged gags of whatever type; supervises and/or triggers the special effects during each take involving special effects of any kind; supervises, or does, the removal of all special effects rigging and any unactivated explosives and incendiary devices following the final take of the setup in which such matériel was utilized; otherwise carrying out the duties normally required of this craft.

Assistant Special Effects Technician Responsibilities and Duties. The Assistant Special Effects Technician is directly responsible to the Key Special Effects Technician and assists in the performance of special effects duties, which consist of picking up, loading, unloading, preparing matériel for transportation and rigging and operation of special effects matériel under the supervision of the Key Special Effects Technician.

Considerations. Because of the potential danger inherent in special effects rigging and execution, certain precautions are taken: When any explosives are used in a production, a Key Special Effects Technician, licensed by the State of residence as a Powder Expert, must be used to supervise such rigging and execution; a qualified Key Special Effects Technician is used to handle, rig and operate any special effects rigging of a hazardous nature to cast, crew, livestock, or property; and finally, a take or rehearsal which involves special effects is not started until the Key Special Effects Technician has given the Director a prearranged and clearly acknowledged clearance to proceed (as well as a signal to abort the process), because it is imperative that the timing and pattern of the activation of the special effects during a take involving personnel and/or animals not vary a whit from that of the final rehearsal.

This last aspect is so vital in preserving the safety of those actors, technical personnel and livestock participating in special effects sequences that Directors, inexperienced (or relatively so) in special effects shooting, have been known to turn the execution of such sequences over to an experienced Second unit Director or to the Key Special Effects Technician.

Summing Up. Special effects and stunt sequences are currently proliferating in motion picture production—theatrical and TV programming. Special effects and stunts have a predictable effect in drawing audiences into the action. While physically safe to see displayed on a screen, capturing the ambience and excitement of such action often requires close proximity of camera crews to the special effects and/or stunt. This, in turn, requires careful consideration regarding safely positioning and/or protecting operative camera crews from physical injury while shooting such sequences.

THE VIDEO COLORIST

The Video Colorist is a Telecine Operator who specializes in the transfer of film images to video tape. During this process, and on a scene-by-scene basis, the Colorist adjusts the color (hue and chroma), the brightness (density), image positioning (headroom and sideroom) and image size (to free the framing of any extraneous matter) in order to maintain a visual consistency throughout the transferred material.

The function of the Colorist is similar to that of the Timer at the film lab in so far as the timing adjustments for density and color are concerned. For resizing and repositioning of framed images, film-to-film must go through the optical printing process; whereas the film-to-tape process does it all in one pass.

The work of the video Colorist may well have a more profound effect upon the work we do as Cinematogaphers and Camera Operators than we are aware. Because of the efficiencies of electronic post-production techniques, film has found its way onto the flying spot scanner and into the sophisticated computerized editing bays.

It is during the transfer process that the work we do as film artists/technicians—our lighting and framing—can be, and often is, modified by another or others who may or may not have our subjective sensitivities.

A Director of Photography whose work is destined to be transferred to video tape is therefore well advised to be present during the transfer and colorizing process in order to provide the Colorist pertinent subjective input for color, density and sizing adjustments which he or she deems necessary. Short of being there in person, it pays for the DP to send written instructions to the transfer house detailing the desired "look" for each scene and sequence, and how "problem shots" are to be handled.

Most film shows transfer to tape directly from camera negative to save both time and money. A few shows transfer from print film in order to protect the negative and/or to get a heavier, more contrasty look.

The Colorist, using the provided grey scale/color chart registered on the material to be transferred, should work to maintain a consistency in the visual look of the transferred material in keeping with the intent and/or instructions of the Director of Photography. From the Camera Operator's standpoint, the material should be transferred at a one-to-one size ratio, unless special reframing is specified or required.

Because the Colorist can also resize and reposition the framed images to a limited degree, it behooves the Camera Operators to document their framing positioning by shooting a 1.33 aspect ratio color chart, framing it carefully within (but filling edge to edge) the TV-safe scribe lines on the ground glass of the ocular. Then, should a problem arise regarding framing, especially headroom on closeups, it can be quite easily determined whether the fault lies with the Camera Operator (for the original framing) or with the Colorist (for the resizing or repositioning).

Once the color and density (set by reference to the greyscale/color chart) and frame positioning parameters have been determined, these are usually set for the entire show. The transfer is made one scene at a time in order to maintain sync with the sound track. At any time and for any scene, the need to reposition or resize images in frame may become necessary. The process works something like this: First, the picture and sound tracks are put in timecode sync and interlocked; next, the take is run in its entirety to see whether problems exist which need attending to; if so, correcting modifications are cranked into the computer and the take is run again; if it looks all right, then it is run a final time and transferred to tape; after which, the next take is put in sync, and the process continues.

In addition to the preset functions, there is also a variable dynamic sizing control which can enlarge or diminish the size of an image while repositioning it frame by frame, as the take runs, much as you would during a pan/tilt-and-zoom shot.

The Colorist is responsible to the Supervisor of the post-production facility, is responsive to the client and is responsible for effectively and efficiently analyzing and appraising the material to be transferred, determining and setting the appropriate parameter controls (in accordance with the Director of Photography's instructions and intent), and transferring the film images to video tape.

The Colorist is assisted by the Telecine Operator who logs in and prepares the film and audio tape footage to be transferred, mounts the footage on reels (as necessary), threads the film on the telecine transfer machine, puts the audio tape on a sound dummy, places a video cassette in the VCR, and puts these machines on-line to the appropriate editing bay.

During the transfer process, the Telecine Operator logs the beginning and ending time code numbers of each transferred take along with any color, density, resizing and repositioning modifications which are made by the Colorist.

Film is the predominant and ever-increasing medium of choice for television programming origination. Syndicators for the foreign market prefer and even specify the highest quality tapes (transferred from film origination) for the superior quality display systems (625-line PAL and SECAM) in their television markets. With talk of high definition **digital** television/video recording and display systems being approved and in place in the not too distant future, no one wants inferior quality product on their hands. Originating on film keeps all options open insofar as high definition (and particularly the inevitable visual digital) systems are concerned.

As more TV programming goes to film, the work of the Colorist and the Video Editor seems certain to proliferate.

THE FILM LABORATORY

As camera people, it is a good idea to have at least a conversational knowledge of what happens to the film we shoot when it enters the domain of the motion picture film laboratory.

The film lab is the processor of, and often the repository for, exposed and developed negative and positive film stocks. Extreme care and attention in every phase of the handling and processing of the precious camera negatives in order to preserve and, when necessary, enhance the images placed there by the Director of Photography, is the fundamental concern of the film lab and its personnel.

The exposed film represents a considerable investment in production time, studio sets, and the performing and technical talent who collaborated to produce the latent images on the camera negative. Careless handling, resulting in damage or loss of the negative or negative images, inevitably results in costly solutions, provided reshooting is possible.

Basically, a roll of exposed camera negative goes through the following process when it arrives at the film lab: First, it is logged into receiving and sent to negative development, then, either routed to sonic cleaning and to video transfer or to negative assembly, then to color timing, on to sonic cleaning, to printing, to positive development, to positive assembly, and finally, to either shipping or to vault storage.

Receiving. The function of receiving is to carefully enter into the facilities computer data bank all pertinent information about the delivered exposed film stock and to prepare a routing sheet for the material for its trip through the lab.

Exposed film is delivered to the receiving department of the film lab, where the date and time received, the client's name, the title and/or number of the production, the type of film, the number of rolls, the camera number for each roll, special development instructions and requests for damage checks noted on the Camera Reports, attached to each can of film, are logged into the facilities computer data files. The negative then goes to . . .

Negative Developing. Order and tracking comprise the shepherding process. Each delivered batch of film cans are grouped by company, production, shoot date and camera roll number, as noted on the attached Camera Report forms. Rolls to be forced-developed (pushed or pulled) or flashed are kept separate.

During **the darkroom phase,** the Negative Developer takes the canned film into the darkroom, opens each can, removes its roll of exposed film and assembles each roll, end to end, into a larger roll while hand-checking the film edges for tears and other damage. Any torn edges and/or perforations are repaired prior to putting the film through the processor.

The film is placed on the feed end of the processing machine, attached to the leader or the end of the preceding roll of negative, on its way into the pre-bath, then past the REM jet removal unit, on into the developer, and through the stop (development) solution, which completes the darkroom phase of the developing process.

Film requiring special push or pull processing will be sent through the processor after its linear flow speed is reset to accommodate the special developing requirements.

From the stop solution, the film emerges **out of the darkroom** into normal room light for the remainder of the trip through the processor. The film goes through a wash, then a ferricyanide or "UL" bleach solution, another wash, then a fixer, another wash, a final rinse, then into the dryer and off the processor. At this point, the Negative Developer rolls the processed film onto a takeup, identifying, breaking down and carefully reassembling the film by camera roll number, then separating and placing each roll in its respective can and noting the time and date the film came off the processor, then on to negative assembly, or to . . .

Video Transfer. At this point, film destined for video transfer is routed directly to sonic cleaning and then on to the transfer house where the negative will be transferred and colorized (timed) in telecine to 1″ video tape.

Negative Assembly. The developed negative scheduled for printing to film is then leadered, measured and identified by the Negative Assembler who then fills out a daily work order form specifying the type of print—color or B&W, blowup or reduction, wet or dry, low/high contrast, dupe negative or interpositive—to be made from the negative. The negative then goes to . . .

Color Timing. For the timing process, the negative is run through a color analyzer, a telecine device with video monitor and three knobs, one each for red, green and blue values, with intensity increments on each knob of 1 through 50 (a range equivalent to approximately five stops), representing printer lights. If a best-light/one-light print is desired, the Timer, in viewing the monitor with the negative in place, adjusts the color displayed by turning each knob until a combined and satisfactory setting of the RGB values is visually arrived at. These settings are then inputted into the facilities computer system. Normally one-light prints have a best light for each film emulsion used—one-light values for each of the following: For interiors, exteriors, night-for-night, day-for-night, process and special effects work. For a properly exposed negative, the one-light RGB values generally will fall between the mid-20s and mid-30s. From then on all daily printing will use those established one-light settings for that particular production.

For the Director of Photography who wishes to maintain control over, and consistency of, the imaging process from concept and production through preparation of the release print, it is essential that he or she be present during the timing of the cut negative (or at the colorizing process during telecine transfer to tape).

Scene-by-scene timing, usually done for intermediate or release printing, will sample the first frame of the first scene and of each incoming scene in order to set the

RGB for each scene at a level which will optimize the color rendition of each scene and insure consistency from scene to scene and throughout the entire length of the print entity. Each setting is inputted to the computer which stores the color balance settings and the exact footage and frame for each scene change on the roll of negative to be printed. The computer then outputs two punched printing control tapes—one for RGB and another for footage and frames. The negative then goes to . . .

Sonic Cleaning. The negative is placed on a conveyor-type film transport and is put through a sonically vibrating solvent which removes any foreign particles from the film surfaces. Dried, the negative, accompanied by its punched control tapes, now goes to . . .

Printing. The negative is placed in the printer and is bi-packed with the print stock. The punched tapes are inserted into the tape reader on the printer. The printer will properly expose the print raw stock through the timed negative and will also print the sound, if any, on the edge of the film stock. The negative is sent to shipping for pick up or storage and the exposed print stock in the printer film magazines goes to . . .

Positive Developing. During **the darkroom phase,** the Positive Developer takes the magazines holding exposed film into the darkroom, opens each magazine, removes its roll of exposed film and assembles each roll into a larger roll. Any torn edges and/or perforations are repaired prior to putting the film through the processor.

The film is placed on the feed end of the processing machine, attached to the leader or to the end of the preceding roll of positive, on its way into the pre-bath, then past the REM jet removal unit, on into the developer, and through the stop solution, which completes the darkroom phase of the developing process.

From the stop solution, the film emerges **out of the darkroom** into normal room light for the remainder of the trip through the processor. The film goes through a wash, then the first fixer, another wash, then a bleach accelerator preceding a persulfate bleach solution, another wash where film needing sound track development is transported through a sound track developer applicator and a wash box, after which it then returns to enter the second fixer, another wash, a final rinse/stabilizer, then into the dryer and off the processor. At this point, the Positive Developer rolls the processed film onto a takeup, identifying, breaking down and carefully reassembling the film by printer roll number, then separating and placing each roll in a film can, noting the time the film came off the processor, and then on to . . .

Positive Assembly. The developed print is then leadered, measured and identified by the Positive Assembler, who then enters this information on the daily work order form, verifying the type of print that was made and whether the film is to be mounted on reels or cores for the customer. The film is then projected at high speed, during which it is inspected for any quality imperfections. At this time, the print, or prints, will be mounted on cores or reels, as specified by the customer. The film is placed in appropriate containers and is then sent to . . .

Shipping. The Shipping Clerk collects and sends all paperwork to the billing department and the film is shipped, stored or held for pick up as per instructions from the customer.

Special appreciation to Bert Leibee of Technicolor Labs for his constructive input.

PRODUCING & PRODUCTION MANAGEMENT

Producing is about gathering the wherewithal—concept, scenario, finances, creative, technical and administrative personnel—necessary to develop, produce, complete and market a cinematic product. Producing takes strong belief in the project and its outcome and a sense of dedication, determination and perseverance to gather the details and see it through every phase from concept through pre-production, production, post-production and marketing.

The production management team is there to support the Producer's vision and day-to-day decisions, to develop and maintain a budget and shooting schedule, to plan and arrange the logistics, to provide the Producer constant feedback on the progress of the production, and to help keep the work on schedule and within budget.

With a more complete picture of the many responsibilities of the Producer and his or her production management team, the extent and importance of the collaborative effort becomes clearer and more meaningful.

PRODUCERS

What with the proliferation of people receiving Producer credit on most film and video sitcoms, some episodics and a few features, one needs a scorecard to tell who is doing what for whom and when (not to mention, why). Producer credits are in danger of becoming meaningless.

It was simple in the not-so-olden days. A Producer produced the picture or series and got due credit for the effort. If two people equally shared in the responsibilities and duties, the Co-Producer credit was given each person.

During the halcyon days of movie-making, the studio heads (the movie moguls) took very personal interest in all their product and in every aspect of the production process. The major studio system was in full sway. Each major studio had its stable of salaried Producers, Directors, Writers, actors, Cameramen, Department Heads, and technical personnel. What made this possible was each major studio owning its own theater chains, thus controlling the distribution and exhibition of its product. This arrangement, along with enforced block-booking of "A" and "B" (high- and low-budgeted) product into the independent theaters and chains, assured that each picture would make a profit and that firm economic control of the above-the-line talent would be maintained. With a more-or-less guaranteed cash flow, having the money to produce more product was not a problem for the majors during this period. On the other hand, independent producers had a difficult time getting their wares into theaters.

Then, in 1956, came the so-called "**Consent Decree**" which, in effect, separated the major production studios from their theaters—production from exhibition— and the studio system began to change drastically. Without the previously available and assured financing which the majors had enjoyed, the Producer now had to scurry around, getting a package (Writer, script, principal actors, Director, budget and a distribution plan) assembled to present to a studio head or bank or consortium for financing consideration, and *then* see the project through to completion with no guarantee that the project would be financially successful. Thus, the age of the independent Producer was ushered in. All the while, television production practices (key Writers were being accorded Producer credit for "producing" their writings) were having their effect upon Producer credits on programming made especially for release on television.

Today, there are approximately eight classifications within the motion picture Producing Category. The hierarchy is as follows: Executive Producer, Producer, Co-Producer, Associate Producer, Supervising Producer, Segment Producer, Coordinating Producer and Line Producer. Even now, with some imagination (and financial and/or ego incentive) several more Producer titles could be developed.

The Executive Producer. The Executive Producer is generally the studio or production company head and is responsible for all product output bearing the studio logo. He or she approves each project (and each phase thereof) and the creative personnel involved (the Producer, Writer, Director and cast), arranges and controls the financing, production plan, marketing and distribution, and follows the progress of each project through the acquisition and development, pre-production, production and post-production (including the marketing and distribution) phases, replacing above-the-line creative personnel and even pulling the plug on a production when necessary.

The Producer. The Producer has the responsibility of putting a production project together and seeing it through from beginning to end, from inception through completion and, often, exhibition. If working for a major studio or an independent production company with multiple concurrent production in place, the Producer is responsible to, and works under, the Executive Producer. If an independent, single-production company, doing it all, including: Arranging the financing; developing a story; hiring a Writer to prepare a scenario; assembling a budget; hiring a Director, sub-Producer(s), Production Designer/Art Director, actors, Cinematographer, Music Composer and Editor; supervising, coordinating and controlling every facet and every phase of the complex motion picture-making process.

The Co-Producer. The Co-Producer shares the overall responsibilities and duties with the Producer and thereby shares the credit.

The Associate Producer. The Associate Producer is directly responsible to the Producer. This credit is given when the Producer needs assistance in watching over certain specific aspects of the production process, such as financing or accounting, or to coordinate certain aspects of special visual effects, second unit, location management, ADR for a foreign version, or the editing or re-recording sound mixing processes.

The Supervising Producer. The Supervising Producer is directly responsible to the Producer and oversees the activities of those producing discrete portions of the overall production. It is a title often used for episodics or sitcoms as indicating a special area of production expertise and/or responsibility during production (supervising those producing second unit, special effects and/or stunts) or post-production (supervising those responsible for editing, ADR, Foley or final re-recording sound mixing).

The Segment Producer. A Segment Producer is responsible to the Producer and is directly responsible to a functioning Coordinating Producer for producing one or more portions of multiple-portioned production in an efficient manner consistent with the visual look desired by the Director for the particular show and/or the established look of the series.

The Coordinating Producer. The Coordinating Producer is directly responsible to the Producer for coordinating the functions and efforts of two or more Segment Producers in order to help achieve a consistent and unified aesthetic look of an episode, show and/or series.

The Line Producer. The Line Producer is directly responsible to the Producer, or to the Supervising Producer, if so charged. This is a title often given the Unit Production Manager for having done a particularly good job managing logistics and the shooting schedule, keeping the Production on time and under budget.

Producer titles for television film or video programming (following a television tradition) are often given Writers on sitcoms as an added monetary and recognition incentive symbolic of their on-going writing contributions to the show. But no matter how Producer titles are shared and fragmented for television or theatrical programming, there remain the basic responsibilities and duties which must be attended to (by one or more people) in order to efficiently and effectively produce a viable result.

Producer Responsibilities. The Producer is responsible for protecting the financial investment in the production by selecting, and surrounding him/herself with, key collaborators who will contribute creatively and technically to the development, production, completion and marketing of a viable and financially successful cinematic product.

Producer Duties. In **Phase 1 (development)** the Producer does or oversees the following: Acquires and/or develops a story idea; hires a Writer to write a screenplay; develops a package by getting commitments from key principal actors with proven box office appeal, a Director with a good track record of successful pictures, shows or programs brought in at or under budget, and a Director of Photography with similar credentials; prepares a preliminary shooting schedule and budget for the proposed project; prepares a detailed proposal with potential costs, a release, marketing and distribution plan along with a profit projection; presents the package—script, cast, Director, Art Director or Production Designer, Cinematographer, budget and a marketing/release plan—to prospective and appropriate financial sources for funding consideration.

Once funding has been accomplished, the Producer begins **Phase 2 (pre-production planning)** duties: Enlarges and augments the administrative production staff; sees that the production is fully protected by legal advice and insurance coverage; signs with unions and guilds; signs up the lead actors and supporting cast; signs on Writer(s) to refine the screenplay; selects and hires a Director; hires a Production Manager to refine the budget and prepare a viable shooting schedule; hires a Production Designer/Art Director to start planning and begin execution of set and overall production design; signs the Director of Photography; hires a Costume Designer to start work on costume design and execution; hires a Composer to start work on the musical score; arranges studio facilities for shooting; hires a Location Manager to scout for, find and recommend location sites appropriate for the production; completes the casting process; approves the hiring of technical personnel; hires an Editor, or editorial service; makes arrangements with a film laboratory for processing, printing and negative cutting, and with a sound transfer facility; engages a post-production service for transfer of film images to video tape; has numerous meetings with the creative and administrative staffs requiring decisions that will affect either budget and/or shooting schedule.

Phase 3 **(production)** begins the process of principal photography and the following duties: Regularly reviews budget expenditures and shooting schedule status; views dailies and rough cuts; coordinates publicity releases; coordinates the shooting schedule of special visual effects and/or second unit photography with that of the first unit principal photography; sees that all category departments are keeping within their allotted budget at all times; approves or denies any category departmental requests for additional personnel or matériel; hires or fires staff, cast or crew, as necessary; makes decisions as to change of schedule or location due to weather, cast illness or replacement, or other reason; has more meetings with creative staff, production management and key technical personnel requiring decisions which affect budget and/or shooting schedule.

Phase 4 **(post-production)** is when the following duties apply: Continues the publicity campaign and marketing plans; sees that the editing process is keeping pace with the scheduled release date; approves the final cut; coordinates the completion and delivery of all elements—special visual effects, animation, second unit, inserts, stock footage opticals and title art—to editorial for inclusion in the finished product; arranges facilities for music recording and re-recording, ADR, Foley and the final mix dubbing; arranges sneak previews as needed; acquires additional funding, as necessary; sets exhibition schedule; sees that the negative and printing elements are stored properly and safely; orders release prints and press kits.

During *Phase 5* **(marketing—release/distribution/exhibition)**, the Producer does the following: Continues careful coordination of the publicity campaign with the marketing plans; makes deals for ancillary markets income; sees that all rental and lease items are returned and that all bills are paid; checks final status of budget expenditures; checks box office reports and distribution income; makes provision for residual payments; prepares regular status reports for the financial sources during the economic life of the picture.

Summing Up. As you can see, the Producer has myriad details to attend to, and must carefully select a contingent of collaborators to assist in preparing, producing and delivering a cinematic product which will entertain audiences and return its investment—along with a profit for good measure.

ABOUT BUDGETING, STAFFING AND COST-ACCOUNTING

In the early days of movie-making, everyone worked on a flat weekly or daily salary with no overtime pay or fringe benefits, so budgeting was a relatively simple matter. As motion pictures expanded in production time, size and production values, as unions, in establishing working rules in their agreements with producers, had their effect on crew size, job descriptions, overtime and fringe benefits, cost-accounting became an ever more important function in order to monitor and keep productions on budget.

Budgeting. A budget is broken down into **above-the-line** costs (creative and artistic personnel and expenses) and **below-the-line** costs (technical personnel, matériel purchases and rentals, and running expenses). On a low-budget picture the average proportion of above- to below-the-line costs might be close to one-to-one. On a higher-budget picture or series, the ratio might grow to two-to-one, four-to-one, or very much more, depending upon Producer, Writer, Director and starring actor(s) fees and/or salaries and/or guaranties and/or participation points and other amenities and perks. Below-the-line costs, insofar as production employes are concerned, tend to remain fairly fixed. The real variable is above-the-line costs which can vary from union scale to amounts well in excess of that amount.

Staffing. From the point of view of the Producer/Employer, the only justification for the addition of production personnel has been to save money (1) by helping expedite the production process by speeding up the camera-ready process or (2) by sharing certain duties which would cut down the risk and/or rate of error (and hence, expensive reshoots). From the viewpoint of the camera crew, having an Assistant help with certain duties saves crew energy and allows for much more efficient and accurate work output. The bottom-line questions should always be: Will the addition of an Assistant (or a piece of equipment) save actual (cost-per -hour) production cost or raise it? If raised, will the quality of the production suffer or improve? If improved, has the added cost been worth it?

Cost-Accounting. Cost-accounting is very important to the health of the motion picture industry. Financing is the life blood of this business. Some might say that whoever holds the financial spigot has creative control. But too often the budget sheets are examined for cost, item by item, without considering the impact which that item (person or piece of equipment) might have on **cost-per-production-hour**. Items are often arbitrarily reduced in number or eliminated in order to "save money" on the budget breakdown, without considering the full impact of that action on the overall pace of the production.

It has been said that at least one major studio will go to any expense to save a dollar (on the budget breakdown). For example, when a Western dolly was used in the morning on the backlot exteriors for a sitcom, production management wouldn't spring for a crab dolly for the interior stage work to be done that afternoon. As a result, the company saved about $50 in equipment rental (on paper), but because the Western dolly didn't track well, the additional takes took a half hour longer which translated into several hundred dollars of added expense. It's always the end of the shooting day, the overtime hours, when production time becomes very expensive and that is when reimbursement in full is made for shortchanging the immediate needs of the production.

Another case of misplaced attention was the Production Accountant (an apparent film production neophyte) in examining the Call Sheets of current productions on the lot who asked who PeeWee and Hustler were and why were they on call every single day, on several productions simultaneously. [For the uninitiated, PeeWee and Hustler are camera dollies.]

Lack of knowledge of, and seeming disinterest in, production processes and requirements (which vary with each production project) is largely responsible for the present state of affairs.

Budget items contributing to the cost-per-production-hour are: All rental items, all purchase items, all salaries and wages paid, all expenses and reimbursements laid out, including taxes and labor fringe benefits. Only those items expended and personnel employed **during actual production** should be factored into the cost-per-production-hour figure, which is derived by dividing total production costs by the total number of production hours scheduled. For example, a $6 million production scheduled for six sixty-hour weeks in the studio and on local locations with production time costs of $4 million comes to approximately $11,000 per production hour.

Once the cost-per-production-hour is determined, it becomes a very important tool in weighing the advantages and disadvantages of hiring an extra Assistant or so or renting a piece of equipment. If an extra Assistant at approximately $1,200 per 60-hour week (plus about $500 per week for food and fringes) saves the production just fifteen minutes a day, hiring that Assistant has saved the production company approximately $12,000 for that entire week. Even if the Assistant saves only fifteen minutes cumulatively during a week, the company has saved more than $1,000 above the cost of that Assistant for that week. The same consideration applies when evaluating a useful piece of production equipment.

Since it seems that unit costs are presently the focus of attention in production accounting, and since cost-per-production-hour should be a principal criterion in judging item-by-item expenditures, it does not seem logical that production management would consider (let alone propose) having a Director of Photography operating the film camera in addition to essential lighting duties and responsibilities. Certainly those two functions cannot be handled as well and in the same amount of time as each function handled by a separate person. Having one person do two jobs does not save production money. Considered from a strictly cost-accounting cost-per-production-hour point of view, the actual time it takes to do the two jobs should be the determining factor; combining the two functions will not save a production either time or money.

Cost-per-*pre*-production-hour averages about one-tenth that of the cost-per-production-hour. **Cost-per-*post*-production-hour** varies, depending upon the number and type of optical, digital or animation effects and whether film or electronic editing procedures are followed.

In the meantime, perhaps more attention should be paid by all concerned to the ballooning above-the-line costs.

A LOOK AT PRODUCTION MANAGEMENT

The purpose and principal function of production management is to accurately estimate and then to tightly control and account for all cost items (personnel wages and matériel rentals and purchases, etc) utilized in a production project, making sure that each expenditure is approved and does not exceed the planned-for limit. Production management is the official guardian and caretaker of budgetary finances. (Of course, it is the Production Accountants who neatly place all figures in columnar categories for convenient access and reporting purposes.) It is the Production Manager, the Producer's detail person, who sees that the detailed proposed production schedule (time) and expenditures (money), as represented in the shooting schedule and budget, are adequate to serve the production needs at hand.

The classifications which make production management function are headed by the Producer's principal line representative and supervisor, the Production Manager, who in turn may under certain circumstances be assisted by the Unit Production Manager and the Location Manager.

Production Manager Responsibilities. The Production Manager (PM) is directly responsible to the Producer, is the Producer's representative and works in close cooperation with the Unit Production Manager and the First Assistant Director. The PM is the **behind-the-scenes expediter** and is responsible for arranging and scheduling all production elements—cast, crew, matériel, food, lodging and transportation—in the most efficient manner practicable and arranging payment therefor in a timely manner.

Production Manager Duties. The Production Manager does the following: Reads and analyzes the script; budgets production projects—estimating total budget based on itemized categorical or departmental estimates, plus a duration-of-shooting estimate; prepares a comprehensive categorical/departmental breakdown of the approved script from continuity tear sheets and a shooting schedule strip board for budgetary and production scheduling purposes; schedules productions; requests and/or hires production personnel of the various film and/or video craft technical specialties required for the production(s); (if the Company is signator to a craft union contract) determines that each production employee is a Union member in current good standing, operating in the classification granted by the Union, and available for work during the period set for employment; (if the Company is signator to a performers guild contract) determines that each actor is a Guild member in current good standing; demonstrates a comprehensive understanding of Union and Guild working rules and of the responsibilities and duties for the technical craft categories and classifications; has a thorough understanding of contracts signed with performers, particularly those sections affecting scheduling and perks granted; arranges for selection, clearances and permits regarding location shooting sites, supervising the preparation thereof; approves cast and crew start slips, time records, pay vouchers, deal memos, box rentals and reimbursement (mileage, per diem and cash pay-outs) authorizations; sees that necessary contracts, clearances and permits are prepared, signed and adhered to; selects, arranges for and supervises preparation of the sound stage(s); orders sets and props built and dressed; expedites and coordinates the work of all departments at all times; prepares the production board, arranging scenes and sequences to be shot in the most expeditious, efficient and economical order practicable; gives daily notification to staff, cast, atmosphere, stand-ins and crew regarding work calls, scenes to be shot, sets and/or locations to be used, as well as the operational matériel required; sees that supplies and matériel are procured and rentals returned; arranges transportation for staff, cast, crew and matériel; arranges for food and lodging for staff, cast and crew; authorizes all purchase orders and expenditures; disburses Company funds and/or petty cash for the production project(s).

The Production Manager should know the cost-per-hour for pre-production and post-production time on every production project, but especially for the very costly production time, in order to make educated decisions regarding the economical impact on the budget of whether or not to add personnel or a piece of production equipment and for what period of time.

Unit Production Manager Responsibilities. The Unit Production Manager (UPM) is directly responsible to the Production Manager and is responsible for helping carry out the production plan (as set for a production project by the PM) in the most efficient, cost-effective manner practicable.

UPM Duties. The duties of the Unit Production Manager are essentially those of the Production Manager while the UPM is on a production project under the supervision of the PM, such as an assignment to one of several television shows at a studio, or managing a second unit.

The UPM keeps the Production Manager currently apprised of the status— on, over, or under schedule as well as time and cost overruns—of the production project to which he or she has been assigned.

Independent Productions. In the independent production field, features, series, miniseries and specials are each managed by a Production Manager, with a Unit

Production Manager being brought in to handle second unit production.

Major Studio production. In the major studio process, wherein several projects may be shooting simultaneously, a Unit Production Manager is usually assigned to each television series, miniseries, pilot or special under the supervision of a Production Manager.

Production Manager Expectations. The Production Manager is responsible for hiring most of the production crew—some with the recommendation of their respective department head. The PM is primarily interested in putting together a competent crew of caring professionals who will work well together, under pressure when necessary, and who will help keep the production process on schedule and within budgetary constraints. Both the PM and UPM are ever alert for personnel who fit in well and help make the production process flow smoothly, effectively and efficiently.

Summing Up. Money/time/people management is what production management is all about. The Production Manager needs a good working knowledge of all three elements in order to function effectively plus, of course, a thorough understanding of the picture-making process, including the responsibilities and duties of the various crafts personnel involved in that process.

Special thanks to Rusty Meek (PM) for his constructive input.

THE LOCATION MANAGER

Selecting appropriate location shooting sites is a task as important to a production as casting performers. Knowing where available and appropriate shooting sites are located, then making arrangements for permission to shoot on those premises, and finally, seeing that those arrangements are lived up to by all parties (and/or renegotiating when necessary in order to help keep everything and everyone on track), require an expertise which has become ever more valuable to a film or video production company.

This function falls to a very important and relied-upon member of the production management team—the Location Manager.

Location Manager Responsibilities. The Location Manager is directly responsible to, and reports to, the Production Manager and is responsible for locating and making arrangements for appropriate location production sites, both interior and/or exterior, in order to help facilitate pre-production scouting and the ensuing production process.

Location Manager Duties. The Location Manager does the following: Reads the script, noting geographical locations which are cited, along with the time of year and day during which the action occurs; consults with the **decision group**—the Producer, Director, Production Designer and/or Art Director, Director of Photography and Production Manager—as to any parameters they might have in mind regarding the geographical location, the polar orientation, the architectural style and the physical dimensions of the shooting site, both exterior and interior; prepares for preliminary location scouting by researching appropriate publications and pictorial files for potentially usable shooting sites; plans preliminary scouting trips for the purpose of selecting several possible shooting sites which most closely satisfy the parameters set by the decision group during preliminary conferences; arranges the itinerary, transportation, food and lodging for all personnel involved in all scouting trips; personally inspects each proposed shooting site, shooting polaroids and/or stills thereof showing north, south, east, west views of the exterior and surroundings and of each side of each structure and of each wall of each interior room to be utilized; prepares a planned layout drawing of the property and a floor and elevation plan of the structures to be utilized, indicating the location of doors, windows and skylights, practical electrical fixtures and outlets and the main power supply terminal, noting the voltage and amperage available; notes all dimensions of the exterior and interior (those areas to be utilized and/or photographed), the polar orientation of the property and of the structures thereon, the path the sun tracks across the property, approximate time of sunrise and sunset at the time of year planned for production at each site, area and seasonal weather and wind patterns, distance to transportation terminals, food and lodging accommodations, and the state of the roads connecting the location sites thereto; lists all conditions placed on the use of the property by the owner(s) as well as federal, state and/or local regulations concerning the use of public property, streets and walkways; arranges all location data in appropriate order for presentation to the decision group for its collective consideration and selection of specific locations for the principal scouting group; leads the scouting group, which often consists of the Director, the Production Designer and/or Art Director, and the Director of Photography.

Once the decision has been made regarding the location shooting sites, the Location Manager firms up the arrangements made with owners and local and state officials for utilizing the shooting sites and their environs, such as contractual understandings and permits—among which are fees and/or rental/lease arrangements, duration of use, access to the property and its structures, care and responsibility for furnishings and accoutrements, and liability insurance; negotiating extensions for location rights when production shooting will not be completed within the agreed-to time period or when additional shooting will be required at a later time.

When shooting at each location site has been completed and the location(s) released by the Production Manager, the Location Manager sees that the location sites are returned to agreed-upon order and condition. A Location Manager generally works through pre-production and during production until shooting at each location site has been completed and the location sites have been put back in agreed-to order and condition.

Summing Up. Discovering, selecting and recommending appropriate location shooting sites and the management thereof is a skill which contributes greatly to the collaborative effort of making a film or video production successful and effective; the Location Manager is a key contributor to a smooth, efficient and effective location shoot.

PRODUCTION TYPES

There are several types of productions, each requiring a particular production technique, from single-camera features, episodics, documentaries or TV commercials to film or video multiple-camera audience sitcoms, soap operas, specials and sporting events.

It behooves a film or video craftsperson who is interested in remaining busy and advancing in his or her craft to know as much about these varying production techniques as possible. The opportunity to work in any of these production genres can emerge at any time. With persistence and perseverance, a competent and dedicated craftsperson can learn, adapt to and advance in any of these specialized procedures. Preparation is the key to opportunity.

COMPARING FILM SITCOMS AND EPISODICS

There are substantial differences between operating on a single camera episodic show and on a multiple camera situation comedy, just as there are substantial differences in operating on a film sitcom and on a video sitcom.

Let's consider the differences between operative camera work on a single camera episodic show and on a multi-camera film sitcom.

Number of Cameras. A single camera can go its own way, unimpeded by other cameras, to get its assigned shot from the best angle possible.

On a multiple camera sitcom, filmed before an audience, the cameras need to be carefully choreographed in order to avoid playing bumper-cars during a take. This is where the Technical Coordinator comes into play, and earns his or her keep in advising the Dolly Grips over headset intercom when to move the cameras to the next position.

Coverage. On **episodics**, the single camera usually takes the wide establishing/master shot first, then is moved in for medium and tighter group shots, and finally, with a longer lens up, goes for the opposing closeups. A second camera—"B" camera—is frequently used at the same time with the principal camera for added coverage in order to assure matching action, and is either paired with the main camera while using a longer lens or is set to get the closeup which opposes that being taken by the "A" camera. Multiple cameras are used when shooting broad or violent action sequences involving numerous people, livestock, rolling or floating stock, vehicles, aircraft, and those scenes involving destruction of an elaborate set, and the like, in order to cover the essentials of the action taking place. Episodics are generally shot out of sequence.

Multi-camera usage on **sitcoms** is an attempt at blanket coverage of the action. Most often the center camera(s) obtain the wider angle master coverage for major movement or group shots while the two wing cameras get opposing overs (over-the-shoulder shots) and closeups.

Depending upon whether three or four cameras are used for a sitcom, no one camera will be used much more than for 25% to 40% of the final show length, whereas the total responsibility for overall coverage is, of course, on that one camera in a single camera show, when a "B" camera is not used. Therefore, during a sitcom filming, every portion of each take need not be perfect (although the Director and Script Supervisor should be apprised if there has been a coverage problem during the take), because another camera usually has the action covered from a usable angle. For example, the coverage by the master camera(s) which hold the wide angles is generally used for crossing movements and group mixes, while the coverage from the wing cameras is cut to when the movement stops for face-to-face dialogue. Planned and unplanned pick-up shots take care of those closeups and other angles not covered during certain portions of a scene (which may run as long as eight or nine minutes with as many as six or eight principal players involved in the action). Audience sitcoms are always filmed in sequence, which doesn't hold true for block-and-shoot sitcoms—or episodics, for that matter.

Camera Movement. On **single camera shows**, camera moves can often be finessed that cannot be easily done (if at all) on multi-camera sitcoms. For example, pan/tilt, zoom or rack-focus moves, when used as transitional devices for scene changes, can be planned and executed quite precisely on a single camera show, whereas there is little time (or inclination) to match, perfect and execute such moves in a multi-camera sitcom.

The added production value of a **crane shot** is common to the single camera show, but rare indeed in a multi-camera sitcom. The design of both the sets and the lighting and the restricted shooting area of a sitcom pretty much preclude any but the smallest of studio cranes, when it is possible to use one.

Lighting. Lighting for a **single camera** is constantly adjusted for the camera angle which best captures the facial contours, the direction of the look, the expression, the gesture, the action, the composition and the mood for each shot setup. However, lighting for **multi-camera** sitcoms is of necessity a compromise. With the two wing cameras spread wide, at times describing a 160° angle relative to the respectively framed subject, the modeling is set and the several back-cross key lamps must be carefully diffused and masked in order to avoid lens flares. The relatively low-hung front fill lighting on sitcoms limit both high camera rises and moving a camera very far into a set in order to avoid camera shadows falling onto the settings, set props and/or actors.

The recent technique of bouncing **all** the front fill light off 4´x8´ foam core boards softens the light to such an extent that it, in effect, wraps around any intervening object such as a camera, thereby creating no discernible shadow. With this type of front lighting, the cameras can be moved well into the set when necessary.

Actor Positioning. Actors are expected to hit their marks, uncover for the camera(s) and stay out of another actor's key light, whether on a single camera episodic or multi-camera sitcom. When they don't, they either block each other's key light, thereby casting an unattractive shadow on each other, cover each other from camera view, and/or disrupt the planned compositional arrangement. Depending upon the Director's preference, the Camera Operator can advise either the Director or the offending actor as to the problem involved and how best to position themselves to avoid the problem.

Prop Repositioning. Resetting props and set dressing is a common occurrence whether single or multiple camera shows. A foreground object may be too intrusive or may block some essential action or camera movement, or a background prop or set dressing may appear to grow out of the head of an actor standing or sitting downstage of that prop or set dressing. (Just be sure to check with the other Camera Operators before having the offending piece moved.)

Operator and Director of Photography Perspectives. On a single-camera show the Camera Operator can be working either under the constant control of the Director of Photography or with the Director in setting the shots (setups) which are then lighted by the Director of Photography (as in the British system), depending upon how the DP wishes things handled.

On a multi-camera sitcom, the Director of Photography concentrates on the lighting and seldom gets involved in camera or actor positioning unless lighting is being affected.

Operator-to-Operator Perspective. Some single camera episodic shows carry a second active camera and Camera Operator for double camera coverage throughout the show. The cameras are usually positioned by the Director or by the Director of Photography, and placed in such a way as not to interfere with camera operation or get into each other's field of view and still hold enough difference in position, perspective and sizing to afford a pleasing intercut.

With multiple camera sitcoms, a great deal of cooperation is required among the Camera Operators. The wing cameras have to pull back a bit and go with a longer portion of the zoom lens in order to clear the field of view of the master camera(s). In general, there is much more give-and-take adjustment required among the Camera Operators on a multi-camera sitcom than on an episodic using multiple cameras.

Operator and First Assistant Perspectives. Compared to single camera shows there is much more communication (largely soft talk) between the Camera Operator and First Assistant Camera Operator during rehearsals and takes on sitcoms. This is partly because of the long and complex takes in sitcoms, and partly because the sitcom performers do not always precisely hit and stay on their marks, so quick adjustments in lens sizing and/or focus have to be made in order to avoid retakes.

Operator and Dolly Grip Perspectives. The same would apply to communication between the Camera Operator and Dolly Grip on multi-camera sitcoms, although such communication is usually signalled by the Operator by hand, finger, elbow or body English, which translates to the following principal adjustments: To adjust the dolly left, right, in or out, arm up or down, speed up or slow down, start or stop, get ready, no, okay.

Summary. The principal difference between filmed episodics and filmed sitcoms is the greater number of active cameras being used on each take for sitcoms, on which are filmed fewer but longer-running takes with relatively complex camera/dolly moves, in sequence, while making constant adjustments to accommodate any actor mark-missing. Cooperative flexibility among sitcom Camera Operators is expected and essential.

COMPARING MULTI-CAMERA FILM AND VIDEO SITCOMS

Just as there are substantial differences in operating a film camera and a video camera, there are equally substantial differences in operating a camera on a film or video audience sitcom. By comparing several aspects of multiple-camera film and video audience sitcoms, we can focus on some of these differences for those who may be interested in moving over from one discipline to the other.

The Camera. The **film camera** is a *mechanical* marvel that moves film intermittently through a gate, past an aperture, behind a lens to accept a latent image exposure on a chemically light-sensitive emulsion. With a fully loaded 1,000 foot 35mm film magazine on each studio camera, filming at a frame rate of 90 feet per minute at the standard sound speed of 24 fps, a scene up to eleven minutes in length can be photographed without a break.

The **video camera** is an *electronic* marvel that converts an optical image coming through the lens and forming on the surface of a picture tube (CRT) or charge-coupled device (CCD), which is then transformed into an electronic signal which wends its way through a network of signal modifiers—correcting color, enhancing image outline, adjusting brightness and contrast—and is then transduced in the picture monitor(s) to an optical image while at the same time being recorded onto magnetic video tape. Studio video on-line shooting time is limited to the amount of tape loaded onto a video tape recorder (VTR) which is normally 90 minutes of one-inch tape per reel at 30 fps, but can be either one- or two-hour reel length, as desired.

The Operative Film Camera Crew and Support Personnel. The personnel manning a film camera are: A **Camera Operator** to manipulate the geared head wheels in order to frame and follow the action; a **First Assistant Camera Operator** to mark actor positions, tape, slate, size, follow focus, load and unload film into and out of the camera; a **Second Assistant Camera Operator** to set the clap sticks and/or electronic time-code slate later used by the Editor for synchronizing the film which has moved through the three to four cameras; and a **Dolly Grip** to mark dolly positions, move the dolly and raise or lower the riser arm during a take. Supporting the operative camera crew are: A **Loader** to load and download film magazines used for filming the show; and the **Film Laboratory Personnel** who assemble, develop and prepare the negative for printing and/or transfer to video tape.

The Video Camera Setup. The studio video camera, mounted on a friction head and mobile pedestal, is manned during rehearsals and takes by a **Camera Operator** who pans and tilts, sizes and focuses the zoom lens, while trucking and also on occasion raising or lowering the camera on the pedestal—a veritable one-man band. Directly supporting the video Camera Operator is the **Utility Person** who sets up and wraps camera equipment and cable, clears and dresses the video cable (which connects each camera to the camera control unit—CCU) from the operational area around each camera. Supporting the video-imaging process behind the scenes are: A **Video Controller (VC)** who monitors and makes fine-tuned adjustments (often in close consultation with the **Director of Photography—DP)** to insure the quality of the electronic image; the **Video Tape Operators (VTOs),** normally two who load, operate and unload the video tape recorders (one for each studio camera and one for the switched, intercut on-line version plus a 3/4 inch VTR on-line back-up); the **Technical Director (TD),** who is in charge of the technical video personnel and who does the camera switching, fading, dissolving, wiping, chroma-keying and other electronic matte and applied visual effects; and a **Maintenance Engineer** to keep the system operational.

Camera Coordination. Film sitcoms have a **Technical Coordinator (TC)** who directs the Dolly Grips over RF headset intercom when and to what mark to move each camera. The camera positions for given compositions are set by the **Director** during camera blocking. Numbered tape marks are placed on the stage floor by each **Dolly Grip** for his or her respective dolly, while the **Camera Operator** makes notes regarding who or what is to be framed and sets the sizing for that composition, and the **First Assistant Camera Operator** tapes, marks and records the measured distance(s) from the camera to each marked position for each actor as well as noting the focal length setting for the zoom lens at each dolly position.

During a **video sitcom**, the **Associate Director (AD)** calls the shot numbers (which have been designated by the **Director**), which appear on a duplicate shooting script, over PL headset intercom to alert the Camera Operators for each upcoming shot which the Director is ready to have the **Technical Director** (the **Switcher**) put on-line. Each **Camera Operator**, having received a shot list from the AD prior to on-camera rehearsals, has made a notation for each on-line shot expected of his/her camera on his or her **shot card** as to who or what should be in frame, the movement and sizing thereof, and any necessary pedestal moves, but seldom marks the floor for actor or camera positioning.

Video Monitors. An emerging trend in **film** sitcoms is to employ video-assist—a CCD video tap in the ocular system of each film camera—thereby sending a video signal by radio frequency (RF) or hard wire to a cluster of black and white monitors (one for each camera), and/or quad-split monitors, so that the framed images can be observed from the stage floor by the Director, the Technical Coordinator, the Producers/Writers and the Camera Operators (for more precisely conforming closeup image sizes framed by the wing cameras). With the video-assist set-up, a video image can be sent to the audience monitors during program filming.

In **video**, each camera has a black and white electronic viewfinder. Each camera has its own color monitor in the control room and there is usually a color floor monitor displaying either on-line shots, or in a quad split-screen configuration, showing what each camera is framing at any given time.

Cranes and Dollies. Whether film or video, there is little difference in the way cranes are used during sitcoms. In a video set-up, the **Crane Grips** and **Dolly Grips** use video monitors mounted on the equipment to facilitate the executing of moves.

Transfer to Editing. At present, nearly all sitcom film is sent to the lab for development only, then transferred via flying-spot scanner by the **Colorist** (re-sized, re-positioned and color-corrected, as necessary) to one-inch video tape, then transferred to laser disc for rapid computerized editing.

Video, if not shot on one-inch video tape, goes to one-inch and then to laser disc or to the CMX system for computerized editing.

The **Director of Photography**, whether for film or video, often sits in at this stage to oversee the colorizing and image-repositioning aspects of the transfer process.

Summary. So far as multi-camera sitcoms are concerned, video requires somewhat more equipment and personnel support in the image-capture process than does film. Film requires a great degree of cooperation and coordination among the Camera Operator, First Assistant Camera Operator and Dolly Grip in getting the shot, whereas the video camera Operator is a veritable one-man band. Because of the manpower differential, much more extensive, rapid, complex and precise moves can be made by a fully coordinated operative film camera crew using a dolly than by a video camera Operator maneuvering a mobile pedestal.

Moving Over. Moving from film camera operation to video camera operation, or vice versa, is a matter of familiarizing oneself with the equipment and production techniques of each system. In going from **film to video**, complete visual and audial concentration, a high degree of eye-ear-hand-body coordination, and a light touch on the controls are necessary to a successful transition. From **video to film**, calls for a light and sure touch on the controls and learning to rely on and coordinate the efforts of the other members of the operative camera crew.

MULTIPLE CAMERA FILM SITCOM TECHNICAL PROCEDURES

Multiple-camera film sitcoms have been around ever since Desi Arnaz successfully inaugurated the technique, with a studio audience, for "**I LOVE LUCY**" on 8 September 1951 on Stage 2 at General Service Studio. Subsequently, this half-hour comedy format style has proved to be a viable and profitable addition to prime time and syndicated television programming.

System Description. The film sitcom technique is composed of three or four 35mm (or 16mm) studio film cameras. Each 35mm camera is loaded with 1,000′ of color negative film (11 minutes of running time at 24 fps), or 2,000′ of color negative film (22 minutes of running time at 24 fps); or if 16mm, each camera is loaded with 1,200′ of color negative film (33 minutes at 24 fps). Each camera is mounted on a geared head (for smooth and exact pan-and-tilt operation) and that configuration is in turn mounted on the crab dolly riser arm. ·

A compact CCD video tap, inserted into the ocular system of the film camera, shares the image entering the taking lens and sends an RF (or cable) signal to the floor, operations (directorial, camera coordination, sound) and audience monitors. The monitor display is either in quad-split or 4-gang cluster—a split-screen monitor, or a separate monitor for each of the four cameras.

Staffing the Camera System. The **Director of Photography** heads the camera crew but also directs the efforts of other technical personnel in their functions, as related to preparing the lighting configurations and to the photographic aspects of the presentation of costumes, makeup, set dressing, props and special effects to the cameras.

The **operative camera crew** on each camera (the personnel operating the camera and dolly during rehearsals and takes) consists of the Camera Operator, the First Assistant Camera Operator and the Dolly Grip. Rounding out the camera crew are a Second Assistant Camera Operator and Loader, who service all four cameras.

The **Camera Operator** might be considered "captain of the camera ship," insofar as his or her duties are to see that the collaborative efforts of the three operative camera crew members are smooth, responsive and fully integrated and coordinated with the action taking place and being photographed.

The **First Assistant Camera Operator** sees that: The assigned camera is properly assembled and set up, and that all components are in place, clean, functional, checked out and ready to operate; position tapes or floor marks for the actors are properly identified and placed; the static position of the assigned actor(s) is measured from each static dolly position; the designated framing sizes are carefully noted along with the focus distances; the assigned camera is loaded with the correct emulsion, properly threaded and ready to shoot; the camera report information is complete and clear; and the camera equipment is properly wrapped, following the show.

The **Dolly Grip** is the operator of the mobile camera platform and it is encumbent upon that person to manipulate the dolly with every bit as much care and attention as the Camera Operator and First Assistant devote to their functions. The Dolly Grip marks each assigned dolly floor position and the vertical repositioning of the riser arm for each take and makes a note thereof.

The **Second Assistant Camera Operator**: Assists each of the First Assistants, as necessary; operates the clap sticks or electronic slate prior to each take; is custodian of all loaded film magazines; distributes an unexposed magazine to each camera along with an attached camera report form; with each reload, collects an exposed magazine and its completed camera report from each camera; checks that the camera reports are properly and completely filled out and that each is attached to its proper film magazine; sees that the exposed film gets to the Loader for down-loading.

The **Loader**: Carefully loads sufficient magazines with the designated emulsion type, specifically indicating footage on any short end roll; numbers each magazine with a roll number; enters the basic information on each camera report; attaches that report to the proper magazine; delivers, or orders delivery of, the unexposed film to the Second Assistant at the shooting site; downloads exposed film magazines; specifies the type of processing required ("develop and print," or "develop and prep for video transfer," "push" or "pull" development, "flashing," and so forth); cans and IDs each exposed roll, attaching its camera report to the can; sends the exposed film to the laboratory for processing; cans, IDs and dates each unexposed short-end roll and delivers this to the production company.

TECHNICAL PROCEDURES

Although there are no hard and fast rules regarding every aspect of the technical procedures employed in multiple camera film sitcom production, the following is presented as a representative composite of the procedures which have been followed by a cross-section of film sitcoms, both early and recent.

Directorial Preparations. During the five days normally allotted the **Director** for each half-hour sitcom show, the first three days are devoted to actor preparation, which involves script reading, character interpretation, interaction and delivery, preliminary actor blocking, rewrite adjustments, and setting final business and blocking. The **Script Supervisor** and **Technical Coordinator** are usually in attendance, observing and annotating the script, during third-day activities. All this is in preparation for the fourth day, which comprises camera blocking and rehearsals with the actors, in real time. The fifth and final day sees reblocking for rewrites, refinements in actor/camera blocking, dress rehearsal, then filming the show before a live studio audience.

Lighting. The **Director of Photography**, assisted by the Gaffer and Key Grip and their Assistants, install, focus, set and modify the light from each lighting unit for each setting. In general, the **DP** endeavors to set a lighting pattern which will accommodate an angle sector of up to 160°, from wing camera to wing camera. In order to achieve an acceptable lighting ratio balance from camera to camera, shooting simultaneously, the Cinematographer lays a soft front fill across the entire set. To present a modicum of modeling to each camera, and to keep mic and boom shadows off the walls and thrown to the downstage areas out of camera view, back cross-keys are set far enough upstage to cover each static position of the actors. Emphasis lights are set to cover areas such as entrances, corners, set pieces, special set dressing, or for eyelights. Cycs, translights, drops, backings and "exterior" lighting is adjusted to balance with the on-set lighting.

Equipment Setup. Each of the four **Dolly Grips** affix a geared head on the assigned crab dolly, fully charge the air pressure system, and then make an incremental reference mark scale, related to the vertical positioning of the dolly riser arm, placing it along the riser arm well. Attaching a pointer on the riser arm then provides a convenient reference indicator.

Each of the four **First Assistant Camera Operators** mounts a camera on the geared head of the assigned dolly. The First Assistant then checks and installs a zoom lens, its motor and zoom control, and the matte box assembly. After checking the camera and lens for cleanliness and operation, the Assistant installs a film magazine and threads film in the camera prior to the take.

Each of the four **Camera Operators** adjusts the camera ocular eyepiece diopter to his or her eye, adjusts the tension and ratio of the geared head control wheels, and sets the seat and side boards for maximum operating comfort and flexibility.

Camera Blocking. The **Director** assigns the floor positions for each dolly, and the lens/framing size(s) for each camera, in order to achieve the desired coverage of the assigned actors and their movement. The dolly positions and framing sizes for one or more of the cameras change with each substantial move made by one or more of the actors. The four cameras are designated, L-R, as **A, B, C,** and **X,** respectively. In general and most of the time, cameras **B** and **C,** the center cameras, hold the master (wide angle) shots in order to include most or all of the group of actors on stage as well as the staged movement of those actors; cameras **A** and **X,** the wing cameras, more often than not, are assigned closeup coverage, to be "**on-air**" when the actors stop their movement to interact with dialogue.

Dolly Grip Concerns. At the start of blocking on each set for each show, each **Dolly Grip** (wearing an RF headset, in communication with the Technical Coordinator) will place a line-up tape of the assigned color (either black, blue, green or red) in order to align the dolly chassis with respect to the action area of the set. When given the first dolly floor position by the Director, the Dolly Grip places a tape to mark that position for that sequence. Marked on each tape in the assigned color, and for each subsequently assigned position, is the sequence letter (**A, B,** or **C,** etc) followed by the position number (**1, 2,** or **3**, etc). Also on the position tape is an arrow (straight or curved, depending upon the available and/or intended pathway) pointing in the direction of the next static dolly position, with a subscript number indicating the footage distance to that position. A special color code may be added to indicate either a more rapid move, a variable-speed move, or an **on-air** move. The Dolly Grip also places reference marks along the riser arm well to register (by a reference pointer on the riser arm) the various rise heights requested by the Director or Camera Operator during each sequence take. The Dolly Grip must know: **When**, with what **velocity, how far,** and to what **exact position** to move the dolly (and riser arm), as well as the **direction** and **path** in which the dolly must be moved to get there.

Dolly Grip notes include: The sequence letter and set description with the starting height of the riser arm; each dolly position number with a description of any actor moves which trigger any subsequent riser arm height variations and/or dolly moves; any on-air move designated by the Director; and the velocity and configuration of each dolly move.

Camera Assistant Concerns. To begin camera blocking for each sequence, the Director will present the actors, moving about and performing in the action blocking plan, for the benefit of the operative camera crews, the Technical Coordinator and the stand-ins. While this more or less stop-and-go process is going on, the **Camera Assistants** place a small, thin strip of tape (appropriately color-coded by character, and identified by sequence letter and chronological position number) on the floor, at the static position of each actor, after each move, until the entire scene/sequence has been run and floor-marked.

Camera blocking follows, usually using stand-ins wearing character name tags. As the stand-ins move stop-and-go through the scene, replicating the action and positions of the cast members, the Director determines the positions for each camera in order to provide the desired coverage and composition from each angle for the entire scene. At each dolly position, each First Assistant Camera Operator determines, by tape measurement, the distance from his or her camera film plane to the target subject matter, then records the dolly position number followed by the exact distance figure(s) and zoom lens position setting(s) (framing size) for each actor move on a note pad for ready reference during the rehearsals and takes.

Each **First Assistant Camera Operator** changes film magazines and threads film in his or her assigned camera, sets or resets the footage counter, sets the T-stop as received from the Director of Photography, places required filters in the matte box or behind the lens, operates the zoom motor control for image-sizing, manually follows focus during each rehearsal and take, rebalances the camera after each take, and keeps a camera report of each take on each film roll load.

The **Second Assistant Camera Operator** presents the grey scale/color chart to each camera at the start of each fresh roll and/or prior to the first take on each set, voice slates and operates the electronic time-code slate or giant multi-camera clapper sticks for each take, checks camera reports on each camera, delivers unexposed film magazines (each with its camera report form attached) to the First Assistants and picks up exposed film magazines (each with its filled-out camera report attached) during each camera reloading sequence.

The **Loader** sees that sufficient film magazines are properly loaded with the specified emulsion and that each exposed magazine is carefully down-loaded, canned, ID'd, and forwarded, with properly filled out camera report copies, to the film laboratory for processing.

Camera Operator Concerns. With the start of the camera blocking process, each **Camera Operator** (wearing an RF headset, in communication with the Tech Coordinator) takes appropriate notes regarding the singles or cast groupings to be held in frame, their location on the set, and their movements, the coverage of which is the responsibility of his or her camera from each static or moving camera position during the entire scene. The Camera Operator makes sure that the movement of the dolly and/or its riser arm, zoom sizing movement, and any panning and/or tilting required to follow the action is coordinated to smoothly start and stop with the movement of the subject matter in frame. It is the Operator's responsibility to coordinate the efforts of the operative camera crew and, if faulty, to devise means of correcting the problem as promptly and unobtrusively as possible.

Technical Coordinator Concerns. The principal concerns of the **Tech Coordinator** is to: Maintain a comprehensively annotated script, with notes carefully made during camera blocking, regarding each move, position and coverage of each camera and the cueing point in the script for each move; keep track of and verbally cue the Dolly Grips (by means of RF headset communication) for every move, for each dolly; assure that each dolly is on its appointed position, at its appointed time; monitor relative sizes of opposing closeups, advising the Camera Operators to have the First Assistant adjust the sizing; give special cues to a Dolly Grip or Camera Operator, at their request; make note of any and all changes or modifications in the original actor/camera blocking and individual camera coverage, as designed and assigned by the Director.

Summing Up. The multiple-camera film sitcom technique is a hybrid system borrowed in part from the multiple electronic camera coverage and fathered by live television production programming. The innovation of using film cameras, inaugurated by Desi Arnaz and sustained by the economic viability and popularity of the half-hour, live-audience format, will likely be around for a long time to come. It does require a high degree of collaborative effort in coordinating the discrete movement of the dolly, the camera and its lenticular elements, as manipulated by the Dolly Grip, the Camera Operator and the First Assistant, respectively, in concert with the Tech Coordinator, and in harmony with the movement of the actors. However, the precision with which the film cameras can be moved and the composed shots delivered by top-notch operative camera crews is unequalled by other multiple-camera techniques.

SPECIALIZED PRODUCTION TECHNIQUES

Wherever there is action, whatever the action, there is camera equipment which has been designed and developed to record that action in its environment and a willing Camera Operator to turn the camera on and focus and frame that activity.

Whether in the arctic, tropic, equatorial regions, desert or temperate zones, in space, the air or at sea, in the jungle or on glaciers or ice floes, in caves or on mountain tops, or underwater, appropriate equipment and experienced personnel are available, willing and able to do the job required.

For those who might be interested in functioning in any of these specialized camera techniques, it might be well to review some of these and become acquainted with a few of their principal procedural parameters at this time, insofar as health, safety, matériel, and wearing apparel are concerned.

Temperate Zone Shooting. The best of all worlds. The equipment and personnel function well without special weatherizing and without working in, and the constant concern for, extreme temperatures, blowing sand, sea spray, precipitation or high humidity.

Generally speaking, weather is not ordinarily a problem to deal with throughout a shoot, depending upon the time of year and the location being utilized. Communications facilities, transportation, lodging and feeding accommodations, medical facilities, equipment and expendable resupply sources are all arranged to be relatively readily available at or near most location sites. Logistically, shooting in a temperate zone is not the problem it can become when working in the arctic or tropics, on the ice or in heavy jungle bush or desert sand. Relative to other climatic zones, moving matériel and personnel in the temperate zone is a breeze.

Arctic Zone Shooting. Sub-zero weather, blowing snow, and 24-hour or nonexistent daylight hours (depending upon the time of year) are the bane of working in the arctic or antarctic regions.

Cameras must be winterized with special lubrication for all moving metal parts (with plastic replacement for some) and with heating elements installed internally in order to insure operational dependibility. Personnel require heavy-duty clothing suited for sub-zero temperatures. Equipment must be kept in the temperature range in which it will be used in order to avoid condensation on metal and glass elements. If kept in a much warmer environment overnight to be stored or serviced, it must be allowed sufficient time to cool down in the temperature of the shooting environment for maximum operational efficiency.

Because of the generally extremely low humidity, static electricity can streak the frames as the film travels through the film gate. A little light lubrication such as nose grease applied to the gate can help reduce this problem. The film also tends to become quite brittle in extremely cold temperatures, so great care must be taken to avoid cracking or breaking the film when threading it in the camera.

For the Camera Operator and Camera Assistant, silk gloves (worn inside heavy outer gloves) can make the job of threading film much more convenient and comfortable while still protecting the hands and fingers from sticking to the freezing metal parts during the handling process.

Wearing apparel includes: Thermal underwear and socks; waterproof, lined boots; thermal glove liner and heavy gloves (with hand-warmer units); thermal face mask and fur-lined cap; fur-lined pants, vest and hooded parka; snow goggles. A chap stick can come in handy.

Be prepared to consume a lot of liquids.

Tropical/Equatorial Zone Shooting. Hot, humid, rainy and insect-ridden is the shooting experience in the tropical lowland jungle regions. Fungus tends to form on leather, film, lens elements and the human body. This is a case where cleanliness is indeed next to godliness. Equipment must be kept clean and dry. Personnel soon get in the habit of bathing and changing clothes several times a day. Sleeping under draped mosquito netting or in jungle hammocks is a must in order to keep biting insects and (in some areas) vampire bats at bay.

Equipment or film maintained or stored in an air conditioned room must be given sufficient time to acclimatize to the much warmer and more humid shooting environment prior to use, otherwise heavy condensation will form on surfaces and optical elements. The very high humidity can transform the film emulsion to the consistency of taffy, causing the film to stick in a firmly pressured gate.

Wearing a wide-brimmed hat and long-sleeved shirt, with pants tucked into waterproof boots and developing a full beard (if you can) helps protect against the sun, mud and insects.

Using a native guide, someone totally familiar with the topography, flora, fauna and customs of the area, is a very good idea to help keep production personnel out of harm's way from: Treacherous rivers, trails, terrain and weather; potentially hostile natives and their territory; poisonous reptiles, insects, plants and water sources; dangerous animals; and inappropriate interaction with the locals.

Be prepared to consume a lot of liquids.

Desert Terrain. Shooting in arid, sandy terrain presents the problems of a great temperature differential from day to nighttime as well as blowing particles which can work their way into the working parts of a motion picture camera. The film gate should be pulled and examined immediately following each print take to be sure the gate is clear of any debris. Following the shooting day, cameras and magazines should be field stripped and thoroughly cleaned.

A broad-brimmed hat, desert boots, long pants and sunglasses are appropriate articles of attire for desert shooting. Loose-fitting clothing (in layers) will be more comfortable while working in this environment. Sunglasses, a chap stick and sun screen lotion are also appropriate.

Working personnel should protect themselves from dehydration and heat stroke during daylight desert shooting by consuming sufficient quantities of liquids and wearing appropriate head gear and clothing.

Again, a native guide who knows the terrain and local customs can be quite useful in helping protect production personnel and making their work and relaxation time safer, more comfortable and productive.

Be prepared to consume a lot of liquids.

Marine Shooting. Marine shooting can be on the water surface and/or underwater and/or on ship to shore to ship. Shooting at sea is not for those with a queasy stomach or fear of water.

The environment is relatively moist and, if at sea, there is blowing spray carrying salt (and sometimes oil) residue which can coat lenses and camera bodies and corrode metal surfaces. So constant attention must be paid to protecting and thoroughly cleaning these items daily after they have been used and exposed to the elements.

Recommended surface attire includes: A billed cap; sun glasses; deck shoes; shorts and T-shirt (unless subject to sunburn, then a wide-brimmed hat, long-sleeved shirts and long pants are in order); a chap stick for the lips and an ample supply of sunscreen; a windbreaker; and foul weather gear.

Underwater gear includes SCUBA equipment and a wet suit or even deep sea diving apparatus and support paraphernalia. Great care must be taken to always dive with a buddy, and when diving at depth to be careful to avoid techniques which might bring on the bends.

Camera stabilizing equipment such as a gimbel head are often useful in shooting from undulating surface platforms. underwater shooting, of course, requires watertight camera housings appropriate to the types of cameras being used and the depth range of the shoot.

Aerial Shooting. Shooting aerials is a specialized field for people with no fear of, but rather a love of, flying. A high degree of coordination, quick reflexes and a steady stomach are assets for the Aerial Camera Operator. Aerial maneuvers in following or holding a target can be rather abrupt, and swooping moves can produce significant G-forces which can drain blood from the head, causing grey-outs, black-outs, or nausea.

Depending upon the type of aircraft and the operational altitude for the shoot, appropriate clothing must be planned for. If the camera position is to be exposed (shooting from an open hatch or safety-belted in a doorway), thermal underwear and socks, a fitted flight suit, thermal gloves, boots, ski mask, and fleece-filled jacket and pants (if needed) should be considered. Loose-fitting outer clothing should be avoided. Take a chap stick along.

One dehydrates quickly when working at altitude in an open environment, so sufficient liquids should be taken before and during the mission. Of course, one should attend to elimination functions prior to each sortie, for there are no comfort station facilities on most aerial camera platforms.

Shock-mounted, vibration-dampened, camera stabilizing systems are widely used for aerial cinematography. Cameras used can be 8mm, 16mm, 35mm, 65mm or electronic. Remotely controlled, stabilized mounts attached to fuselage and/or airfoils are also widely used. Film cameras should be winterized when shooting in very low and sub-zero temperatures which, at higher altitudes and with a substantial wind-chill factor, are quite common.

Be prepared to consume a lot of liquids.

Other Types of Specialized Shooting. There are many more types of specialized camera techniques. Nearly anywhere you can physically place yourself you can take a camera to record and thereby share that experience with others.

Alpine, or mountain climbing, camera work requires specialized climbing gear, an excellent and fully conditioned physique, and handheld cameras. Work in snow or on glaciers requires winter clothing and winterized cameras. Rock climbing gear may also be necessary. Your sleeping accommodations, food (dehydrated), camera equipment and film are carried with you. Skiing ability may also be a requirement.

Space, for now, is the domain of astronauts who routinely record their exploits with film and electronic cameras. However, some day ordinary production crews as well will be plying their crafts in that environment.

Underground. Shooting in excavations, mines or caves requires specialized techniques, clothing and support matériel. Hard hats and miners' headlamps are protective and useful in these dark, dripping and often confining environments. Working mines usually have means of transporting personnel and equipment deep into their interiors. Deserted mines, excavations and caves more often require all equipment to be carried in by foot, so it should be lightweight and compact. Underground temperatures are in the comfort zone so clothing and footwear should be rather light and for protection against abrasions caused by the rough and uneven floor, wall and ceiling surfaces. Dust, dirt and falling fragments or cave-ins are to be expected in mines and excavations. Potentially lethal gases must be guarded against in deep and extensively developed mine tunneling, so breathing apparatus may be needed.

Summing Up. Since cameras and their crews can be sent into any region, climate, and topography to live, work and record production images, it behooves those interested in this type of location employment to maintain an updated passport and to learn as much as possible about the particular specialized production technique(s) of specific interest. The better prepared one is for working in various or specific locales throughout the world, the more rewarding the experience and the results thereof are likely to be.

SHOOTING STAGE INSERTS

Inserts shooting on stage is a type of cinematography which can help prepare a Camera Operator for the more demanding work and responsibility of directing photography for a full-blown production.

Other types of inserts shooting include inserts shot from a camera car, aerials, underwater, and those done by second units, utilizing photographic doubles for the principal performers.

Camera car, aerial, aquatic and underwater inserts are second unit work, involving photographic doubles and/or stunt personnel in place of the acting principals. Inserts are planned for in order to save valuable production time during principal photography and/or to expedite completion of a production within the shooting schedule and/or to help an editing problem.

Other second unit inserts shooting are shots which use photographic doubles in stunts, or for distant location establishing and transition shots (normally taken of the double's backside and with substantial apparent distancing), and the shooting of scenics and process plates.

Highly specialized inserts shooting include tabletop, special visual effects and models or miniatures.

Shooting stage hand/body/objects inserts is a matching process and requires a good eye for discerning and reproducing the same visual values which the first unit Director of Photography intentionally has included in his or her lighting/filtration/exposure plan.

Strictly speaking, stage inserts shooting is done without the principal performers, with closeup views of important details (either not shot during expensive production time, or to replace insert shots already made, or to provide a means of modifying the length of a scene), and with stand-ins body-doubling for the principals.

In shooting inserts, the idea is to match and merge perfectly in all respects with elements in the originally shot scene or sequence so that the insert will fit in unobtrusively with the leading shot and the following shot, between which it is to be juxtaposed.

In several respects, this very exacting kind of photography is more difficult and demanding than the original photography. It requires an analytical eye for detail and the patience and perseverance to accurately and completely duplicate the work of another.

Preparation. When you are given an assignment for shooting inserts, you need to know (by getting the info from the production DP) or ascertain (by getting the info from production shots, or clips therefrom) the following: The film gauge and emulsion used; the make and focal length of the lens used; lenticular modifiers used;

the aspect ratio used; the required length of the insert; the filter pack and diffusion (if any) used; the position, direction, quality (color temperature; and diffusion and color gelling, if any), and relative intensity of the key, fill, top, back, kicker, eye, accent, foreground, midground and background lighting; color gels or diffusion used on specific lamps; smoke, steam or hot ice for effect; and, when applicable: the frame rate (fps), shutter angle setting and special matting.

The inserts shooter, with the help of a compact crew, operates the camera, directs the placement, focus, intensity and quality modification of each lighting unit, determines the exposure and all other camera/lens settings and, with input from the inserts Director, camera placement and moves.

First, the inserts shooter is usually given a film clip of the scene preceding and a clip of the scene following the point where the insert shot is to be placed. More often than not, a 1/2″ video cassette is provided showing the flow of the shots and scenes and the exact insert point and its duration as represented by a "**MISSING SCENE**" slug.

At this point, the inserts shooter and the inserts Director should be sure that: All props, settings, set dressings and costume items are present and in appropriate condition for handling and presentation to the camera; the body doubles (people whose limbs and portions of their bodies may be shown in frame) are present and appropriately selected and costumed, for handling the props and replicating the action to be matched, in order to properly conform to the already shot and edited preceding and/or following scene(s), between which the inserted shot will he placed.

Camera Positioning. The position of the camera, in consideration of the nature and magnitude of the insert action, is then set, along with the selection of the taking lens and any dolly, pan/tilt or zoom moves necessary.

Lighting. Determining from the film clips the positioning, filtration, diffusion, color gelling and relative intensity of the lighting units set by the Director of Photography during the principal photography, the inserts shooter strives to match exactly the lighting plan established by that DP for each scene in which an insert shot will be placed.

Of prime importance are the lighting ratios used to expose the production footage—key to fill, and midground action areas to both foreground and background—which need (when included in frame) to be closely replicated in the insert shot. In addition, the intensity and color quality of the light as well as the amount of color gelling, if any, and the degree of diffusion used are important visual and metering considerations. The inserts shooter must determine from the production footage—film clip or video tape—where each light was placed in order to replicate that setup relative to the normally limited area in which the insert is to be staged and shot. But beware of relying on the tape as a dependable guide for color, optical diffusion or contrast rendition. Use only film clips for this purpose.

Shooting. At this point, the emphasis is on precisely matching the action at the tail end of the lead-in shot and that of the head end of the follow-up shot. In addition, the screen direction of the action—whether static or dynamic—must be consistent with the production footage action. Assuming that the lighting for the insert has been a perfect match (in all respects), and that the props, settings, set dressings and costume items which are to be included in frame, as used and/or worn by the body doubles, are the same as (or an acceptable match for) those items which were used or worn by the principals in the action footage to be matched, the insert is ready to be shot.

Because of the exacting requirements of the action, which frequently requires a high degree of coordination between the insert double (positioning), the Camera Operator (framing) and the Camera Assistant (focus and sizing), several takes are usually made in order to insure an appropriate match. Video assist can help speed the process so the Director can see exactly what the camera is framing during each take, making it possible to make an immediate and informed decision on each take.

Inserts can also include an entire sequence of tightly framed hand/body/object shots wherein subject/action selection and shot duration are determined by the inserts Director.

The Acid Test. In the final analysis, does the insert match—fit in as an unobtrusive, integrated element in the sequence of shots in the finalized production? If it does, then you've succeeded in your endeavor as an inserts shooter, and have taken another important step toward preparing yourself for greater responsibilities and challenges.

A Final Word. Shooting hand/body/object inserts is similar to watchmaking, in that precise, analytical attention to and execution of myriad detail is key to a successful shoot. If the insert fits into the principal photography so well that it is not noticed, then the insert shooter has accomplished his or her mission faithfully and well.

PHOTOGRAPHIC SURVEILLANCE

Surveillance work by its very nature is done furtively, without the knowledge or consent of the person or persons being observed. To be effective, motion picture, video and/or still shots of the subject(s) are employed and should record clearly the observed action (and sound and dialogue when required), in order to document the specifics and nature of the surveilled activity, the place(s) of occurrence, the time(s) of day each observation occurred and the person(s) participating therein.

The objective is to dispassionately and accurately record the actions and reactions of an individual or individuals—visually, on film or video tape, and (on occasion) audially on tape, without the subject(s) being aware of the surveillance.

Surveillance can be of several types, involving civil, criminal or espionage activities. Each type has its own agenda and requirements for staff and matériel, depending upon the nature, scope and location(s) of the activity(ies) to be documented. Generally federal, state and local law enforcement agencies have their own specialists who plan and execute surveillance assignments. These can take the form of a so-called "sting" operation where a person or persons are visually and audially recorded participating in an unlawful act in a prearranged environment. The use of one-way glass and hidden microphones is a common practice in this type surveillance. Occasionally, outside technicians are contracted for to staff these operations.

Most work of this nature is derived from private investigators and attorneys and involves civil suits dealing with divorce action or bodily injury and insurance claims. A surveillance assignment may be day or night, interior or exterior, local or distant location.

Bodily Injury Cases. Since bodily injury cases frequently require surveillance work, it is well to consider whether this type work is for you, during off-days and seasonal production down time. In bodily injury cases, the principal contention between the claimant (the injured) and the defendant (the insured) is the extent of the claimed injuries and the extent of physical incapacitation suffered by the claimant. In order to establish this, particularly when there is reason to believe that the claimant is not suffering the disabilities claimed or is indeed faking injury, the defendant orders surveillance of the claimant. Once the private investigator has determined that the claimant is engaging in activities beyond his or her claimed limitations, a surveillance specialist is hired to surreptitiously and photographically document the claimant's activities.

Matériel Required. The camera person needs a vantage point from which to observe and record the subject. This vantage point is usually a van with either one-way glass or neutral density-tinted window ports, parked in front of the residence or work place of the subject where activity of the subject can be conveniently observed and recorded. The view should not be impaired by van window curtains or other intervening objects (parked vehicles, telephone poles, trees, shrubs, etc).

Super 8mm, 16mm or 35mm film cameras are used; however, since Super 8 is reliable and the least expensive film system to run, it is widely used for this purpose. Video CCD cameras are also economical and acceptable. The camera should be mounted on a tripod in order to minimize camera shake during recording. A 10X zoom lens will suffice in most cases. A T/1.5 lens (or even image-enhanced or infrared system) may be required for night shooting along with a high speed film emulsion. Shooting color is preferable to black and white. No filters should be used to enhance or modify the subject image (such as corals or diffusion); however, color balancing and neutral density filters are appropriate. An ample supply of film or video tape, camera batteries, and food and liquids is essential, as is a portable facility for relieving bodily functions. The wait and the work can be long, hot, demanding and enervating—and sometimes physically dangerous.

Procedures. Since only unedited original film or tape will be admitted into evidence, it is essential that certain procedures and precautions be observed in the recording process.

It is important to tie the subject in to his or her surrounding environment where the documentation is taking place. It is well to record the subject exiting his or her residence. (An exterior bug is often used to alert the photographer that the subject is about to exit to pick up the morning paper, take out the garbage, open the garage or engage in yard work, etc.) Long, continuous takes are the order of the day. The camera should be started early in order to record the entrance into frame of the subject and the complete ensuing action, cutting the camera only after the action of the subject has been completed and/or the subject has exited the photographic area. Jump cuts—cutting and starting the camera during an action (with or without changing the image size)—must be avoided. Jump cuts, when displayed, can make an action appear to be more rapid than it actually was. Camera movement—panning and tilting—should be done smoothly with, and only in order to follow, subject movement. Zoom resizing can be done during a take in order to more closely examine a portion of the action. No color filtration should be used on the lens which might make skin tones more ruddy, or healthy-looking, than normal. The camera should be rock-steady during static shots. Focus should be on the subject. Exposure should be correct and consistent from shot to shot. Film should be exposed at 24 fps; however, 16 fps is acceptable if no other frame rate is used during the surveillance. The important thing is that the projecting frame rate and the taking frame rate be the same so that the recorded action is not distorted when projected for the court.

Generally, in physical injury cases, the subject should be framed in full figure in order to record the movement of the entire body at all times. Jump cuts and extraneous camera movement tend to impart a false appearance of vitality to the subject. To avoid the appearance of a jump cut, when the camera is cut, the lens size should be adjusted a few millimeters tighter or looser for the next shot (particularly when the subject remains in the same specific area—i.e, the porch or the front yard). Very short takes should be avoided. Camera pan and zoom moves should be unobtrusive and follow the action in order to keep the subject in frame while in the photographic area.

A complete record must be kept of the film emulsion used, the EI rating used, the frame rate (fps), the T-stops used, the filters used and the camera and lens used. Each exposed roll should be numbered, dated and identified with the case assignment number. Equally important is logging the address, the date and the in and out time for each location site, identifying the subject(s) of each recorded activity and the time of day that activity occurred.

If these procedures are not closely followed or if "creative" license is taken by the photographer, the court may not allow the film or tape into evidence, or an opposing expert witness may well destroy or diminish the validity of the visual recording. The court is interested in just the unvarnished visual and documented facts. Visual embellishments should be reserved for purely fictional projects.

APPENDIX

Here you will find the very first article written for the "Operating Tips" column in *International Photographer* magazine, followed by a survival technique and an historical survey of technical innovations affecting camera operation.

IMPROVING VIEWFINDER COMFORT

Ever had your camera eyepiece fog up during a long take in a cold studio, or during a cool night shoot?

Well, there may be a way out of this dilemma short of taking a hand off the controls to swab the condensation from the surface of the ocular while the shot is in progress.

Try placing a nubby-knit cotton tennis wristband over the rubber fitting of the eyepiece. This allows ventilation past your eye and across the surface of the glass viewing system thereby reducing or eliminating the buildup of condensation on the outer surface of the glass elements.

This procedure will work on moderately cold camera bodies. An electrically warmed eyepiece is necessary in very low temperature shooting.

Yet another use for the wristband is on a hot and humid day, when the rubber, plastic or chamois eyepiece cover is getting saturated with perspiration (from each and everyone who looks through the lens). The wristband will keep the viewing eyepiece relatively comfortable by absorbing the perspiration (of all lookers).

By turning the wristband end-for-end and later inside-out, at periodic intervals, a relatively clean and dry surface can be presented to the eye. Daily changing and laundering of the used wristband(s) is recommended.

A COOLING AID

The warm months arrive and many of us will be sweating it out on hot and humid location exteriors and interiors. Even working high on a fully lighted stage can leave one overheated, dehydrated and drained after a while.

We can each think of environmental production situations we've been in that made us sweat like we were in a sauna, joining cast and crew in putting away gallons of liquids, and yet not finding any lasting relief from the discomfort of the heat. To keep relatively comfortable under these conditions, while getting the job done, can be a real challenge.

Well, there is a way out of this dilemma. It entails utilizing a small plastic container (quart-size and covered), two neckerchiefs or bandanas, water, ice and the skin antiseptic SEA BREEZE. Add a pint of water to an equal quantity of cracked ice or cubes, then add one or two tablespoons of SEA BREEZE to the water. Place the two neckerchiefs in the ice water solution and when thoroughly chilled, remove one, wring it out and tie it around your neck. When that kerchief dries out or gets too warm, replace it in the water and remove and apply the other kerchief.

Although not a cure-all, you'll find this technique a refreshing aid while getting your work done in an uncomfortably hot environment.

TECHNICAL INNOVATIONS FOR CAMERA OPERATION

Every Camera Operator relies upon his or her Assistants and upon the equipment and accessories which are used to capture the desired images on film or video tape. Then there are the "hidden assistants," those who develop, introduce, maintain and supply the tools of the trade. The innovations and improvements in the camera equipment, accessories, material and techniques utilized in production over the years have steadily helped advance the art and craft of operating cinematography.

There have been advances in cameras, lenses, remote and electronic operational controls, viewfinders, oculars, fixed and mobile camera mounts, operating heads, and ancillary accoutrements. A review of these technological advances in the cinematic media will show a steady trend of innovation and improvement in tools, materials and techniques of production. In this writing, we will list just those innovations and improvements which have significantly helped accommodate the art and craft of the Camera Operator.

Criteria for Selection. The criteria which have been applied to the selected technical achievements advancing the cause of the Camera Operator are: **1)** Introduction and first use or application of the technical development of an equipment item, a component of that item, a tool, product or technique; **2)** the further significant development and refinement of an important innovation; and **3)** the adjudged value and importance of the technical development in relation to the state of the art and craft at the time of its introduction. **For those innovative tools which were given technical achievement awards by either the Academy of Motion Picture Arts and Science and/or by the Society of Operating Cameramen, an asterisk (*) has been placed immediately following the name of the product or technique.**

The reader may feel that certain items in the following listing could be considered more or less deserving of recognition, or that certain items should have been included, but were not, and that others should not have been included at all. In addition, dates and model designations not confirmed have been excluded. Consider this a starting list which will be continually updated and will serve to keep us aware of the progress of innovative development which encourages and nurtures the art, craft and skill of operating cinematography.

CAMERAS

There have been numerous advances in motion picture and video cameras which have been developed by many manufacturers throughout the world during the past hundred years or so. Although the Camera Operator operates the film camera by turning it on and manipulating it in order to maintain appropriate framing while the First Assistant Camera Operator maintains focus and sizing, and although the video Camera Operator does all that in addition to physically moving the camera, not every working component of the film camera is directly controlled by the Camera Operator and the First Assistant , or of the video camera by its Operator. Nevertheless, whether controlled on-board or off-board, it remains a synergistic process of collaborative synchronization of expertise and effort.

The 35mm Production Film Camera. From the early compact hand-cranked production cameras, the development toward/of high-precision blimped cameras with multiple controls was inevitable and constant. The controls were conveniently access-ible to the Camera Assistant, thereby freeing the Camera Operator to concentrate on following and framing the action. (The massive Edison "**Kinetograph**" [USA] in 1889; the compact Lumière camera/printer/projector "**Cinématographe**" [Fr] in 1894; Eberhard Schneider [Ger] in 1896; Demeney [Fr] and Kine-Messter [Ger] in 1897; massive Mutograph [USA] in 1898; Gaumont [Fr] in 1900; Empire [Eng] in 1902; Lubin [USA] and Ernemann [Ger] in 1904; Pathé [Fr] and Moy/Bastie [Eng] in 1905; Schustek [USA] and Cinex [Fr] in 1906; Chronik [USA] and Thoronton-Pickards [Fr] in 1907; DeBrie "**Parvo**" [Fr] and Prestwich [Eng] in 1908; Williamson [Eng], Ensign [Eng] and Barker Bros [USA] in 1909; Bell & Howell [USA] and the Proszynski "**Aeroscope**" [Pol] pneumatic pressurized camera in 1910; Olikos glass-plate [Fr], Prevost [Aus] and U S Cinematogaph "**DeLuxe**" [USA] in 1912; Bell & Howell **2709B** [USA] in 1912; American [USA] and Geyer [Ger] in 1913; Simplex [USA] and Vista [USA] in 1914; Kinograph [USA] and Wall [Eng] in 1915; Akeley [USA] in 1916; King-Barker camera-projector [USA], Davsco [USA] and Universal [USA] in 1917; Eagle "**No. 5**" [USA] and Newman-Sinclair [Eng] in 1918; Wilart [USA] in 1920; Koehler [Ger] in 1921; Sept [USA] in 1922; Warwick "**Biokam**" [Eng] in 1923; Barnack [Ger] in 1924; Bell & Howell "**Eyemo**" [USA] in 1925; De Vry [USA] and Wall [USA] in 1926; Acme [USA] in 1928; Moreno-Snyder [USA] in 1931; ARRI **35*** [Ger] in 1932; Mitchell [USA] **NC*** in 1933 and **BNC*** in 1934; Eclair 16/35mm "**Cameflex**" AKA "**Camerette**" [Fr] in 1938; 20th Century-Fox "**Silenced Camera**"* [USA] in 1940; Cameraflex Corp "**Cameraflex**" [USA] in 1943; 20th Century-Fox "**Cinemascope**"* in 1953; Paramount "**VistaVision**"* [USA] in 1954; Mitchell **Mark II*** [USA] in 1962; Panavision [USA] **PSR*** in 1968 and "**Panaflex**"* in 1972; ARRI [Ger] **35BL*** in 1973, **35-3*** in 1979, **35BL-4S*** in 1990, and **535*** in 1995; Bauer "**Moviecam**"* [USA] in 1982; ILM "**Empire**" [USA] in 1981 and "**Vistaflex**" in 1984; Fries Engi-neering "**Fries BNC Reflex**" in 1983; UltraCam in 1986; Wilcam **WII VistaVision 25db*** [USA] in 1989; Aaton* [Fr] in 1990; ARRI **535*** in 1994, and others.)

The Hand-Held 35mm Production Film Camera. Freeing the Camera Op-erator from the constraints of a tripod-mounted, ultra-heavy studio camera with geared head control ushered in a new era of flexible and imaginative camera coverage. The light-weight, compact camera could now be conveniently carried by the Camera

Operator while filming the requisite action. (Steedman **"Rifle"** [USA] in 1920; Sept [USA] in 1922; Warwick **"Biokam"** [Eng] in 1923; Bell & Howell **"Eyemo"** [USA] in 1925; ARRI **35*** [Ger] in 1932; Eclair **CM3** **"Camerette"** AKA **16/35** **"Cameflex"** [Fr] in 1938; Cunningham **"Combat Camera"** [USA] in 1941; Cineflex [USA] in 1944; Mitchell **"Mark II"*** [USA] in 1962; Todd-AO/Mitchell* [USA] in 1968; Panavision **"Panaflex"*** [USA] in 1972; ARRI [Ger] **35BL*** in 1973; Ferrra **Ferraflex Eyemo** in 1985; Bauer **"Moviecam"*** in 1985, **"Moviecam Compact"*** in 1992 and **"Moviecam SL"** in 1995; Aaton **35 III*** [Fr] in 1990; and others.)

The Hand-Held 65mm Production Film Camera. This development made hand-held 65mm production shots possible for the first time. (Panavision 65mm hand-held camera,* 1968.)

The 16mm Professional Film Camera. Professional versions of the 16mm camera provided the professional Camera Operator a dependable and in most instances, lighter-weight package with nearly all the bells and whistles of the 35mm camera. (Kodak **"Cine Special"** in 1933; Mitchell in 1936; Keystone, Victor, Maurer and Bell & Howell **70DA** and **"Specialist"** in late 1940s; ARRI **16St** in 1952; Eclair **NPR** in late 1950s; Kodak **"Special Reflex"** in 1961; Auricon, RCA, Pathé, Revere, Bolex, Kodak **K-100** and Eumig in 1960s; Cinema Products **CP16** in 1971; Panavision **"Elaine"** in 1984; Aaton in mid-1980s; and others.)

The 65mm Production Camera. This large negative format originated in the mid-30s and the cameras used to shoot this format have evolved with the state of the art. (Fox 65mm **"Grandeur"*** camera in mid-1930s; **Todd-AO*** in 1957; MGM **Camera 65*** in 1959; Fries 65 in 1958; Cinema Products **"Showscan"** **CP-65*** Camera System in 1986; Panavision **System 65*** and ARRI **765** Camera System* in 1989; IMAX **15-perf*** in 1985 and **MSM9801 15-perf*** in 1994.)

Spring-Loaded Camera Drive. This development freed the Camera Operator from the constraint of hand-cranking the film through the camera. (Bell & Howell 35mm **"Eyemo"** in 1925; 16mm, from 1923-27: Keystone; Victor; Kodak **"Cine Special"** and **K100**; Bell & Howell **70DA**; Bolex.)

The Electric Camera Motor. This development made possible longer takes while eliminating frame rate (and therefore, exposure) fluctuations. (First camera to use an electric motor was the Kinetograph in 1889; then the Mutograph in 1898; then Bell & Howell in 1912; Akeley; and many others.)

The Variable-Speed Motor. The development of efficient, light-weight electric motors for driving professional film cameras at variable or constant speeds made possible either a constant frame rate (to accommodate the requirements for sound recording) or a variable-rate undercranking (fast-motion) or overcranking (slow-motion), thereby adding another tool to the creative shooting arsenal. (Bell & Howell in mid 1920s; ARRI in 1932; Mitchell in early 1930s; Panavison in 1967.)

Variable Speed Control*. This innovation allowed the camera to be run at varying speeds during a take while automatically changing the aperture to maintain a consistent exposure. (Preston Cinema Systems in 1994.)

The Crystal-Controlled Motor. The accuracy and dependability of this innovation assured a constant, unvarying frame rate and, with a crystal-controlled sound recorder, the "umbilical cord" connecting the camera motor to the sound recorder was no longer necessary. (Cinema Products* for ARRI 35 in 1968; ARRI in 1975; Eclair "**Beala**" motor* [Nagra crystal synchronizing control for the sound recorder]; Cinematography Electronics **Precision Speed Device*** in 1983.)

Motion Picture Camera Systems. The concept, design and continuing development of a completely integrated camera system of camera bodies, lenses, filters and other accessories greatly facilitated the setting up, operation and wrapping of camera equipment. (Panavision **Panaflex Motion Picture Camera System*** in 1978; ARRI in 1980; Bauer **Moviecam Camera System*** in 1987.)

The Panavision Camera System*. This integrated camera-accessory concept began development in 1972 with the introduction of the Panaflex camera and became a true system in 1978. This system is especially helpful for the Camera Assistants in their work of assembling, co-operating, and wrapping the camera gear and placing and replacing lenses, filters and film magazines.

The High-Speed Camera. Frame rates in excess of 100 fps on up to several hundred or several thousand frames per second are used to slow (at the standard projection rate of 24 fps) actual movement time for either dramatic effect or for scientific analysis and evaluation of an event. (35mm: Bull in 1904; DeBrie in 1927; Wilcam **Image 300*** in 1988. 16mm: Bell & Howell "**Fastax**" in 1924; Milliken and Photo-Sonics in the 1950s.)

The High-Speed Reflex Camera. Introduction of reflex view and video assist capability has aided the Camera Operator in monitoring frame content and focus during high-speed takes. (Photo-Sonics 35mm **4ER*** in 1988; Wilcam **W7-Image 300*** in 1989.)

An Optical Camera System. The first motion picture cameras were used to record, then print/duplicate, and finally to project the finished product. Optical camera systems were subsequently developed, first to copy from the developed camera negative, making dupe negatives or screening prints. Then, by combining and copying several negatives onto a strip of film, with holding mattes selectively placed, magical optical effects could be obtained. (Bell and Howell in 1912; Acme in 1920s; Mitchell in 1933; Industrial Light & Magic **Empire Motion Picture Camera System*** in 1981; and others.)

The Professional Video Camera. Introduction of the electronic camera ushered in a revolution in the broadcasting and the motion picture media. (RCA **TK** series in mid-1930s; Philips-Norelco **PC70/90*** series in 1972; Bosch-Fernseh in 1973; Thomson in 1975; Ikegami and Hitachi in 1980s.)

The Hand-Held Video Production Camera. Developments in electronic engineering and circuitry miniaturization finally reduced the size of the video camera. Recently the portable video camera has been greatly reduced in size and is getting more and more Operator-friendly. (From 1968: the Philips-Norelco **PCP70*** & **90**; RCA **TK76**; Bosch-Fernseh; Hitachi **SK70**; Ikegami **77** & **79** series; BTS; Sony "**Betacam**."*)

VIEWFINDER SYSTEMS

The viewfinder, whether optical or electronic, is the Camera Operator's visual connection with what he or she is composing and framing. Early viewfinders were often crude side or top finders, requiring parallax compensation, and only approximated what the camera was actually capturing. The introduction of true reflex through-the-lens viewing has changed all that.

The Side-Mounted Parallax Correcting Finder. Mounted on the side of the camera, level with the taking lens, the viewfinder only needed to be adjusted to correct lateral parallax when framing and focusing on a subject. As action became more extensive and cameras became more mobile, a number of early hand-cranked cameras had these swing-out or incrementally scribed oculars to compensate for parallax between the finder and the taking lens while following and framing the action. Later, specially shaped cams were developed for the lens complement which, with the finder connected to the follow focus gear train, kept the viewfinder centered on the action. (Simple hinging finder: Bell & Howell **2709B** in 1912; adjustable cam system: Mitchell **NC*** in 1934.)

The Spinning-Mirror Shutter Viewing System. The spinning-mirror shutter reflex viewing system was developed by Arriflex in 1932, and for the first time made it possible for the Camera Operator to see clearly and exactly what was being framed and whether or not it was consistently in frame and focus while the shot was being made. (ARRI "**Spinning-Mirror Reflex Viewing System**"* in 1932; Cunningham "**Combat Camera**" in 1940; Mitchell "**Mark II**"* in 1952 and **BNCR*** in 1968; Panavision **PSR*** in 1968.)

The Rack-Over Ocular System. Permitted the camera body to be shifted to one side thereby placing the ocular in alignment with the taking lens in order to line up a shot or to check focus before and/or following a take. (Mitchell **NC*** in 1933.)

The Prismatic Viewing System. A beam-splitter prism was used to provide reflex viewing on a modified Mitchell NC camera used to record kinescopes. (DuPont, 1959.)

The Pellicle Viewing System. The optical pellicle, a light-sharing reflex viewing system, made possible through-the-lens, flicker-free viewing while the take is in progress. (Cinema Products pellicle conversion* in 1968.)

The Adjustable Parallax Side Finder. Removable, incrementally shaped cams, each used with a specific taking lens, maintain proper vectoring of the viewfinder to the coverage of the taking lens. (Mitchell, 1934.)

The Zoom Finder. The PSR was the first silent reflex camera to have zoom finding. (Panavision **PSR***, 1966.)

The Adjustable Ocular Diopter. A viewfinder ocular diopter adjustment brought most Camera Operators' vision to 20-20, thereby avoiding the need for eyeglasses during a take. (Mitchell, 1933.)

The Eyepiece Condensation Eliminator. Eliminates the formation of condensation on and in the ocular elements, assuring clear vision for the Camera Operator. (Panavision "**Panaclear**," 1980.)

The Eyepiece Leveler. A stabilized viewfinder-leveler positioning device which maintains a constant eyepiece position during tilt moves of the camera head. (Akeley in 1917; Panavision in 1974.)

The Orientable Multi-Positioning Swingover Viewfinder. This development made possible convenient viewfinder positioning at virtually any 360° position, horizontally and vertically, around the camera. (ARRI, 1975.)

The Ground Glass Magnifier. Allows the Camera Operator to fine-check focus and framing details imaged on the ground glass. (Mitchell, 1933.)

The Illuminated Ground Glass. Clarifies for the Camera Operator the aspect ratio frame limits when framing night exteriors or other contrasty scenes with dark or deeply shadowed background. (Panavision "**Panaglow**"* in 1978.)

The Selective Aspect Ratio Electronic Ground Glass Imager. Useful for night shooting and for contrasty scenes where multiple aspect ratios are in use. (ARRI "**ARRI Glow**" in 1988.)

Video Assist Monitoring. Introduction of the charge-coupled device (CCD) made efficient through-the-lens image transmission feasible. The development of the video tap, placed in the film camera ocular viewfinder, made convenient reference possible for Camera Operators (as well as Directors, Producers, Writers, DPs, and others) on multiple-camera shows to check floor monitors and match shot sizing with the other cameras. (Roos "**Video Assist,**"* 1988, and others.)

Color Video Assist Camera*. A reflex video tap used to transmit color images to the viewfinder, to a VTR and to floor monitors. (Denz, 1996.)

Flicker-free Video Tap Imaging*. Reduces or eliminates image flicker displayed on floor monitors, caused by the spinning mirrored shutter in the film camera. (Cinematography Electronics Inc in 1990.)

The Electronic Viewfinder. Believe it or not, this visual aid was added to early electronic cameras as an afterthought. (RCA in mid-'30s; thereafter, Bosch-Fernseh; Broadcast Television Systems; Philips; Thomson; and others.)

Adjustable Electronic Reticle Lines. A useful development, the adjustable illuminated reticle lines on the electronic viewfinder, provides the Camera Operator with framing limits. (Broadcast Television Systems in 1989.)

Split-View of Multi-Camera Coverage. Enables the Camera Operator to punch up a display on the electronic viewfinder of the external video shot coverage of each video camera on a multiple-camera show. (Broadcast Television Systems in late 1940s.)

LENSES & FILTERS

The taking lens provides the Camera Operator with a view of the scope and perspective of the imagery which will be recorded by the camera. Certain lenses with specialized applications can make the work of the Camera Operator and Camera Assistants more efficient, effective and productive.

The Zoom Lens. Development of the variable focal length lens made possible, for the first time, numerous fixed focal length positions from a single lens as well as dynamic movement through the focal length range of that zoom lens. (For film: The first in the late 1920s, then the Angénieux **10-1*** in 1964; then Cooke, and Canon "**Macro Zoom**"* in 1971; Zeiss **Primes*** in 1991; Panavision "**Auto Panatar**"* in 1958 and 1993 and the "**Primo Zoom**"* in 1991, "**11-1 Primo**"* in 1992, and "**3-1 Primo**"* in 1993; Nemenz Intl*, Clairmont Camera* and Century Precision Optics* in 1991. For video: The Bach "**Zoomar**"* in the late 1950s; then Taylor-Hobson; Angenieux; Canon; Fujinon.)

The Super-Speed Lenses. The super-speed lenses transmitted more light through the reflex viewfinder, making it possible for the Camera Operator to see the framed subject matter more clearly in low light levels. (In 1976: Zeiss*, Canon*, and Panavision*.)

Enlarged Incremental Two-Sided Lens-Settings Numbers. This innovation significantly helped the First Assistant Camera Operator, who could now conveniently set aperture stops, set and follow focus and make zoom moves—from either side of the camera. (In 1976: Panavision; then Angénieux; Cooke; Nikor; and Zeiss in 1987.)

The Dynalens. An image-stabilization device which smooths out vibration and the visual bumps and bounces of a mobile camera platform as it moves over an uneven or rough surface, thereby improving the look of the framed subject matter. (Dynasciences "**Dynalens**"* in l969.)

The Snorkel Lens. A lens extension used with a prime lens which, with its combination of internal optical elements and mirrors, makes possible extremely low, floor level camera angles and tight, precision work in photographing tabletop displays, models and miniatures. (Kenworthy "**Snorkel**"* in 1977; then Century Precision Optics; Laikin.)

The Low-Angle Prism System. An obliquely arranged set of prisms placed in front of the taking lens makes possible extremely low tabletop surface angles. (David Samuelson of Samuelsons, London in early 1980s.)

The Periscope Aerial Camera Lens*. An obliquely arranged set of prisms in a housing placed in front of the taking lens, allows aerial photography to take place without exposing the camera to external elements. (Continental Camera Systems, 1977.)

The Pitching Lens*. This device is a tiltable/swingable lens element on the front end of a periscopic lenticular arrangement which allows additional tilt (50° zenith and 180° nadir, totalling 230°) and pan (360°) latitude to an otherwise non- or limited-tiltable configuration. (Continental Camera Systems [John Carroll, inventor] in early 1981.)

The Swing Shift Lens Set. This bellowsed lens mounting configuration is used with specifically designed prime lenses to control and/or alter subject position and perspective in frame as well as depth of field by means of swings, tilts, rises, falls and shifts of the lens mounting board. (Clairmont Camera in 1988.)

Lens Calibrating System.* Properly calibrating a lens based on actual light transmission is important to maintain consistency of exposure. (20th Century-Fox in 1942; Basco **system of lens collimating*** in 1973.)

The Slant Focus Lens. This lens configuration permits tilt of object plane focus in any azimuth, which in effect extends the depth of field along a vertically and/or horizontally skewed subject plane alignment. (Panavision* in 1991.)

Filters. Optical filters designed to control the amount and quality of light passing through the lenticular system are useful tools. (Tiffen **Laminated color filters*** in 1984; Harrison & Harrison **Diffusion filters*** in 1985; Iso-Optic "**Ultra Star**"* in 1988; Tiffen "**Ultra Con**"* in 1992.)

The Pola-screen.* Used to control polarized light by selectively screening the light to reduce reflections and glare. (Eastman Kodak in 1935.)

Lightflex Contrast Control*. A system of controlled light washing across the surface of the taking lens in order to minimize contrast. (Lightflex in1983.)

Zoom Lens Control Motor*. The motor attached to the zoom lens along with a variable control device made possible to make a variety of smoother sizing adjustments during a take. (Cinema Products in 1971.)

The Anamorphic Lens. Either a lenticular attachment placed in front of a prime taking lens (Cinemascope) or a specially designed lens (Panavision) each of which compresses a scene of more than twice the usual width onto the standard film width. (20th Century-Fox/Bausch & Lomb "**Cinemascope**"* in 1952; Panavision* in 1968; Todd-AO* in 1972.)

MOTORIZED CONTROLS FOR
CAMERA & LENS SETTINGS

Starting with manipulating and riding the lens settings by hand, the need arose, particularly for the video Camera Operator, to be able to change lens settings—zoom and focus—while operating the camera. Two flexible cables ran from the lens to hand controls attached to the pan handles, one flexcable connected by a rotating gear to a geared focus ring and the other flexcable connected by rotating gear to a sector gear on the sizing lever on the zoom lens. Because of a degree of lag and slop in many of the mechanical controls, the way was open for the more precise electronic controls, either hard-wired or controlled by RF, IR, sonar or MW transmission, actuated by the Camera Operator and/or First Assistant Camera Operator.

The Zoom Control. An electronic controller provides smoother execution of zoom lens movement than mechanical controls. (Cinema Products **J-series*** in 1971; Preston Cinema Systems "**Micro Force**"* control [with Hayden micro-servo motor] in 1980; Panavision "**Panazoom**" in the 1980s.)

The Focus Control. An electronic controller provides precise focusing. (MGM **Semi-automatic Focus Control*** in 1937; Cinema Products and Preston Cinema Systems "**Micro Servo**" servo control in 1982.)

The Automatic Focus Control. Automatic focus control by use of a recently developed laser radar technique allows the First Assistant to point the light-ranging device at the subject to achieve proper focus. (Preston Cinema Systems "**Light Ranger Auto Focus***," 1992.)

The Aperture Control. An electronic controller provides smooth and precise movement and setting of the lens aperture. (Panavision, Cinema Products, Preston Cinema Systems in 1983.)

The Frame Rate Control. An electronic controller provides precise control of the frame rate. This is particularly useful when varying the frame rate during a take. (In the early 1980s: Panavision and Preston Cinema Systems, with Cinematography Electronics, 1983.)

The Frame Rate-Aperture Control. By means of computer and micro servos, consistently even exposure can be maintained during changes in the frame rate while making a take. (Preston Cinema Systems "**Speed-Aperture Computer**"* in l983.)

The Camera Actuation Control. Developed to actuate the on-off switch when the camera is in a remotely controlled configuration. (Cinema Products in early 1980s.)

The Film Magazine Take-up Motor. This slave, or torque, motor minimizes film breakage and jams by maintaining take-up tension as the exposed film re-enters the film magazine. (ARRI in 1960; Panavision "**Panaflex**"* in 1972.)

INTERNAL CAMERA CONTROLS

Film cameras have all had a certain number of internal controls which can be adjusted to keep the camera running and operating properly. Now many of the adjustments that used to be handled externally are controlled by integrated electronic circuitry, often tied into an internal mini-computer.

Integrated Shutter Angle/Frame Rate Settings. Makes possible continuing exposure compensation by automatically adjusting the shutter angle when the frame rate has been manipulated. (ARRI, 1990.)

Behind-the-Lens Filter Slots. Filter-holding slide-frames make it convenient for the First Assistant to cut and place gel filters behind the taking lens. (Mitchell, 1933.)

Pitch Control. Adjusts the pull-down cycle range of the pull-down claw to conform to the perf size and pitch of the film being used. (Mitchell 1933, Panavision 1968.)

REMOTE CAMERA HEAD CONTROLS

Controlling and operating a camera which is remotely situated from the operating position can be accomplished today either by hard-wiring the control mechanisms from the control console to the camera, or by sending an RF, IR, MW or sonar signal to a receiver at the camera and control head. The remotely controlled camera configuration makes possible placing a camera in an advantageous position where there is not room for a Camera Operator and Assistant, or in a potentially physically hazardous position without endangering operative personnel.

The Camera Remote Controls. Provides a technique which, while providing full, fluid control of camera operation by control wheels or joy-stick, physically separates the operative camera crew from the camera, thereby providing a great degree of safety as well as a variety of heretofore unavailable camera angles. (MGM "Grand Prix"* radio-activated electronically controlled head in 1965; "**Louma Head**"* in 1975; A & C Ltd for Technovision "**Hot-Head**" in 1979; Nettmann "**Cam-Remote**"* in 1983, "Mini-mote" in 1992, a "Micro **mini-mote**" in 1995 and "**Gyron**" in 1996; Kaleidescope "**Power Pod**" in 1987; Shotmaker "**Scorpio II 3-axis**" in 1996.)

Witness/Video Assist Cameras. The use of small video cameras mounted on the remotely controlled camera to send back readouts on lens stop, focus and zoom positions as well as video assisted through-the-taking-lens view of the coverage. (John Stephens in 1965*; Louma in 1975; Sony in 1994; Panavision "**Panaview**" in 1995.)

Triple-Axial Remote Control. Extends the function of the remotely controlled head with pan, tilt and roll capabilities. (Louma in 1989; Nettmann "**Cam Remote**"* in 1994; Shotmaker "**Scorpio**" in 1995.)

The Remotely Controlled Aerial Camera. Housed in external configuration on an aircraft, the camera control head is manipulated by servo/selsyn drive from hand wheels or joy-stick control. (The Wescam mount in 1973; Matthews "**Astrovision**" in 1975 and "**Vectorvision**" in 1987 by E F Nettmann, inventor; the Preston "**Gyrosphere**" in 1985.)

The Louma Arm. The remotely controlled camera on this modular camera crane can be manipulated, moved and placed in otherwise difficult or impossible configurations and vantage points. (The Louma Camera Crane* was created by Jean-Marie Lavalou, Alain Masseron and David Samuelson, Sam Alga Cinema, Paris & London in 1975.)

The Python Crane Arm. Extends the vertical and swing limits of remotely controlled camera movement and placement. (Chapman, 1986.)

The Sky Cam. Further extends the overhead mobility and placement of the remotely controlled camera. (Garrett Brown and Skyworks, 1984.)

Flying-Cam*. This remotely controlled flying miniature helicopter provides a mobile camera mount for unusual camera angles. (Flying-Cam in 1994.)

CAMERA CONTROL HEADS

The camera control head determines to a substantial degree the facility with which the Camera Operator can manipulate the pan and tilt movement of the camera. The design of the camera control head has steadily advanced from the early friction heads to the current state-of-the-art fluid, fluid/spring, geared and electronic control heads.

The Friction Head. Provided smooth, dependable manual pan and tilt movement for early cameras and later, for the heavier studio cameras. (Méliès and Eastman in early 1890s; then Waltindaw; Pathé; DeBrie; Akeley; Mitchell; Birns & Sawyer; CECO.)

The Nodal Point Head. Places the vertical, horizontal and rotation axes precisely at the nodal point of the taking lens. (Paramount **"Nodal Point Head"*** in 1944; Nemenz International in 1991; Louma in 1994.)

The Hand-Cranked Positioning Head. A turning handle geared into the azimuth plate pivoted the camera horizontally and a second turning handle provided a vertical tilt adjustment. (The Waltindaw and others, 1890s and early 1900s.)

The Geared Head. Introduction of the 2-speed geared head (triple mode with neutral or free-wheeling) with its rotating control wheels provided a smooth and dependable operation for pan and tilt movement of the heavy studio cameras while exposing film and subsequently for lighter-weight cameras. The current 3-speed (quadruple mode with neutral) geared heads are state-of-the-art. (Worrall Geared Head* in 1933; Moy in 1940s; Cinema Products **"Mini-Worrall"** in 1976; Mitchell **"Light-weight Head"*** in 1978; Technovision **"Technohead"** in 1990.)

The Chain-Driven Head. The chain-driven 3-speed/4-mode head with rotating control wheels and adjustable horizontal swing positioning of the tilt control. (ARRI **"ArriHead"*** in 1986.)

The Belt-Driven Head. The belt-driven 3-speed/4-mode head with rotating control wheels. (Panavision {**PanaHead"*** in 1982.)

The Spring-Loaded Fluid Head. Adjustable hydraulic and spring tension aids in controlling and smoothing out pan and tilt movements. (Miller [for 16mm only] in 1948; O'Connor **100*** in 1949; Cartoni* in 1973; Sachtler* in 1984; Ronford* in 1985; Baker* in 1990; Vinten **"Vector 70"** in 1996.)

The Gyro Head. Particularly useful in smoothing out extensive camera panning moves with an extreme telephoto taking lens in place. (Akeley in early 20s; Cartoni in 1945; Sachtler in 1946.)

The Gimbal Head. An especially appropriate camera mount for shooting on or from floating marine conveyances or from a construction crane platform during a vertical swing rise or from a swinging or swaying camera platform. (Mitchell in mid-1930s.)

The Offset Head. The 360° tilt capability along with adjustable skewed or "dutch" orientation, permitting movement 45° or more either side of vertical, makes possible a wide range of heretofore nearly impossible-to-make effect shots. (O'Connor offset in 1958 and dual-sided offset in 1964; Weaver/Steadman tube frame head in 1972; Nemenz International "Dutch" head in 1988; Louma "Dutch" head in 1989; Cartoni in 1992.)

Rotating Rig Head. The extended capability of this head allows continuing 360° rotation of the camera on its lenticular axis during a shot. (Nemenz International in 1991.)

The Extended Tilt Range Head. This heavy-duty fluid head has extended the tilt range for a large camera to 180° movement, straight down to straight up, without benefit of a tilt plate. (O'Connor **2575*** in 1989.)

The Tilt Wedge & Adjustable Tilt Plate. A tilt wedge or adjustable tilt plate affixed to a control head can be adjusted to place a mounted camera in a position which extends either the effective vertical down or up tilt range of a friction or geared head. (Worrall in the late 1930s; Mitchell, Panavision and others.)

The Rotating Offset Plate. Makes possible mounting the camera in a position off the center vertical axis of the mounting ring on the dolly. This is particularly useful for wing cameras, working close to set walls, on multi-camera film sitcoms. (Fisher **"Ubangi"** in 1987.)

The Electronically Controlled Head. [See Remote Camera Head Controls above.]

STATIC CAMERA SUPPORTS

Ever since the photographic camera was invented, there was a need for a sturdy support on which to mount it. The still camera required lengthy exposures and a rock-steady mount. The early motion picture cameras required both hands—one to crank the film through the camera, and the other to manipulate the external iris and/or the lenticular diaphragm, or to crank-pan the camera—during a shot. In both applications, a tripod was the support of choice because of its ease in setting up, secure mounting and efficiency in leveling the camera on a variety of surfaces and terrain. As the camera became more mobile, other means of stabilizing the camera during filming were developed.

The Tripod. This three-legged mount was the support of choice of the early Camera Operators, many of whom were Still Photographers. So it was a natural choice for the production cameras at that time. (Méliès and Eastman in early 1890s; then Waltindaw; Pathé; DeBrie; Akeley; Mitchell; Birns & Sawyer; CECO; Miller; O'Connor; Cartoni; Sachtler; Ronford; and others. Paramount **Nodal Point Tripod*** in 1954.)

The Unipod. The unipod, as the name implies, is a single support element. It can be an adjustable length apparatus; or it can be a pole, stick, dowel, or plastic pipe used to support the camera during a shot. (Origin unknown.)

The Rope/Chain Pod. The rope or chain pod is a camera support system which consists of one end of a rope or chain attached to the top or base of the camera. If the other end is from the camera base, it is stepped on and the camera raised until the tension in the rope or chain is sufficient to steady the movement of the handheld camera. If the rope or chain is attached to the top of the camera, the other end can be affixed to a ceiling, roof eave or overhanging tree limb and downward pressure can be applied until the camera is quite steady for a shot. (Origin unknown.)

The Body Pod. The body pod is a device for stabilizing the camera during essentially static camera shots. It can, however, be used to make moving shots in lieu of a purely handheld mode.

MOBILE CAMERA PLATFORMS

Mobile camera platforms have freed the camera from the earthbound static positioning of the early days. The camera can be, and often is, placed on various mobile platforms, some developed especially to carry the camera, its Operator and the Assistant in a variety of specially designed configurations and moves.

The Wheeled Tripod. Developed to conveniently move the camera from one shooting position to another. (Edison Co in late 1880s; the Waltindaw Studio Tripod in the 1890s; the Thomas "**Sputnik**" stomp-up, 1960.)

The Studio Crane. These electric-powered, silent-operating cranes are capable of moving and placing the camera, Camera Operator and First Assistant in or at heretofore difficult or impossible configurations and vantage points. (Fearless in the 1920s and 30s; MGM "**Mobile Camera Crane**"* in 1939; Chapman electric-driven cranes: **#1** through **#5** [22′ to 40′ lens height] from 1947-52, the "**Crab Crane**" elec [9′] in 1958, "**Electra**" elec [12′] in 1960, "**Nike**" elec [14′] in 1963, "**Zeus**" elec [16′] in 1965; Brooker crane in 1960; Matthews "**Tulip Crane**"* in 1982; Deats "**Little Big Crane**"* in 1982; Camera Platforms Int'l "**Shotmaker**" gas/elec in 1986; Matthews, thereafter.)

The Exterior Location Crane. These gas- and/or electric-powered cranes are capable of moving and placing the camera, Camera Operator and First Assistant at any position through a substantial elevation range while the crane body is in a static, slow or rapid mode of movement. (Chapman: "**Hercules**" gas/elec [27′] in 1953, "**Atlas**" gas/elec [19′] in 1954, "**Titan**"* elec/gas [27′] in 1961, "**Apollo**" elec/gas [19′] in 1962, "**Super Nova**" elec [27′] in 1989; Camera Platforms Int'l: "**Shotmaker Elite**" in 1986 and "**Premier**" in 1991.)

The Louma Arm. This modular camera crane enables the remotely controlled camera to be manipulated, moved and placed in otherwise difficult or impossible configurations and vantage points. (The **Louma** Camera Crane* was created by Jean-Marie Lavalou, Alain Masseron and David Samuelson, Sam Alga Cinema, Paris & London in 1975.)

The Adjustable Length Crane Arm. The length of the crane arm can be quickly changed by adding or removing modular lengths of support arm structure. Lengths more than 16′ are for mounting a remotely controlled camera only. (Louma [3′-25′] in 1970; Chapman "**Python**" [11′ or 20′] in 1988, the "**Lenny Arm**" [7′-25′ in 4′ lengths] in 1992; and the 70′ Akela crane in 1994.)

The Extendable Length Crane Arm. The extendable length crane arm provides another axis of movement, thereby avoiding arc movements when desired, while making a shot and/or can place the camera at a desired position without moving the crane body. (Technovision Cameras "**Technocrane**" in 1989.)

The Jib Arm. The jib arm is an extension device available in various lengths which can be used to mount and manuever a remotely controlled camera on a crab dolly or other support. (Fisher, Jonathan, Chapman and others in the 1980s.)

The Cable Cam. The camera platform, holding a Camera Operator and Assistant, or remotely controlled camera only, moves horizontally on a heavy-duty cable strung between two towers and has a substantial vertical fall and rise capability below that cable run. (The Grip House, 1991.)

The Camera/Insert Car. Made possible the convenient and secure placing of cameras and operating personnel during the shooting of high-speed moving shots. (Others in 1920s through the 50s; Caspar Camera Cars in 1960s; Mitchell Insert Systems* **in 1980;** Camera Cars Unlimited in 1983; Camera Platforms Int'l Shotmaker: "**Standard**" camera car in 1986; the "**Elite**"* elec/gas [23′ boom arm] in 1986, and the "**Premier**" elec/gas [21′] in 1991.)

The Camera Dolly. A variety of four- and three-wheeled platforms have been placed in service to move the camera, its Operator and Assistant while making a shot. (Houston-Fearless "**Panaram**" in 1940; Hogue Dolly in 1948; Chapman "**Doorway**" and "**Western**" dollies in early 1950s; Fisher **Model 8** [a 3-wheeler 2-way] in 1963.)

The Crab Dolly. Introduced a significant contribution to the controlled mobility of the camera and its Camera Operator. (First crab dolly with 3-way steering and hydraulic lifting arm* designed by Steve Krilanovitch for McAlister in 1946, and an advanced 2-directional dolly for McAlister in 1950; King 2-directional in 1955; Moviola bi-directional in 1957; Elemack "**Spyder**"* in 1963 & "**Cricket**"* in 1978; Fisher: **Model 8** 3-wheel 2-directional in 1963, **Model 9*** 2-directional in 1966, **Model 10*** 3-directional in 1978, and **Model 11** in 1994; **Stindt*** 2-directional [by Art Brooker] in 1966; Chapman 2-directionals: "**Sidewinder**" elec [10′] in 1970, "**Hustler**"* [6.5′] in 1974, "**PeeWee**"* [6′] in 1981, "**Hybrid**" [7′] in 1984, and "**Olympian**" elec [14′] in 1984; Panther 2-directional "**Super Panther MS-180**"* in 1987.)

The Mobile Studio Pedestal. A significant contribution toward facilitating the controllable mobility and positioning of the electronic camera while on-line. (Fearless in the 1930s, TVP in the 40s, Vinten "**Fulmar**"* in 1989, Chapman "**Pedolly**" in 1996.)

Mobile Studio. The first mobile studio and camera platform was developed to accommodate efficient location work. (Fouad Said "**Cinemobile**"* in 1965.)

CAMERA STABILIZING SYSTEMS

Keeping the camera steady and vibration-free when hand-holding or shooting from a moving conveyance has long been a criterion of camera operating excellence. To take the effort out of operating such shots, special mounts have been developed to smooth out balance, vibration, sway and bounce.

The Tyler Counter-Balanced Stabilizing System. This revolutionary (when introduced) system is shock-mounted, counter-balanced and spring-tensioned for smooth, effortless and reliable manual camera operating during aerial photography, principally from helicopters. (Tyler Camera Systems **Helicopter Mount*** in 1962.)

The Continental Helicopter Mount*. This system is shock-mounted, counter-balanced and spring-tensioned for smooth and reliable aerial camera work. (Continental Camera Systems in 1974.)

The Wescam Gyro Stabilized Remotely Controlled Mount*. Wescam's remotely controlled, self-contained camera sphere, which uses a joy-stick and video monitor display from a CCD camera video tap, is primarily a helicopter mount but can be installed on other type aircraft for aerial photography. (Wescam **Stabilized Camera System** in 1973.)

The Gyrosphere. A remotely controlled camera placed in a spherical enclosure is mounted so as to neutralize the force of gravity on its fast pan and tilt movement during aerial photography. (Preston Cinema Systems, 1985.)

The Spacecam Mount*. A remotely controlled, enclosed aerial camera mount. (Spacecam, 1990.)

The Space Gyro Mount. This configuration combines counter-balancing with gyro stabilization. (Tyler Camera Systems, 1992.)

The Steadicam™ Spring-Loaded Stabilizing System. Takes the bounce out of the physical movement of the Camera Operator and makes possible smooth-looking walking or running shots as well as up-and-down-the-stairs shots. (Garrett Brown, SOC, inventor, and Cinema Products, developer, of **Steadicam*** in 1975.)

The Panaglide Spring-Pneumatic Stabilizing System. Accomplishes the same mission as the Steadicam™ System, but with heavier load capability. (Panavision, 1979.)

The Pogo Cam™. This counterbalanced, leveraged camera stabilizing system helps the Camera Operator achieve smooth following moves, particularly with the camera in the low configuration mode. (International Camera, 1989.)

ANCILLARY ADVANCES

Not every helpful development concerns the eyes and hands of the Camera Operator. Other areas of the anatomy also have been considered, as well as light measuring and shot lineup devices.

The Sliding and Adjustable Height Dolly Seat. The variable vertical and horizontal positioning capability makes possible conveniently adjusting the Camera Operator's seating position to the height and framing direction of the viewfinder. (Houston-Fearless "**Panaram**" in the early 1940s; McAlister in 1956; Moviola in 1957; Fisher in 1962; Chapman; and others.)

The Rotating Dolly Seat. This innovation saves wear and tear on the posterior of the seated Camera Operator during extreme panning moves. (J L Fisher, 1991.)

Exposure Meters. Light measuring devices are a valuable aid when the Camera Operator is sent out to do second unit work. (Norwood "**Director**"* in 1968; Photo Research "**Spectra Tri-Color**"* in 1972 and "**Spectra II**"* in 1979; Spectra-Cine "**Spectra CineSpot**"* in 1988; Belco Assocs "**Cinemeter**"* digital/analog in 1990.)

Director's Finder. An optical device which aids the Director in lining up a shot and choosing the best lens for the camera position. (Alan Gordon Enterprises "**Director's Finder**"* in 1996.)

TECHNIQUES

Applicable techniques which affect the mode of operation of the Camera Operator must also be acknowledged when such procedures contribute to the art and craft of camera operating.

The Quick-Change Magazine Technique. Uniquely designed film magazines can be removed and replaced on Eclair cameras while the camera is running. (1949.)

The Wide Screen Systems. Wide screen systems require special framing attention—the wider the framing area, the more information there is to check and compose. Most employ the full camera aperture. Some of these systems use spherical lenses with either a scribed ground glass or hard aperture of 1.65 aspect ratio or greater. Other of the systems utilize anamorphic taking lenses framing aspect ratios of 2.0 to 2.55. (Standard—non-squeezed 1.66-1.85 35mm 4-perf pull-down; CinemaScope* and Panavision 35—squeezed 35mm 4-perf pull-down; Techniscope*—non-squeezed 35mm 2-perf pull-down; 1.78 hi-definition TV 35mm 3-perf pull-down; VistaVision—non-squeezed 35mm 8-perf horizontal pull-across; Todd-AO* and Super Panavision 70*—non-squeezed 65mm 5-perf pull-down; Ultra-Panavision—squeezed 65mm 5-perf pull-down; Showscan*—65mm at 60fps; IMAX*—65mm, 15-perf, horizontal feed)

The Multiple-Camera Film Sitcom Technique. The situation comedy format, performed in continuity before a responsive studio audience, brought about a great degree of cooperation and collaboration among the three to four operative film camera crews on each show. (Desi Arnaz, 1935.)

The Mixed-Media Technique. This technique features a modified version of a professional film camera mounted on a mobile studio pedestal and operated as a video camera would be. This is made possible by a feed to an electronic viewfinder from a CCD video tap in the closed-off camera optical reflex viewfinder. The configuration includes the zoom and focus controls, one control on each of the two pan handles. (Panavision "**PanaWard System**" in 1990.)

The Underwater Camera Housing. The underwater camera housing made possible cinematography at varying depths without damaging camera or film. From the first box-like housings to the current fluid-dynamic, stabilized designs. (Jacques-Yves Cousteau 35mm box square-port housing in mid-1950s; the football-shaped Samson-Hall Eyemo housing with built-in batteries, exposure metering, accommodating a 400´ 35mm mag with a sports finder in the 1960s; also in the 1960s: Eclair, Alan Gornick and the Ribicoff cylindrical; Milliken 16mm housing in the 1970s; Hydroflex Systems* in 1992.)

IN CONCLUSION

There has been continuing progress by our corporate colleagues in the development, introduction and refinement of the technology relating directly to camera operation, the application of which directly supports and nurtures the art and craft of the Camera Operator. Every technical component under direct control of the Camera Operator, the First Assistant Camera Operator and other Camera Assistants has undergone some degree of change and refinement by technicians, manufacturers and suppliers. More of the same is certain to be in store for us in the future. So by giving them our input we will be certain to profit from their output.

Special acknowledgement for their helpful input goes to: Wes Lambert, Grant Loucks, Denny Clairmont, Ed DiGiulio, Bob Nettmann, Tak Miyagishima, Chuck Mallory, Jim Fisher, John Hora, and Jay Nefcy.

GLOSSARY

3D—three-dimensional motion picture system

A

"ACTION!"—Director's command to cast and crew to begin the action for the rehearsal or take

action line—the imaginary line connecting interacting players

AD—Art Director, Assistant Director, Associate Director (depends on context)

ADR—automatic dialogue replacement; used in a process called voice dubbing

AFL—American Federation of Labor

anamorphic—an extremely wide viewing aspect ratio, often 2:1 to 2.5:1

anomaly—any deviation from planned procedure, framing or shot production

ASA rating—an American Standards Association rating system of the sensitivity to light of a given film emulsion

ASC—American Society of Cinematographers

aspect ratio—the outer dimensions within which captured imagery is composed and framed [expressed as the relationship of width to height, i.e., 1.33 to 1, 1.33:1, or simply 1.33]

atmosphere—the extras (people in addition to the cast) used to populate the settings

B

backpanning—panning the camera in reverse to the movement of the mobile camera platform

"banana"—banana-shaped movement of performers or mobile camera platform

bellows—a folding enclosure which connects the taking lens to the camera body

bi-packed—two film stocks, one the unexposed negative, the other the developed negative or print, are run through a camera or optical printer emulsion to emulsion

"bird"—a microphone shadow

blimp—a camera housing which dampens and confines sound emissions from a running camera

block-and-shoot—the process of blocking the camera moves for a shot after which immediately taking the shot on film or tape

blocking—the process by which the Director moves and positions both performers and the camera

boom—a lengthy mechanical counterbalance beam connected to a post to support or guide the camera and/or personnel to be lifted and manipulated

buckle switch—the internal leaf plate which turns the camera off when film fails to feed into the film magazine and buckles into the film chamber pressing against the buckle plate

bug—a union logo; a symbol that represents the end of an article in a magazine or newspaper; a hidden microphone placed surreptitiously to record sound for surveillance purposes; to irritate

C

call—the time and place to report for work

call sheet—the paper prepared by the UPM on which is noted the call times for each member of the crew and cast, the scenes to be shot, the time for makeup, etc

camera—a light-tight chamber through the lens of which a controlled amount of light is introduced to record an image on a light-sensitive medium—a film emulsion, CRT, or CCD

camera accessories—items which can be attached to the camera and which can contribute to the process of image capture

camera angle—composed of the position of the camera and the choice of taking lens

camera components—the essential, constituent parts of the camera; the camera body, the film drive and transport mechanism, the film gate, the lens port

camera control head—the mechanism which allows the camera to be panned, tilted and/or canted

camera platform—any surface, static or mobile, upon which a camera can be positioned and from which the camera can be operated

camera support—any device on which a camera and its control head can be mounted and operated

cams—a shaped metallic template designed for each taking lens used in cameras with parallax viewfinders in order for the cam follower to adjust the finder to the particular taking lens while following focus

cant—to slant or tip a camera sideways

cat-bird seat—the safe spot where all can be viewed omnisciently

CCD—charge-coupled device, the TV picture chip

CCU—Camera Control Unit for video production

"CGI—character-generated imagery

cheating"—subtle repositioning of the head or body by a performer to allow better framing

"chinese"—a movement of the mobile camera platform directly across approaching movement or that of a stationary facing performer

choker—a closeup, framing the top of the head to the throat

ciné camera—a motion picture film camera

Cinematographer—one who is in charge of directing the photographic aspect of a cinematic production

CIO—Congress of Industrial Organizations

CLC—Canadian Labour Congress

"clear the field"—move out of the field of view covered by the taking lens

"clear the lens"—move away from in front of the camera

CMX—an electronic video editing system

collaborative—working together synergistically

color chart—a chart displaying the red, green, blue, yellow, magenta, and cyan color chips along with the greyscale chips, which is shot at the head end of each fresh film roll prior to filming principal action; used by the Timer or Colorist to set exposure and color values during printing or transfer to video tape. *See* lilly

composition—the arranging of subject matter in frame, or the selection of the frame size and position around existing subject matter

contact printer—a film printing machine which exposes print stock that has been bi-packed, emulsion to emulsion, with exposed camera negative and run past a controlled light source

coverage—varied shots of people, props and set dressing, of their placement and movement

crabbing—when the camera dolly wheels are positioned to move the platform in a relatively lateral or sideways direction without changing the alignment of the chassis

crane—a mobile camera platform from which the camera can be positioned—raised or lowered, or swung to either side—at varied heights

CRT—cathode ray tube, the TV picture tube

"CUT!"—Director's command to stop the camera, the sound recorder and the action

cutaways—shots of other staging elements, such as reaction shots of others in the scene, which can be used to break up, shorten or lengthen a scene

cyc (pronounced "sike" to rhyme with "bike")—cyclorama

D

dailies—work print of accepted takes made the previous working day

dampen—to check or restrain movement in a camera control head

deal memo—the agreement made between a craftsperson and production management which deals with areas not specifically covered in the union contract such as special above-scale rates, guaranteed working hours, box rentals, screen credit, etc

depth of field—the area between the nearest and farthest objects from the lens which are in acceptable focus

depth of focus—the extremely finite area between the surface of the rear element of the taking lens and the film focal plane where light rays converge to form points on the surface of the film emulsion; the degree at which the points of convergence are on the film plane determines the sharpness of the imagery; if the point of convergence occurs either before or after the light rays reach the film plane, the imagery will be less sharp and well-defined.

diffusion—the passing of light through a translucent medium or the reflection of light from a rough or textured surface

diopter—an auxiliary lens which, when placed in the lenticular system, modifies the characteristics of the taking lens; also a setting on the eyepiece to provide the viewer visual conformity of the displayed image

diving board—an extended side board used on a camera dolly to provide added standing surface for the Camera Operator.

dolly—a compact mobile camera mount and/or platform with multiple directional modes

dollying—to move the camera on a camera dolly while rehearsing or making a take

double—a close look-alike who takes the place of a principal performer in risky and second unit staging

doubler—a lens accessory added to the mounting end of a lens, which effectively doubles the focal length of a lens

DP—Director of Photography

dry-run—a runthrough rehearsal in real time with the cast or with stand-ins

"dutching"—a canted or rolling movement *or* positioning of the camera control head to one side or the other

duvetyn—a heavy, black cloth material used to dampen light reflection

E

EI rating—exposure index which rates various emulsions for their sensitivity to light

electronic time-code—a system of identifying each frame of film in order to expedite the process of electronic transfer and editing

emulsion—the light-sensitive material which coats the film base and upon which latent imagery is captured

encroachment—unplanned appearance or entry into frame of extraneous objects or personnel

exposure—the amount of light which will be allowed to reach the light-sensitive surface—film, CRT or CCD

extension tubes—lens accessory added to the mounting end of a lens which extends the focal length of a lens; requires additional exposure compensation

extras—people, in addition to the cast, used to provide atmosphere during rehearsals and takes

F

f-stop—an arithmetic calculation and setting based on the relationship between the size of the opening in the lens aperture to the focal length of the lens

FAX—the process of setting up, checking and aligning video cameras and the entire CCU chain; preparation of video components for shooting

field of view—the entire area covered by the taking lens

film gate—the component of the camera through which the film passes and which presses and holds the film flat during the exposure interval

film test—exposing film to determine its exposure range, color rendition, grain and resolution, or to test actors, makeup or wardrobe

filter—a lenticular device which absorbs or modifies color, intensity, quality and/or direction of light rays

finder—the eyepiece; ocular; viewfinder

fisheye—an extreme wide angle lens

fishpole—a lightweight, handheld mic boom

focus—the process of keeping the captured imagery in acceptably sharp resolution

focus control—the electronic or mechanical system of rotating the lens to the desired focal length

Foley—the system of recording live sound effects performed in synchronization with picture

following—moving the camera in a manner to keep dynamic action in frame at all times

foreshortening—the effect of forcing the perspective by use of wide angle lenses in order to visually manipulate the apparent sizes of objects in frame

fps—frames per second [standard US frame rate is 24 fps; standard European rate is 25 fps]

frame—the basic linear element in cinematic structure

frame rate—the rapidity with which the film passes through the camera; the number of frames per second which are exposed in camera

framing—the process of manipulating the camera in a way that will carry and hold specific imagery in frame as seen through the viewfinder

friction head—a camera control head on which control surfaces interface and rub against one another when being moved

G

Gaffer—the Key Lighting Technician

gate—See *film gate*

geared head—a camera control head which uses gears and gear ratios to control pan and tilt modes of movement

gimbal head—a camera control head which maintains plumb while the support is freely tipped or inclined in any direction

greyscale—the chart holding the six chip values from pure white through 20% increments to pure black, used to help the Timer or Colorist determine exposure and density values

Grip—a technician who moves sets, camera dollies and cranes and controls lighting patterns

ground glass—positioned in the viewfinding ocular in alignment with the film plane, the image from the taking lens is formed on the optically ground surface of the glass, on which is etched the aspect ratio within which the imagery is framed

H

hand-cranked—turning the film transport mechanism by hand [in the early days, all portable film production cameras were hand-cranked]

hazard—any shooting setup which places production personnel at risk

headset—a device, worn on the person, for sending and receiving verbal communications

hyperfocal distance—the nearest distance from the film plane at which the subject will be in acceptable focus with the lens focused at infinity

I

IATSE—International Alliance of Theatrical Stage Employees

ID'd—identified

inching knob—the external control, located at the rear or side of the camera, which, when manually turned, moves the film through the gate a frame at a time

incident light—light rays emanating from a source

input, inputted—information, suggestions or instructions given or received intercut—shots, or pieces of shots, which are juxtaposed with other shots placed in linear continuity

IR—infra-red

iris—an adjustable diaphragm, with a central opening, which controls the amount of light passing through a lens

J

jib arm—a lengthy tubular device on which a remotely controlled camera can be mounted and which can be attached to a dolly or crane in order to extend the effective camera angle

K

Key...—the Category/Department Head

key light—the principal modeling light, often the light on which exposure is based

L

lead framing ("lead" is pronounced "leed")—allowing more frame space in the direction of the look or movement

lead space ("lead" is pronounced "leed")—same as lead framing

lenticular—all optical devices and elements through which light passes to the light-sensitive surface

lilly—the color/greyscale chip chart. *See* color chart

liquid gate printer—an optical printer which runs the exposed negative through a liquid bath to reduce the effect of surface scratches while exposing each frame on a duplicating stock

location—the geographic area away from the studio where the production will take place

logistics—the transport, lodging and feeding of personnel and the movement of matériel during production

luminaires—the lighting instruments used on a production

M

master—the widest, most inclusive camera angle of an action and/or setting

matériel—the material equipment, company property and expendable supplies needed during the production

mic (pronounced "mike")—short for microphone

mic boom—the extendable arm to which the mic is attached and from which it is manipulated

mini-series—a short-run multi-part series, usually fewer than eight episodes and complete in itself

Mobile Camera Platform Operator—a Dolly or Crane Grip, Aircraft Pilot, Boat Captain, or construction Crane Operator who operates a platform on which a camera is mounted

monitor—the electronic device which displays the output from: the video tap of each of the film cameras; or from each of the video cameras; or used as a viewfinder for each video camera

"monkey"—a microphone shadow

morphing—the process of transforming an image in real time into something quite different

MOS—mit out sound, i.e., without sound, silent

MOW—movie-of-the-week, a long-form of TV programming

MW—micro wave

O

OB/obie light—a small, soft, low-intensity fill light mounted above the lens on the camera; said to be named after Merle Oberon, the first actress to utilize it

ocular—the eyepiece; the viewfinding system of a camera

on-the-air—a camera move or angle which will be used in the final cut

operating apron—the surface between the audience and the set on which the cameras are positioned and move

optical printer—a film printing machine, consisting of a synchronized projector and printer, which projects a negative image into the lens of a printer thereby exposing unexposed film stock a frame at a time

optics—the science of light and its characteristics as applied to vision

P

panning—turning the camera horizontally, either left or right

parallax—the angular deviation of the line of sight through the externally mounted viewfinder from the axis line of the taking lens when both lines are centered on the same object

pellicle—a prism through which light from the lens passes, is split and is directed to the film plane (major portion) and to the ocular (smaller portion).

perf—a perforation in film stock for the sprocketted drive camera mechanism

pickup shot—a take which covers only that portion of a shot which was not adequately covered or that had an audial or visual glitch that needs correcting

pilot—a first-time production of a new show for presentation to the TV or cable networks or syndicators for programming consideration

pitch—the distance from the leading edge of one film perforation to the leading edge of the next

pitch control—the internal control knob which adjusts the pull-down range of the pull-down claw(s) while the camera is running, in order to properly set that distance and minimize excessive noise resulting from an improperly set pitch

PL—phone line

pork chop—a low, pork chop-shaped platform which extends around either front wheel of the camera dolly

post-flashing—exposing exposed film stock to a controlled minimal and even amount of light prior to development

post mortem—the process of discussing and analyzing a project with the goal of understanding its strong and weak points

ppd—pages per day, i.e., the number of script pages to be shot in a day or that are planned to be shot that day

pre-flashing—exposing unexposed film stock to a controlled minimal and even amount of light prior to image capture

principal photography—cinematography during which the principal performers are involved

principals—the lead actors in the cast; the stars

projector—a motion picture machine with a powerful light source which projects the images recorded on each frame of the print passing through the film gate past the lens aperture and projected onto the reflective surface of a display screen

psychical distancing—the *apparent* distance at which the subject matter is located from the camera

pull-down claw(s)—the mechanism which engages the film in the sprocket holes and pulls the film into and through the film gate a frame at a time

R

rack-focus—to change focus radically from a sharply focused foreground object to a fuzzy, more distant object also in frame, thereby causing the foreground object to become quite soft while the distant object has now become very sharp

"realies"—the cast members, not the stand-ins

reflected light—light which is returned/reflected from a surface

reflex viewing—seeing the imagery through the lens as it is being captured

reframing—repositioning framed imagery during the optical or electronic transfer process

registration pin—the mechanism which engages the film in a sprocket hole when the film comes to rest in the film gate, holding the film perfectly steady and in alignment during the exposure interval

rehearsal—a run-through in real time without recording the event

repositioning—moving the imagery in frame, up or down, left or right, during the optical or electronic transfer

resizing—enlarging or diminishing the

imagery in frame during the optical or electronic transfer

RF—Radio Frequency, when headsets are used for communication

RGB—red/green/blue, the primary colors of light

riser—the arm of the dolly on which the camera is mounted which can be made to rise or fall to adjust the camera height in relation to the subject matter being photographed

rising front—by raising the front panel or lens turret of the camera, converging vertical lines can be made parallel

"ROLL SOUND!"—The First AD's command to start the sound recorder

run-bys—where vehicles, boats or animals are photographed as they run by the camera position

rushes—specially processed film which may be prepared for screening later on the same day on which it was shot. See also *dailies*

S

safetied (pronounced "SAFE-teed")—when equipment is secured by a safety cable in a manner which prevents it from falling down or out, getting damaged or injuring personnel

scene—a complete action, which may consist of one or more shots

screen direction—the direction in which performers are facing or moving during a take

second unit—an additional production unit used to shoot doubles, establishing shots, scenics, process plates, stunt action and special effects, all without principal performers involved

sequence—a complete series of actions, which may consist of one or more scenes

set/setting—the construction or environment in which will be used by the production company to stage the action

setup—a camera angle for which lighting, set dressing and sound are arranged in order to accommodate that angle

short-end—the remainder of unexposed film in a film magazine after the exposed footage has been separated and removed

shot—consists of a sequential series of frames and is the continuous recording of an action from a given camera angle

show time—when productions having live audiences in attendance begin the filming or taping process

shutter angle—the open angle of the camera shutter which will allow light to pass on to the film

side boards—a variety of platforms which can be attached to the camera dolly to facilitate Camera Operator positioning

sizing—the process of manipulating the zoom lens to place subjects at an appropriate size in frame

slate—the device on which the scene and take numbers are noted and presented to the camera at the start of each take to properly identify the take

SOC—Society of Operating Cameramen

"SPEED!"—The Production Mixer's response to the 1st AD's "ROLL" command when the sound recorder has attained recording speed

split focus—where the focus is placed at a position which assures that an object in the foreground and another in the background will both have acceptably sharp resolution

stand-in—a person who takes the place and positioning of a cast member during lighting and blocking procedures

storyboard—the device by which a story or sequence is presented shot by shot in order to encourage and clarify visual thinking and production planning

studio system—the system of defined craft specialization and performance

swing/slanting front—a device on which the auxiliary lens can be swung left, right, up or down, thereby altering perspective and skewing depth of field

swish panning—an extremely fast pan to the right or left, usually used as a transitional device

swish tilt—an extremely fast tilt either up or down, usually used as a transitional device

T

T-stop—a standard calculation and setting based on actual transmission of light through a calibrated lens

T's—including the breasts in frame

take—the process of recording an action on film or tape

taking lens—the lens through which a take is made

tally light—the red light on a video camera which tells the performer and Camera Operator which camera is on-the-air

TC—Technical Coordinator

TD—Technical Director

tear sheet—an itemized breakdown sheet, torn from a pad of forms, used by each department to list items required in each scene and sequence the script, noting their availability and cost

telecine—the technical interface where film can be transferred to tape and tape to film

tilting—turning the camera vertically, either up or down

time code—a system which addresses each frame of film or tape for electronic editing purposes

torque motor—the mechanism on the takeup side of the film magazine which maintains tension on exposed film as it is pulled into the takeup side

tracking—a mobile camera platform move which trails the blocked action

transduce—to transform the energy from one system to a form acceptable to another system; TV transforms/transduces light energy into electrical energy then back to light again

trucking—a mobile camera platform move which leads the blocked action

turn-around—the time given production personnel by production management between wrap time and the call time for the next session of work

U

upgrading—moving, or being moved, up a rank in classification

UPM—Unit Production Manager, the person who manages production for the producing company

UV—ultra-violet

V

variac—a variable transformer which controls the amount of current being fed to a variable speed camera, lights or other device

VC—Video Controller

video assist—the feed to floor monitors from a video tap placed in the viewfinding system of a reflex camera

video camera—an electronic camera

viewfinder cutoff—the external control which closes ocular access to the incoming imagery

vignetting—when an improperly positioned matte box, filter or lens shade results in an encircling encroachment into frame

voice dub—the process of placing or replacing dialogue on the sound track

voice slate—where the scene and take are identified by voice only during wild sound pickups

VTO—Video Tape Operator

VTR—video tape recorder

W

whip-pan—an extremely fast pan to the right or left, coming to rest on specified framing

whip-tilt—an extremely fast tilt either up or down, coming to rest on specified framing

wild sound takes—sound which is taken without synchronization to a camera

wrap—the process of assembling and putting things away at the close of a production session

Z

zoom—the process of moving continuously through a given range of the variable focal lengths of the zoom lens during a rehearsal or take

zoom control—the mechanism by which the First Assistant varies the framing size of the captured imagery

zoom lens—a variable focal length lens

INDEX

Directors of Photography, continued

" I like to see a camera operator who is able to instinctually follow and frame the action without my having to specify every compositional moment. Bill Hines' book focuses on that importance." **—John Alonzo** ASC

" Nothing is more important than operating a camera because it is the final distillation of everybody's work. Since it's the essence of the scene that counts, a good operator has to know when that essence has been properly captured in frame. Following the guidance offered in **OPERATING CINEMATOGRAPHY** will help the reader achieve that goal." **—David Quaid** ASC

" I wish I'd had the information contained in **OPERATING CINEMATOGRAPHY** when I was preparing to be a camera operator. All those years of learning by trial-and-error could have been a lot less traumatic." **—Jack Green** ASC

" In **OPERATING CINEMATOGRAPHY**, the essentials of camera operating are listed and codified in a way that is clear, comprehensive and concise, and will help anyone performing, or interested in, the craft do a better job." **—Stephen Burum** ASC

" I have read the '**Operating Tips**' column since its inception and have never failed to get good and useful information from each article." **—Steven Poster** ASC

" **OPERATING CINEMATOGRAPHY** is essential for those interested or working in camera-related activities. Learning or working without this handbook puts one at a distinct disadvantage." **—Robert Primes** ASC

" **OPERATING CINEMATOGRAPHY** is extraordinary information essential in understanding the techniques of operating a film or video camera and in working cooperatively with other crafts." **—Sol Negrin** ASC

" A camera operator who is intuitive—able to go with the flow of the action—and who has a sense of editing—how the takes will cut together as they are being shot—is invaluable to my style of cinematography. **OPERATING CINEMATOGRAPHY** covers these aspects very well." **—Brian Reynolds**

" **OPERATING CINEMATOGRAPHY** will enable the reader to achieve excellence in the best craft the industry has to offer—camera operating." **—Nick McLean**

" William 'Bill' Hines is one of today's premier operating cinematographers. **OPERATING CINEMATOGRAPHY** is required reading not only for all working cameramen and camerawomen, but for anyone who intends to make his or her living in the established motion picture business of today. This book tells not only about camera, but set etiquette and protocol, terminology, and many other pertinent subjects as well." **—Michael A Jones** *more on next page*

Camera Operators

"Much of what the camera operator does depends on feeling. Whether the feeling comes from the heart or gut, without it a person could never be a good operator. Bill Hines' book, **OPERATING CINEMATOGRAPHY for FILM and VIDEO**, captures those nuances. It's a *must read* no matter what your classification."

—Bill Clark SOC

"There is something in Bill Hines' **OPERATING CINEMATOGRAPHY for FILM and VIDEO** for just about anyone, professional or novice, that is of use on the job. The film and video realms have their own set of realities, some overlap, some are unique. The book covers a great deal of both worlds. I found it especially interesting to see his take on the historical nature of our profession and where all the 'traditions' started and why." **—Paul Basta** SOC (Video Cam Op)

"I found Bill Hines' '**Operating Tips**' columns in the *International Photographer* magazine filled with the movie shorthand needed to communicate with the director, camera crew, and other technicians on the set and with its tips for making those unexpected, quick decisions when actors improvise their blocking and you have to make the shot work. **OPERATING CINEMATOGRAPHY** will become required reading for camera operators who want to become successful in Hollywood."

—Eugene M Jackson III

"The advice in the '**Operating Tips**' column has been invaluable to me. It has brought me quickly up to speed with the standards of high-end production without my making too many mistakes along the way." **—Sean Fairburn** (Video Cam Op)

Experienced First Assistant Camera Operators

"Every camera assistant who wants to learn and know more about their craft, and the craft of the camera operator, as well as set etiquette and safety, should study and keep **OPERATING CINEMATOGRAPHY** at hand for ready reference."

—Richard Meinardus

"For a Camera Assistant, learning the secrets of camera operating used to be a hit-or-miss proposition. Now, Bill Hines unlocks the doors, with his comprehensive and thoughtful analysis of the fundamental artistic, technical and practical elements of operating a camera. **OPERATING CINEMATOGRAPHY** is an invaluable tool."

—Jeff Goldenberg

"**OPERATING CINEMATOGRAPHY** will enable one to better understand the techniques and procedures involved with the process of camera operating. It also contains valuable viewpoints and recommendations which, if followed, can further a career in the entertainment business." **—Kevin Haggerty**